China and Japan:

NEW ECONOMIC DIPLOMACY

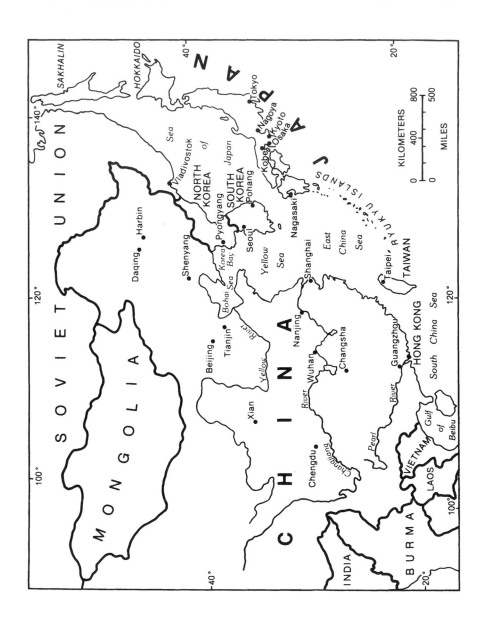

China
and
Japan:
NEW ECONOMIC
DIPLOMACY

Chae-Jin Lee

Hoover Institution Press
Stanford University, Stanford, California

www.hoover.org

Hoover Press Publication 297
Copyright © 1984 by the Board of Trustees of the
 Leland Stanford Junior University

First printing 1984
Manufactured in the United States of America

Library of Congress Cataloging in Publication Data
Lee, Chae-Jin, 1936–
    China and Japan : new economic diplomacy.
    (Hoover Press publication ; 297)
    Bibliography: p.
    Includes index.
    1. China—Foreign economic relations—Japan.
2. Japan—Foreign economic relations—China.   I. Title.
HR1604.Z4J3655   1984   337.51052   84-6602
ISBN-10: 0-8179-7971-9 (cloth)
ISBN-13: 978-0-8179-7971-3 (cloth)
ISBN-10: 0-8179-7972-7 (pbk.)
ISBN-13: 978-0-8179-7972-0 (pbk.)

To my brother, C. D. Lee,
who profoundly influenced
my intellectual awakening

Contents

List of Tables

Chart

List of Abbreviations

API	American Petroleum Institute
ASEAN	Association of Southeast Asian Nations
Baogang	Baoshan iron and steel complex
CAAC	Civil Aviation Administration of China
CCP	Chinese Communist Party
CHINCOM	China Committee
CJLTC	China-Japan Long-Term Trade Committee
CNCIEC	China National Chemicals Import and Export Corporation
CNMIEC	China National Machinery Import and Export Corporation
CNOGEDC	China National Oil and Gas Exploration and Development Corporation
CNTIC	China National Technical Import Corporation
COCOM	Coordinating Committee
CODC	Chengbei Oil Development Corporation (Japan)
CPPCC	Chinese People's Political Consultative Conference
EEC	European Economic Community
Eximbank	Export-Import Bank
Gaimushō	Ministry of Foreign Affairs (Japan)
GATT	General Agreement on Tariffs and Trade
IBRD	International Bank for Reconstruction and Development

IOTC	International Oil Trading Corporation (Japan)
JCEA	Japan-China Economic Association
JCLTC	Japan-China Long-Term Trade Committee
JCODC	Japan-China Oil Development Corporation
JCOIA	Japan-China Oil Import Association
JNOC	Japan National Oil Corporation
JNODC	Japan National Oil Development Corporation
JSP	Japan Socialist Party
Keidanren	Japanese Federation of Economic Organizations
Keizai Dōyūkai	Japan Committee for Economic Development
KMT	Kuomintang
LDC	Less developed country
LDP	Liberal-Democratic Party (Japan)
MITI	Ministry of International Trade and Industry (Japan)
MPI	Ministry of Petroleum Industry (China)
NATO	North Atlantic Treaty Organization
Nisshō	Japanese Chamber of Commerce
NPC	National People's Congress (China)
NSSG	Nippon Sharyō Seizōgaisha (Japan)
ODA	Official Development Assistance
OECD	Organization for Economic Cooperation and Development
OECF	Overseas Economic Cooperation Fund (Japan)
OPEC	Organization of Petroleum Exporting Countries
PCC	Petroleum Company of China
PRC	People's Republic of China
Renmin Ribao	People's Daily (CCP's newspaper)
ROC	Republic of China (Taiwan)
SCCC	State Capital Construction Commission (China)
SGB	State Geological Bureau (China)
SMS	Schloemann-Siemag (West Germany)
Sōhyō	General Council of Trade Unions (Japan)
SPC	State Planning Commission (China)

Acknowledgments

I was fortunate to meet with quite a few scholars and officials in China and Japan who were willing to support my sustained research for this book. They shared their knowledge and perspectives with me, helped me to schedule and conduct interviews of important persons, and helped me to plan and make field trips to many places from Baoshan to the Bohai Sea. I remain deeply appreciative for their friendship and assistance.

In particular, I wish to acknowledge the cooperation provided by President Teng Weizao and Vice-President Wu Daren of Nankai University, Vice-President Tan Jiazhen of Fudan University, Duan Junyi (first secretary of the Beijing Municipal Committee of the Chinese Communist Party), and Hu Lijiao (chairman of the Standing Committee of the Shanghai Municipal People's Congress). I learned much from interviewing Li Wenxue (vice-chairman of the China Council for Promotion of International Trade), Rong Fengxiang (director of the Second Department of the Ministry of Foreign Economic Relations and Trade), Ding Min (deputy director of the First Asian Department of the Ministry of Foreign Affairs), Wu Shudong (commercial counselor of the Chinese Embassy to Japan), Huang Jinfa (deputy general manager of the Baoshan iron and steel complex), and Wu Xunze (deputy general manager of the offshore branch of the Petroleum Company of China). I would also like to thank Professors Gu Shutang, Wei Hongyuan, Yu Xinchun, and Wang Yongxiang of Nankai University.

I can only list the few individuals in Japan who were most helpful to my work: Vice-President Kimura Ichizō of the International Oil Trading Corporation; Dietman Furui Yoshimi; President Ishikawa Tadao of Keio University; Saitō Takashi of the Japan-China Oil Development Corporation; Odagawa Keisuke and Matsumoto Ken of the Nippon Steel Corporation; Hashimoto Hiroshi, Tajima Takashi, and Ikeda Tadashi of the Ministry of Foreign Affairs; Hayashi Haruhiko and Koguchi Motoichi of the Ministry of International Trade and Industry; and Takeuchi Katsushi and Yamada Masaharu of the Overseas Economic Cooperation Fund of Japan. The surnames have been written first for all Chinese and Japanese individuals mentioned in this book.

I am indebted to the Hoover Institution for its support of my work and, in particular, to Dr. Ramon H. Myers, who guided me well in completing this book. The competent and cheerful assistance I received from Anne Wallace, Nancy Kaul, Yoshida Kazunori, Lewis Bernstein, Phyllis McEldowney, and Pam Loewenstein is gratefully acknowledged. I express my special appreciation to Kyung S. Lee and Theodore J. Lee for their invariable support and to C. J. Kim for his friendly encouragement. It must be made absolutely clear that since I am the sole author of this book, none of the persons named here should be held responsible for any aspect of my interpretations or for any omissions.

Introduction

In the late 1960s and early 1970s when the People's Republic of China (PRC) launched a vigorous public campaign against Japanese Prime Minister Satō Eisaku's foreign policy and against what it called the revival of militarism in Japan, a number of distinguished Western scholars confidently predicted the inevitability of conflicts between China and Japan in the years ahead. They cited, as the primary reason for this pessimistic projection, the continuing importance of system differences, economic gaps, colonial legacy, mutual misperceptions, and regional rivalry between the two Asian neighbors. The potentially positive effects of their traditional cultural association, geographic proximity, and complementary economies were largely disregarded in the assessment of the strained Sino-Japanese relationship. In retrospect, the earlier prediction has proved to be less than accurate because China and Japan have achieved appreciable overall progress in policy cooperation since the diplomatic normalization in 1972. Both countries have made concerted efforts to help each other and to strike compromises on policy differences. The acrimonious disputes over Taiwan's diplomatic status, Japan's security dependence on the United States, and the revival of Japanese militarism have been defused, and a combination of pragmatic national interests seems to determine the direction of the new Sino-Japanese relationship.

These achievements and compromises made in Sino-Japanese relations are particularly evident in the functionally specific areas of economic diplomacy—the processes of negotiating and implementing agreements, both intergovernmental and nongovernmental, on economic issues. Since the early 1970s, the volume of two-way trade has increased tenfold, and it has been accompanied by the substantial increase in the number of agreements on technology transfer, plant export, scientific exchange, and financial cooperation. It was almost inconceivable in the late 1960s and early 1970s that China would accept, let alone request, government loans and grants, direct capital investment, economic policy advice, or suggestions for joint ventures or collaborative resource development from Japan. Now China eagerly solicits Japan's increasing participation in all these economic activities, and Japan is no longer passive, reactive, or insecure in its imaginative pursuit of Chinese markets and resources. This new and lively unfolding of Sino-Japanese economic interaction has been and is facilitated by the exchange of diplomatic establishments between Beijing and Tokyo, but it is also built upon the rich reservoir of cumulative common experience and the close personal and organizational networks between China and Japan that had been developing long before their diplomatic rapprochement.

Once the shadow of the U.S. containment-cum-isolation policy that had constrained Japan's economic cooperation with China was eliminated in the 1970s, the United States emerged as Japan's principal economic competitor and, to a lesser extent, collaborator in the China market. Although the Soviet Union strongly supported China's domestic and foreign economic policy during the 1950s, its direct role in current Sino-Japanese economic relations is patently limited. Other industrialized nations, especially West Germany, France, Canada, and Great Britain, seriously challenge Japan's status as the pre-eminent foreign economic presence in China, but the Japanese have effectively utilized their cultural ties, prewar experience, and geographic proximity with China as comparative advantages. In general, the process of bilateral economic diplomacy between China and Japan is intimately linked to their changing regional and global environments, over which the two superpowers, the United States and the Soviet Union, still exert a more credible influence than either Asian country.

In spite of the demonstration of tangible economic and diplomatic cooperation between China and Japan, it must be pointed out that all aspects of their economic diplomacy have not always been smooth, successful, or mutually beneficial. Negotiations for economic agreements or commercial contracts have often been protracted and tortuous, and attempts to implement them have encountered a fair amount of difficulty, setback, and frustration on both sides. The shifting politics of economic diplomacy has indeed been complex, multidimensional, and, at times, dysfunctional. Yet, traditional explanations are not necessarily sufficient to account for the set of substantive and procedural problems associated with the new economic diplomacy between the two countries. Differences of political and economic systems, the lingering effects of the colonial experience, the contrasting stages of economic development, and the conflicting approaches to regional issues are admittedly relevant to the underlying relationship between China and Japan, but it appears that another useful approach to examining the processes and problems of Sino-Japanese economic diplomacy is to focus on domestic bureaucratic politics in both countries. Just as the consensus-oriented resolution of bureaucratic infighting has been amply noted in Japan's policymaking processes, it has been assumed that the way in which China negotiates and implements economic agreements with Japan is to a great extent related to its own bureaucratic dynamics—such as policy differences, factional struggles, interinstitutional conflicts, personality clashes, and central-local gaps. The function and relevance of these intrabureaucratic factors seem to loom larger in proportion to the progress of China's "four modernizations" campaign and to the increasing complexity and pervasiveness of new economic relationships between China and Japan.

In an attempt to examine the achievements and difficulties of Sino-Japanese economic diplomacy since the early 1970s, I pursue in this book three central questions: how China and Japan have conducted (or have failed to consummate) their economic negotiations; what they have accomplished or missed; and why problems and difficulties have arisen and how both countries have attempted to resolve them. Added to these questions are the larger issues of whether this economic cooperation signifies a case of temporary and transitory convenience or progress toward a viable and productive relationship, and whether the two countries will reconfirm traditional images of each other or make serious efforts to learn from and adjust to each other. I will first present a brief historical description of Sino-Japanese economic relations in the postwar era and will then concentrate on a few salient examples of economic diplomacy in recent years: collaborative construction of a multibillion-dollar integrated steel complex in Shanghai's Baoshan County, the long-term joint offshore oil development project in the Sea of Bohai, and Japan's government loans (and grant) provided for several of China's important construction programs. A broad policy assessment will be offered in the concluding chapter.

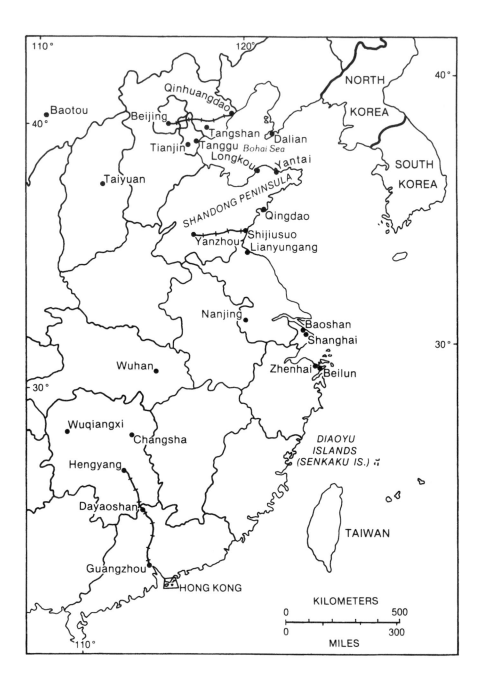

Patterns of
Economic Relations

ONE

The conclusion of the eight-year war (1937–1945) between China and Japan abruptly terminated their close economic relationships, which had been developing since the late nineteenth century; especially during the 1930s and early 1940s, Japan had not only strengthened its exploitative industrial programs in Manchuria (and Taiwan), but had also expanded its substantial economic and commercial activities in China proper.[1] In the immediate postwar period, the possibility of renewing Sino-Japanese economic interaction was effectively eliminated because of the uncertain domestic conditions of both countries and the changing U.S. policy in East Asia. While the United States was embroiled in the abortive negotiations and the military confrontation between the Chinese Communist Party (CCP) and the Kuomintang (KMT), Japan, under U.S. Occupation, was not ready to consider an independent economic policy toward China. The Japanese government was preoccupied with the immense tasks of rehabilitating its war-torn economy with massive U.S. assistance and taking care of the influx of its military and civilian repatriates from abroad, including more than 3 million returnees from China.

When the People's Republic of China (PRC) was established in 1949, it cautiously reopened modest trade with Japan, but any hope for revitalized Sino-Japanese economic relations quickly evaporated after the outbreak of the Korean War in June 1950. As a result of China's direct armed involvement in the war, the United States adopted a trade embargo policy against China and imposed it on Japanese exports to

China as well. The war also accelerated U.S. efforts to transform Japan into an anticommunist bastion in East Asia and to restructure the Occupation in accordance with the emerging bipolar regional alignment. In September 1951 Japan concluded the multilateral peace treaty with the United States and 47 other nations in San Francisco—over the protest of the Soviet Union and China. A U.S.-Japan security treaty was also signed. On the day (April 28, 1952) that both treaties came into force, Japan signed a bilateral peace treaty with the Republic of China (ROC), which voluntarily renounced its right to demand war reparations from Japan.[2] Intense U.S. pressure compelled Prime Minister Yoshida Shigeru to establish diplomatic relations with the ROC, and this relationship made it difficult, if not impossible, for the Japanese government to conduct direct economic diplomacy with the PRC for the next two decades. Hence China and Japan utilized a variety of unofficial or private channels to negotiate and implement their economic agreements.

Unofficial Economic Agreements

O   The list of Chinese complaints against the Yoshida government was long and the charges serious. It was accused of supporting the U.S. anti-Beijing containment policy, colluding with the "remnant KMT reactionaries," and cooperating with the Coordinating Committee (COCOM) and its China Committee (CHINCOM), which were set up to control exports of strategic commodities to communist countries.[3] Yet the PRC showed a degree of economic realism in signing the first private trade agreement with three prominent Japanese individuals in June 1952. They and Nan Hanchen (president of the Chinese People's Bank and chairman of the China Council for Promotion of International Trade) agreed to conduct a barter-based trade until the end of 1952.[4] (From June to December of that year, such trade totaled £30 million.) The agreement was completely devoid of any political message and received a tacit blessing from the Yoshida government, which wished to promote trade with China under the principle of separation of economic and political (and diplomatic) issues.

In the subsequent private trade agreements concluded in October 1953 and May 1955, the Chinese introduced politically inspired demands and obtained various promises and concessions from Japanese negotiators, some of whom were influential leaders of the ruling political parties.[5] The two sides decided in 1953 to exchange resident trade missions and in 1955 further agreed to provide diplomatic privileges to trade representatives. Strongly pressed by China's persistent request, the Japanese negotiators obtained an explicit commitment from Prime Minister Hatoyama Ichirō that his government would "support and assist" implementation of the private trade agreements. However, the Hatoyama government was not yet prepared to allow China's resident trade mission in Tokyo. The prime minister felt constrained by the absence of policy consensus in his own cabinet and among Japan's conservative leaders, and also by the Eisenhower administration's rigid anti-Beijing attitude as exemplified by the U.S.-Taiwan security treaty (1954) and the congressional resolution on Formosa (1955).

The timing of the private trade accords was not conducive to any substantive improvement in Beijing-Tokyo diplomacy, but as shown in Table 1, they stimulated dramatic increases in the amounts of two-way commercial transactions: in 1953, such trade totaled approximately $34 million (121 percent increase over the previous year); in 1954, $60 million (75 percent); in 1955, $109 million (83 percent); and in 1956, $151 million (38 percent). These increases were accompanied by various exchanges of industrial exhibits and economic delegations and by other private agreements on fisheries and cultural programs. However, the value of Sino-Japanese trade remained relatively modest in terms of the countries' respective global trade; the $151 million represented 4.5 percent of China's total foreign trade during 1956 and only 2.6 percent of Japan's total foreign trade.[6]

The inauguration of Prime Minister Kishi Nobusuke (ex-director of the General Affairs Board of Manchukuo and minister of commerce and industry in Tōjō Hideki's wartime cabinet) in 1957 was not welcomed by the Chinese. Kishi was the first Japanese prime minister to visit Taiwan, and he repeated his anti-Beijing rhetoric in his travels throughout Asia and the United States. Premier Zhou Enlai publicly attacked Kishi's collusion with Chiang Kai-shek and cooperated with the Japan Socialist Party (JSP) in denouncing the Kishi government. The growing hostility between the two governments was reflected in the extremely difficult unofficial trade negotiations. After protracted discussions, both sides finally signed the fourth private trade agreement in March 1958, which included the conditions that the Japanese government accept China's resident trade mission in Tokyo, provide Chinese trade personnel with semidiplomatic privileges, and allow them to use their national flag at the mission.[7] Confronted with mounting pressure from Taipei and Washington, the Kishi government then refused to extend any special privileges to Chinese trade representatives, including the right to fly their national flag in Japan. Angered by the Kishi government's negative response, the Chinese seized upon a minor flag incident at Nagasaki in May 1958 to suspend all economic and cultural

TABLE 1
SINO-JAPANESE TRADE 1950–1969
(in thousands of dollars)

YEAR	CHINESE IMPORTS		CHINESE EXPORTS		TOTAL	
	Amount	Percentage Change from Previous Year	Amount	Percentage Change from Previous Year	Amount	Percentage Change from Previous Year
1950	19,633		39,328		58,961	
1951	5,828	29.7	21,606	54.9	27,434	46.5
1952	599	10.3	14,903	69.0	15,502	56.5
1953	4,539	757.8	29,700	199.3	34,239	220.9
1954	19,097	420.7	40,770	137.3	59,867	174.9
1955	28,547	149.5	80,778	198.1	109,325	182.6
1956	67,339	235.9	83,647	103.6	150,986	138.1
1957	60,485	89.8	80,483	96.2	140,968	93.4
1958	50,600	83.7	54,427	67.6	105,027	74.5
1959	3,648	7.2	18,917	34.8	22,565	21.5
1960	2,726	74.7	20,729	109.6	23,455	103.9
1961	16,639	610.4	30,895	149.0	47,534	142.1
1962	38,460	231.1	46,020	149.0	84,480	177.7
1963	62,417	162.3	74,599	162.1	137,016	162.2
1964	152,739	244.7	157,750	211.5	310,489	226.2
1965	245,036	160.4	224,705	142.4	469,741	151.3
1966	313,150	128.6	306,237	136.3	621,387	132.3
1967	288,294	91.5	269,439	88.0	557,733	89.8
1968	325,439	112.9	224,185	83.2	549,624	98.5
1969	390,803	120.1	234,540	104.6	625,343	113.8

SOURCE: Japan-China Economic Association.

relations with Japan and to terminate private agreements on trade, fisheries, steel exports, and other related matters.[8]

Foreign Minister Fujiyama Aiichirō's efforts to relax Tokyo-Beijing hostility failed because the Chinese asked the Kishi government to accept "three political principles": (1) not pursue a policy inimical to China, (2) not join a two-China plot, and (3) not obstruct normalization of Sino-Japanese relations.[9] On the request of the JSP and the General Council of Trade Unions (*Sōhyō*), in early 1959 the Chinese granted a special trade concession to small and medium-sized Japanese companies, which were particularly hard hit by China's trade suspension. However, this action did not arrest the drastic decline of two-way trade to approximately $22 million during 1959—a 78.5 percent decrease from the preceding year.

Friendship Trade and Memorandum Trade

O   The failure of the Great Leap Forward Movement, coupled with the deterioration of Sino-Soviet economic relations, forced China's moderate political leaders (such as Zhou Enlai, Chen Yun, and Deng Xiaoping) to readjust the extreme Maoist emphasis on self-reliance and to follow the pragmatic avenue of increasing economic relations with Japan and other noncommunist industrial nations in the early 1960s. This change in China's ideological and economic orientation coincided with the emergence of Prime Minister Ikeda Hayato, who softened Kishi's hard-line cold war rhetoric and attached a high policy priority to Japan's economic expansion abroad. In his discussions with Japanese business leaders in August 1960, Premier Zhou Enlai initiated the concept of "friendship trade"—the resumption of trade with Japanese companies that China specifically recognized as "friendly" toward its policy positions. The number of "friendly companies" grew from 11 in 1960 to 190 in 1962, but they were limited in their ability to satisfy China's growing requirements for long-term credits and complete industrial plants and to exert political influence over the Liberal-Democratic Party (LDP) government's decision-making process.

Hence, in September 1962, Premier Zhou Enlai invited to Beijing Dietman Matsumura Kenzō, a senior LDP statesman, who advocated close economic cooperation between Japan and China and who had received an explicit blessing from Prime Minister Ikeda. Zhou and Matsumura decided to start comprehensive long-range "memorandum trade" as a gradual and cumulative way to normalize Sino-Japanese economic and diplomatic relations.[10] They also agreed to exchange trade liaison offices and to adopt a method of deferred payment for Japan's exports of industrial plants to China. As political guarantors of this agreement, they appointed their trusted lieutenants—Liao Chengzhi (deputy director of the Foreign Affairs Staff Office in the State Council) for China and LDP Dietman Takasaki Tatsunosuke (ex-minister of international trade and industry) for Japan. Liao had been born and raised in Japan and was educated at Waseda University; Takasaki had served as president of an industrial corporation in Manchuria before 1945 and had met with Zhou Enlai during the Bandung Conference (1955). The subsequent Liao-Takasaki negotiations produced the memorandum on "overall trade" for the 1963–1967 period, in which the average two-way trade was projected to be about $100 million per year. Unlike friendship trade, memorandum trade enjoyed a semiofficial status because it was sponsored by prominent members of the governing LDP and was partially financed by the government–controlled Export-Import Bank (Eximbank).

The initiation of memorandum trade was the first successful move in China's decade-long efforts to establish its resident trade mission in Tokyo. In 1964, Sun Pinghua (one of China's "old Japan hands" and a former student at Tokyo Engineering College) set up the Liao liaison office in Tokyo, and Sōma Tsunetoshi, who had "resigned" from the Ministry of International Trade and Industry (MITI), headed the Takasaki liaison office in Beijing. In the absence of a diplomatic establishment, the Liao liaison office in effect assumed a wide range of political and semidiplomatic activities in Japan. In accordance with the Zhou-Matsumura agreement, the Japanese government was flexible in applying Eximbank funds to finance China trade in 1963, but in 1964 this attitude was challenged by the combined pressure from Taipei and Washington—both vehemently opposed any form of Japanese "foreign aid programs" to China. In May 1964 Prime Minister Ikeda encouraged former Prime Minister Yoshida Shigeru to send a private letter to Taipei; it gave assurances that Japanese Eximbank funds would no longer be used to finance exports of industrial plants to China.

In spite of the Chinese disappointment with the Yoshida letter, the volume of Sino-Japanese trade grew steadily between 1963 and 1966 because China adopted a pragmatic economic policy to expand foreign trade following the disastrous Great Leap Forward Movement of the late 1950s and because the combination of friendship and memorandum trade had positive effects upon their economic relationship. The rates of its annual growth were approximately 62 percent in 1963, 126 percent in 1964, 51 percent in 1965, and 32 percent in 1966. The $470 million figure achieved during 1965 surpassed the declining Sino-Soviet trade ($417 million) and the moderately increasing Japanese-Soviet trade

($408 million). The following year Sino-Japanese trade totaled slightly more than $621 million; it accounted for 14 percent of China's total foreign trade and made China Japan's fourth largest trading partner. The amount dropped to about $558 million in 1967, but Japan still remained China's number one trading partner.[11]

The political environment of Sino-Japanese economic relations markedly deteriorated during the Chinese Cultural Revolution. Radical Red Guards paralyzed the Ministries of Foreign Affairs and Foreign Trade in 1967 and purged the key personnel of these and other central bureaucracies. The two principal promoters of China's economic relations with Japan, Liao Chengzhi and Nan Hanchen, were temporarily removed from their respective positions. A number of Japanese trade representatives and newspaper correspondents stationed in China were arrested on espionage charges or summarily expelled from China; the number of Japanese trade personnel in Beijing had dwindled from 100 to 20 by mid-1968. Shipments of Japanese goods were held up or disrupted at Chinese ports. The Canton Trade Fair was postponed for one month in the fall of 1967. Japanese trade negotiators were required to praise the Cultural Revolution, to study the little red book of Chairman Mao's quotations, and to listen to prolonged political lectures delivered by their Chinese counterparts. The Chinese trade liaison office in Japan was used to direct a public campaign against the Japan Communist Party, which opposed the Maoists and the Cultural Revolution. The Chinese launched a particularly vicious attack against Prime Minister Satō Eisaku for his state visits to Taipei and the United States.[12]

It was in this political context that the Chinese negotiators, headed by Assistant Minister of Foreign Trade Liu Xiwen, refused to renew the 1963–1967 memorandum trade agreement for another five-year period; in 1968, they accepted only its one-year extension and a projected trade volume of $100 million. In return the Japanese negotiators—LDP Dietmen Furui Yoshimi and Tagawa Seiichi (former secretary to Matsumura Kenzō)—were forced to accept China's "three political principles" and to contradict Satō's China policy.[13] The Japanese companies involved in memorandum or friendship trade were required to engage in a variety of explicitly political activities, such as mass demonstrations and the issuance of joint communiqués, in support of Chinese positions. This overt injection of politics into economic matters, plus the chaos created by the Cultural Revolution, caused a two-year (1967–68) decline in Sino-Japanese trade.

The political relationship between Beijing and Tokyo reached an all-time low during 1969 and 1970 when the Chinese assailed the revival of Japanese militarism. As usual, the Chinese exploited trade as a means to articulate and publicize their anti-Satō stand in Japan. In order to extend the memorandum trade for another year in 1970, Dietman Furui was compelled to pay a high political price. In a joint communiqué signed with Liu Xiwen, Furui agreed to condemn the Nixon-Satō joint communiqué of 1969 and pledged to "renounce and smash the revival of Japanese militarism."[14] The LDP counterattacked China's growing criticisms but hesitated to censure or restrain Furui's submissive economic diplomacy.

The Chinese practice of linking trade with political considerations reached a climax in 1970 when Premier Zhou announced that China would no longer trade with any of the following Japanese companies: (1) industries and firms assisting South Korea's rivalry with North Korea or supporting Taiwan's design to "recover" China; (2) large capital investors in South Korea or Taiwan; (3) suppliers of arms to assist U.S. war efforts in Indochina; and (4) joint ventures or subsidiaries of U.S. companies. Once again a majority of Japanese industrial and trading firms related to China followed the historic pattern, accommodating to Zhou's "four conditions" and practicing "unprincipled" economic diplomacy. The episode suggested to the Chinese that they could use economic considerations as an instrument to influence Japan's business communities and their political sponsors and that the imposition of the most stringent political conditions did not adversely affect a significant increase (31.6 percent over the previous year) in Sino-Japanese trade during 1970.

Processes of Diplomatic Normalization

○   As China restored internal political order following the Cultural Revolution and made diplomatic advances to NATO member-states and the United Nations in the early 1970s, a number of significant political and economic developments took place in Japan that directly challenged Prime Minister Satō's anti-China policy. Most important was the organization of a new suprapartisan Dietmen's League for Promoting Restoration of Japan-China Diplomatic Relations in December 1970. It embraced all national political parties and its membership exceeded a simple majority of the members of the national Diet. The league, chaired by LDP Dietman Fujiyama Aiichirō, criticized the Satō government's anachronistic ties with Taiwan and urged it to establish diplomatic relations with China. The fact that one-fifth of the LDP dietmen cooperated with the opposition parties to oppose a major foreign policy principle of their own prime minister was an unusual political development. It signified the erosion of the political base for Satō's China policy.

This interparty coalition on China was formed at the same time that a clearly pro-Beijing tilt occurred in Japan's mainstream business circles. In order not to be left out of the China market, which NATO member-states had begun to penetrate, Japan's key industries, particularly in steel and chemicals, took an unqualified pro-Beijing position and dissociated themselves from Taiwan and South Korea. Further, *Keizai Dōyūkai* (the Japan Committee for Economic Development), one of Japan's four most powerful business associations, showed a distinctly favorable orientation toward China. It is quite clear that even before Nixon's shocking announcement in July 1971 that Special Assistant Henry Kissinger had made a secret trip to Beijing to make arrangements for Nixon's forthcoming China visit, Prime Minister Satō's anti-Beijing policy had been weakened by Zhou's shrewd diplomatic offensive and by the mounting domestic pressure from the Dietmen's League and the *Dōyūkai*-led business community. The Nixon shock made this pressure so pervasive that no responsible Japanese leader could affort to ignore it. Japanese businessmen competed to jump on the bandwagon and to make their pilgrimages to Beijing. The most impressive economic missions to China were organized by the Kansai region in September 1971 and by the Tokyo area in November 1971. These representatives agreed with Premier Zhou that the PRC government represented China and that Taiwan was China's territory. Given their close ties with Japan's ruling political elite, Japan's pro-Beijing business leaders exerted a considerable influence over their government's China policy. In the first half of 1972 the government allowed Japan's Export-Import Bank to finance Japanese plant exports to China. Most important, the politics of economic diplomacy, which had developed in an unofficial or private fashion, was a positive influence on Prime Minister Tanaka Kakuei's decision to establish diplomatic relations with China in September 1972.

Now that the Joint Statement signed by Tanaka and by Zhou Enlai in September 1972 had established diplomatic relations between China and Japan and had eliminated the controversy over Taiwan's legal status that had often constrained the normal development of economic relations since 1945, the governments of both countries fully expected to assume direct responsibility for bilateral economic diplomacy and to replace or complement the already existing private arrangements. Article Nine of the Joint Statement specified that

in order to further develop the relations between the two
countries and broaden the exchange of visits, the Government of
the People's Republic of China and the Government of Japan
agree to hold negotiations aimed at the conclusion of agreements
on trade, navigation, aviation, fishery, etc., in accordance with
the needs and taking into consideration the existing
nongovernmental agreements.[15]

Just as the Republic of China had done in 1952, the PRC renounced "its
demand for war indemnities from Japan," an amount estimated at $50
billion.[16] Indeed, Beijing's (as well as Taipei's) magnanimous decision
contrasted favorably with Itō Hirobumi's forcible extraction of massive
reparations from Li Hung-chang at the end of the Sino-Japanese War
(1894–95) and with Japan's payment of sizable war reparations to some
Southeast Asian nations in the 1950s and 1960s. The Japanese government terminated its diplomatic relations with Taipei and unilaterally
nullified the Japan-Taiwan peace treaty, but it obtained Beijing's agreement that Japan would continue to maintain its economic and other
nondiplomatic relations with Taiwan.

The hitherto semiofficial formula for memorandum trade was to
be incorporated into the new intergovernmental arrangements—
namely, the governmental agreement on trade would replace the
memorandum trade agreement and the embassies would absorb the
trade liaison offices. The Chinese decided to abolish the requirement
that Japan accept Zhou's "three political principles" or "four conditions" and the system for recognizing Japan's "friendly companies."
However, they agreed to continue their trade relationship with those
former friendly companies. The Japanese Council for Promotion of
International Trade (under President Fujiyama Aiichirō) was designated
to represent and coordinate the interests of more than 200 former
friendly companies. Fujiyama also chaired the 411-member reorganized
Dietman's League for Japan-China Friendship.

The Japanese government no longer regarded the Yoshida letter as
politically binding and intended to relax COCOM regulations in regard
to China. Since the demise of the memorandum trade formula limited
the opportunity for Japan's mainstream business entities to enter the
China market collectively and to promote long-term, large-scale, and
barter-based trade with China, *Keidanren* (Japanese Federation of Economic Organizations) Vice-President Inayama Yoshihiro (president of
Nippon Steel Corporation) cooperated with other leaders of *Keizai
Dōyūkai, Nisshō* (the Japanese Chamber of Commerce), and the
memorandum trade office to create the Japan-China Economic Association (JCEA) in November 1972. Partially financed by the Japanese gov-

ernment, this association promised to assume a leading "private" role in future Sino-Japanese economic cooperation. On the other hand, the Japanese government fully financed the Interchange Association, which was set up in December 1972 under another *Keidanren* vice-president (Horikoshi Teizō) to coordinate Japan-Taiwan trade;[17] its Nationalist Chinese counterpart was called the East Asian Relations Association. The two institutions agreed to exchange branch offices in Japan and Taiwan—the functional equivalent of the memorandum trade liaison offices previously stationed in Beijing and Tokyo.

The patterns of economic interaction between China and Japan from the end of the Pacific War in 1945 to the diplomatic rapprochement in 1972 formed the background for the new era of a normalized relationship. They can be summarized as follows.

1. The process of economic diplomacy, even at the non-governmental level, was determined to a great extent by the degree of political hostility or reconciliation existing between Beijing and Tokyo. In general, the relaxation of political tension between the two governments facilitated economic cooperation, and vice versa. The primacy of political considerations was particularly pronounced among the Chinese, who tended to conceive of economic relations as one aspect of their overall policy toward Japan, whereas the Japanese regarded trade expansion per se as a primary foreign policy goal. This conceptual dissonance often compounded the difficulties in resolving what would ordinarily be called purely economic issues.

2. Shifting priorities in China's domestic policies, especially ideologically inspired campaigns (such as the Great Leap Forward Movement and the Cultural Revolution) and economic plans, influenced the extent to which China valued and conducted its economic relations with Japan. Whereas the erratic Maoist ideological exhortations caused a widely fluctuating wave in China's foreign economic policy, the substantive thrust of Japan's international economic policy was relatively independent of its incremental domestic political changes.

3. In most cases, the Chinese took the initiative in Sino-Japanese economic diplomacy. The Japanese positions were largely reactive in nature. This difference indicated that the attitude of Japanese politicians and businessmen toward China was ambivalent due in part to the recent history of Japanese invasion in China; although they wished to revive traditional economic ties with China, they were reluctant to assume an assertive posture lest it heighten China's understandable sensitivity. Hence the Japanese were psychologically predisposed to make concessions or to tolerate abuses in their economic interaction

with China. The fact that associations acted as representatives of private companies and nongovernmental organizations also made it easier than it otherwise would be for the Japanese to accept China's tough political demands.

4. The differences in economic systems did not present an insurmountable impediment to economic relations; both systems—socialist and capitalist—appeared to be adaptable. However, Japan's open, pluralistic, and competitive political system, in contrast to China's authoritarian political system, was both a liability and an asset in economic diplomacy—a liability because it was subjected to China's penetration and manipulation, but an asset because Japan enjoyed a wide range of policy options and organizational channels that made possible flexible economic relations with China.

5. In their attempts to influence Japan's diverse economic and political activities and actors, the Chinese shrewdly practiced a tactic of checks and balances. They encouraged and exploited the appearance of competition or contradictions between Japan and the United States, the Japanese government and private industries, memorandum trade and friendship trade, LDP and JSP, pro-Beijing and pro-Taipei coalitions in the governing parties and bureaucracies, and Tokyo and Kansai. All these balancing operations were useful to China's interests, but its naked political intervention in Japan proved to be counterproductive. Yet the Japanese were both unable and unwilling to find and use to their advantage any contradictions that may have existed in China's political and economic policies and processes.

6. The United States and, to a lesser extent, the Soviet Union exerted a significant influence over the regional political environment that affected both the nature and direction of Sino-Japanese economic relations. Even after the Occupation, the United States insisted that the Japanese respect and follow its policy of containing China militarily and isolating it in the diplomatic and economic fields. The U.S. pressure was effective during the 1950s, but its effect lessened during the 1960s when Japan regained its political and economic self-confidence. Soviet influence, too, declined in the aftermath of China's ideological challenge and Japan's economic ascendancy.

7. The Taiwan factor restricted the Japanese government's ability to conduct direct economic diplomacy with China until 1972. Although the Ministry of International Trade and Industry frequently argued that the Japanese government should adopt a forward-looking economic policy toward China, the Ministry of Foreign Affairs (*Gaimushō*) usually prevailed in honoring Japan's strict adherence to its peace treaty and its diplomatic relations with Taiwan. At times the Chinese took ex-

treme measures (such as trade suspension and presentation of Zhou's "four conditions") to rectify this situation, but they achieved only mixed results.

8. The absence of diplomatic relations between China and Japan did not always prevent them from concluding nongovernmental economic agreements or using the Export-Import Bank funds. In the absence of diplomatic exchange, economic interaction was the most tangible and creative aspect of the Sino-Japanese relationship until 1972. The experiments in economic diplomacy strengthened a system of close personal and organizational networks between the two countries, which significantly contributed to ultimate diplomatic normalization.

Not all of these and other patterns that emerged before 1972 remained intact in the new era of normalization. Some were perhaps inherent in the complex relationship between China and Japan, but others were invented or experimented with as transitional measures given the lack of diplomatic representation. It was fair to assume that the established patterns and the cumulative experience served as a set of precedents and lessons that influenced the subsequent conduct of their economic diplomacy.

Governmental Economic Agreements

○   In order to provide the legal framework for normal economic relations, the Chinese and Japanese governments started negotiating a trade agreement near the end of 1972. This legal arrangement was not an absolute requirement for expanding trade between the two countries, but it was a useful way to agree upon procedural norms and to regularize the dynamics of their bilateral economic diplomacy. A preliminary exploration took place in November 1972 when Japan's first large-scale governmental economic delegation, led by Assistant Minister of Foreign Affairs Tōgō Fumihiko, visited Beijing.[18] The Japanese government leaders, notably Nakasone Yasuhiro (minister of international trade and industry), decided that the intergovernmental trade agreement should encompass all aspects of the private commercial accords and all channels of communication between Japan and China that operated in the absence of diplomatic relations. Although the Chinese had vigorously attacked Nakasone (former minister of defense) as an advocate of Japanese militarism in the 1960s, they welcomed him to Beijing in January 1973 as the first Japanese cabinet minister to visit China since the diplomatic rapprochement. He was accompanied by leading Japanese businessmen, including Inayama Yoshihiro (Nippon Steel president and president of the JCEA). After a round of meetings with

Premier Zhou Enlai and Vice-Premier Li Xiannian, Nakasone promptly agreed with them that the trade agreement should be concluded by the end of 1973 (when the semiofficial memorandum trade agreement would expire) and that representatives of the Japanese and Chinese governments should hold regular consultations on economic matters.[19]

After Nakasone's successful visit to China, it took six months for both sides to prepare and exchange their respective drafts of the trade agreement. The Chinese draft was a relatively brief document that emphasized the general principles of equality and mutual benefits, but the Japanese text was carefully crafted and very detailed. On the basis of these drafts, the two governments conducted substantive negotiations in Tokyo in August 1973. The Japanese negotiators were headed by a diplomat (Takashima Masuo, director of the Bureau of Asian Affairs of the Ministry of Foreign Affairs); the Chinese were led by a trade official (Xi Yesheng, director of the Fourth Department of the Ministry of Foreign Trade). In view of China's bureaucratic system, which was based on a vertical division of specific functions, the Chinese Ministry of Foreign Trade had a greater degree of jurisdictional autonomy and policy responsibility in the area of economic diplomacy than did the Japanese Ministry of International Trade and Industry.[20]

Since the principal purpose of the trade agreement was to facilitate and promote economic and commercial relations, the "most-favored-nation status" clause was a central point of the negotiations. This clause had been absent from the private trade agreements concluded during the 1950s and 1960s. The Japanese proposed to apply it to China to the extent that it was practiced by the General Agreement on Tariffs and Trade (GATT) member-states, but they were not prepared to satisfy the Chinese hope that the COCOM regulations would be lifted for Japanese exports of strategic commodities to China, even though the Australian government had just terminated its adherence to COCOM restrictions in its trade agreement with China (July 1973).[21] Since Japan promised to seek a gradual relaxation of COCOM regulations in its China trade, the Chinese did not insist upon Japan's outright COCOM renunciation, which was not a practicable policy option. Hence the most-favored-nation treatment was extended to the areas of customs duties, internal taxes, and customs rules, formalities, and procedures, but not to "the issue of import and export licenses" as specified in the Sino-Australian trade agreement (Article Four). On the other hand, the Japanese accommodated China's wish that this treatment not apply to "special favors accorded to neighboring countries by either Contracting Party for the purpose of facilitating border trade."[22] China maintained special border trade relations with its neighbors and provided preferential pricing systems to them; for example, China exported Daqing oil to North Korea at a cut-rate "friendship price" as a form of economic assistance.

The two governments struck compromises on other issues: to institute a bilateral subcabinet-level Mixed Committee on economic matters, to submit this administrative agreement on trade to parliamentary ratification procedures, and to include the provision that the agreement, after an initial three-year period, would continue unless either party gave notification of its termination three months in advance. They also agreed upon the forms of payments in yen, yuan, or any other mutually acceptable convertible currencies, arbitration procedures, and exchange of industrial technology and trade exhibitions. The Chinese made it clear in the agreement that they would continue to respect the "achievements thus far accumulated through existing nongovernment trade relations." This was an attempt to placate the fears shown by those "old friends" (especially "friendly companies"), who had conducted business with China before the rapprochement and were afraid of being left out of the new trade arrangements. This unique provision reflected the peculiar postwar pattern of Sino-Japanese economic relations.

On January 5, 1974, the ten-article trade agreement was signed in Beijing.[23] This occasion marked Foreign Minister Ōhira Masayoshi's first, triumphant return to Beijing after diplomatic normalization. Ōhira, despite his cold and fever, met with Chairman Mao Zedong and Vice-Chairman Wang Hongwen; the meeting was prominently reported on Chinese television and on the front page of China's official newspaper (*Renmin Ribao*), accompanied by two large pictures.[24] This publicity signified Mao's approval of Sino-Japanese cooperation as manifested in the trade agreement. Ōhira also had two separate meetings with Premier Zhou Enlai. The two leaders attached a great deal of importance to the trade agreement, not only as a "constitution" for guiding the future of Sino-Japanese economic relations but also as a symbolic reaffirmation of their new diplomatic cooperation; it was the first major intergovernmental legal pact duly signed in the postwar era. (The Zhou-Tanaka Joint Statement was a political document with no binding legal effects.)

On the last day of Ōhira's four-day stay in Beijing, the two governments broke a deadlock in their fourteen-month-old civil aviation negotiations; Ōhira agreed to abrogate the reciprocal agreement between Japan's flag carrier (Japan Air Lines) and Taiwan's flag carrier (China Air Lines).[25] On April 20, 1974, Foreign Minister Ji Pengfei and Ambassador Ogawa Heishirō signed the nineteen-article agreement on civil aviation

and an accompanying three-article annex in Beijing.[26] Japan accommodated China's interests by formally terminating flight and service
arrangements between Japan Air Lines and China Air Lines and by
opening JAL's link with China's flag carrier (Civil Aviation Administration of China or CAAC); Japan also obtained China's tacit concession to
the subsequent resumption of flights between JAL's dummy company
(Japan Asia Airways) and China Air Lines. After both sides ratified the
aviation agreement, the first regular commercial flights were exchanged
between Tokyo and Beijing on September 29, 1974, in commemoration
of the second anniversary of Sino-Japanese diplomatic normalization. A
year later, flights between Tokyo and Taipei were resumed by Japan
Asia Airways and China Air Lines. The CAL flights were allowed to use
Tokyo's old international airport (Haneda), and the new Narita Airport
near Tokyo was to be used for the CAAC flights. The Tanaka government made a substantial concession to China in regard to diplomatic
formalities and procedural matters but gained maximum possible economic benefit from its de facto "two-China" practices in international
civil aviation. The pattern established in these aviation settlements
paved the way for conclusion of a similar governmental agreement on
maritime transport in November 1974.[27]

   This pact covered all practical intergovernmental agreements originally referred to in the Zhou-Tanaka Joint Statement except for the one
on fisheries, which proved to be the most protracted case of Sino-
Japanese economic diplomacy. The Japanese sought to enjoy the free-
dom of fishing operations in China's vast and resource-rich coastal seas,
but the Chinese unilaterally drew various restricted zones in the Yellow
Sea and the East China Sea and declared a 200-mile territorial zone for
the protection of marine resources. The negotiations, which had started
in June 1973, were suspended twice largely because the Chinese insisted
upon Japan's acceptance of the precedents of restricted areas set by the
previous private agreements on fisheries. On August 20, 1975, Japanese
Foreign Minister Miyazawa Kiichi and Chinese Ambassador to Japan
Chen Chu signed an eight-article fisheries agreement and its two
lengthy annexes in Tokyo.[28] The two governments agreed upon the
specific boundaries of fishing activities in the Yellow Sea and the East
China Sea, the numbers and capacities of each side's fishing vessels to
be allowed per year, the establishment of mutual resource protection
areas, and the procedures for communications and assistance in the
event of calamities. They also agreed to disagree on the sensitive political issue of China's unilaterally declared military and protective zones.
In the exchange of notes, the Chinese ambassador specified China's
"military warning area" in the Yellow Sea, "trawl-free zone," and

"military operational area" (south of the 27th parallel in the East China Sea) and limited Japan's fishing operations in all three areas. Foreign Minister Miyazawa reserved Japan's "right" to challenge the Chinese position but promised to discourage Japanese fishing activities in the areas designated for marine resource protection.

The Long-Term Trade Agreement

○   Because the two governments had successfully negotiated four administrative agreements by 1975, a smooth and rapid increase of economic cooperation was expected. Facilitated by the governmental trade agreement, which reduced tariff barriers by one-third on the average, trade between China and Japan grew dramatically after diplomatic normalizaton (see Table 2). The volume of two-way commercial transactions during 1975 (approximately $3.8 billion) was more than triple the volume registered during 1972 ($1.1 billion) and established Japan's undisputed status as China's number one partner in total foreign trade. China became the number three buyer of Japanese goods in the world and the number eight exporter to the Japanese market. About 90 percent of Japanese exports to China consisted of steel, machinery and equipment, chemicals (especially fertilizers), and synthetic fibers. The Chinese in turn sold crude oil, foodstuffs, minerals, and other primary products to Japan. The expansion of trade stimulated an increasing number of visitors from each nation to the other with emphasis on exchanges of specialized economic delegations, industrial exhibitions, and technical information (see Table 3).

Yet, the Chinese were wary of a widening deficit in their Japan trade during 1975 ($728 million in 1975 versus $118 million in 1972). This issue was a key agenda item of the first Mixed Committee meeting held at Beijing in April 1975. The Japanese business community, too, was concerned about this issue as well as about the future of China's Fifth Five-Year Economic Plan (1976–1980). The *Keidanren* delegation (led by President Dokō Toshio) visited China in October 1975 and sought to solve the problem of trade imbalance by encouraging an increase in China's oil exports to Japan. In November Minister of International Trade and Industry Kōmoto Toshio and Vice-Premier Li Xiannian agreed upon the need for China's stable long-term oil supply.[29] Accordingly, the Japanese government, in cooperation with oil importers and energy industries, developed a five-year plan for oil imports from China. Japan agreed to purchase 10 million metric tons of Daqing crude oil in 1977 and to increase the volume each year, to about 15 million metric tons by 1981.[30] The plan was presented to Vice-Premier

TABLE 2
SINO-JAPANESE TRADE, 1970–1982
(in thousands of dollars)

YEAR	CHINESE IMPORTS		CHINESE EXPORTS		TOTAL	
	Amount	Percentage Change from Previous Year	Amount	Percentage Change from Previous Year	Amount	Percentage Change from Previous Year
1970	568,878	145.6	253,818	108.2	822,696	131.6
1971	578,188	101.6	323,172	127.3	901,360	109.5
1972	608,921	105.3	491,116	152.0	1,100,036	122.0
1973	1,039,494	170.7	974,010	198.3	2,013,504	183.0
1974	1,984,475	190.9	1,304,768	133.9	3,289,243	163.4
1975	2,258,577	113.8	1,531,076	117.3	3,789,653	115.2
1976	1,662,568	73.6	1,370,915	89.5	3,033,483	80.0
1977	1,938,643	116.6	1,546,902	112.9	3,485,545	114.9
1978	3,048,748	157.3	2,030,292	131.2	5,079,040	145.7
1979	3,698,670	121.3	2,954,781	145.5	6,653,451	131.0
1980	5,078,335	137.3	4,323,374	146.3	9,401,709	141.3
1981	5,095,452	100.3	5,291,809	122.4	10,387,261	110.5
1982	3,510,825	68.9	5,352,417	101.1	8,863,242	85.3

SOURCE: Japan-China Economic Association.

TABLE 3
EXCHANGE OF VISITORS BETWEEN CHINA AND JAPAN, 1972–1981

YEAR	CHINESE TO JAPAN	JAPANESE TO CHINA	TOTAL VISITORS
1972	994	8,052	9,046
1973	1,991	10,238	12,339
1974	3,161	12,990	16,151
1975	4,441	16,655	21,096
1976	4,018	18,825	22,843
1977	4,039	23,445	27,484
1978	5,951	40,574	46,525
1979	11,622	54,094	65,696
1980	15,328	71,473	86,801
1981	17,550	109,977	127,527
Total	69,095	366,323	435,418

SOURCE: *Look Japan*, September 10, 1982.

Gu Mu (chairman of the State Capital Construction Commission, or SCCC) in January 1976 when a 21-member joint business-government delegation headed by Inayama Yoshihiro visited China.[31]

The timing of this proposal was not particularly auspicious. The state funeral for Premier Zhou Enlai had taken place four days prior to the Inayama delegation's arrival in Beijing, and China experienced a rapid series of dramatic developments in 1976. The tumultuous Tiananmen Square incident, the dismissal of Vice-Premier Deng Xiaoping, the rise of Premier Hua Guofeng, the tragic Tangshan area earthquake, the death of Chairman Mao Zedong, and the arrest of the Gang of Four— these events, taken together, caused political instability and economic disorder in China. In particular, the political ascendancy of the Gang of Four from late 1975 to September 1976 led to a renewed emphasis on the Maoist ideological principles of self-reliance (*zili gengsheng*) and independence (*duli zizhu*) and an autarkically inclined and antiforeign economic policy. The CCP's theoretical journal, *Hongqi* [Red flag], and other publications criticized the policy of reliance upon the most advanced foreign industrial plants, advocated by Zhou Enlai and Deng Xiaoping, and attacked oil exports as foreign exploitation of Chinese natural resources.[32] Deng was accused of adhering to the philosophy of servility to things foreign (*yangnu zhexue*) under the pretext of "four modernizations" (*sige xiandaihua*) and of ignoring the creative ability of China's working masses and the existence of class struggles at the international level. He was also attacked for the "revisionist" and "counterrevolutionary" policy of emphasizing material incentives, profit motivations, and "capitalistic restoration."

When I visited China's industrial plants and people's communes in early 1976, I was aware of the increasingly militant rhetoric of ideological exhortations in economic affairs and the heightened political campaign being launched against Chinese "revisionists." Fearful of this harsh political climate, Chinese economic negotiators expressed a preference to suspend any further discussion on Inayama's proposal.[33] Other ongoing economic negotiations were also suspended. Japanese cargoes were held up at the Tianjin ports following the Tangshan earthquake, and the number of contracts for Japan's principal exports (especially steel and fertilizers) to China was drastically reduced. Consequently, during 1976, Sino-Japanese trade (approximately $3 billion) showed a 20 percent decrease from the previous year (10.5 percent in China's exports and 26.4 percent in imports).

Premier Hua Guofeng (CCP chairman as of October 1976) attempted to legitimize his newly acquired political leadership and to provide a sense of policy direction to the restless nation. In doing so, he chose to rely upon his ability to produce demonstrable economic achievements as much as his claim to the Maoist ideological legacy; his earlier political prominence in Hunan Province was indeed a result of his pragmatic problem-solving and achievement-oriented capabilities in agriculture and finance.[34] Allied with Ye Jianying (CCP vice-chairman and minister of national defense) and Vice-Premiers Li Xiannian (ex-minister of finance), Yu Qiuli (chairman of the State Planning Commission, or SPC), and Gu Mu (chairman of the SCCC), Hua quickly embraced the late Premier Zhou's "four modernizations" slogan and revived the "Outline of the Ten-Year Plan for the Development of the National Economy" (1976–1985). The plan had been drafted by the State Council and adopted by the CCP Political Bureau in 1975 but had been shelved during the Gang of Four era. In early 1977, seeking aid for their ambitious economic programs, which required a massive influx of foreign capital and industrial technology, the Chinese invited Japanese business leaders back to Beijing. Inayama was quite eager to return to China in February 1977 and to resubmit his favorite proposal for long-term trade relations to Vice-Premier Gu and Minister of Foreign Trade Li Qiang.[35] The *Keidanren* delegation, which included President Dokō Toshio, Vice-President Inayama, and all seven other vice-presidents, visited China toward the end of March 1977 and received an unusually enthusiastic red-carpet treatment from their Chinese hosts, including Premier Hua Guofeng. The visit of this delegation marked an important turning point in Sino-Japanese economic relations; the two sides agreed on the basic principles governing Chinese shipments of oil and coal to Japanese industrial plants on a long-term basis.[36] Inayama (president of the JCEA) and Vice-Minister of Foreign Trade Liu Xiwen, who had represented China in the memorandum trade negotiations during the 1960s, were designated the chief negotiators for translating these principles into a concrete agreement. In addition to attaining agreement on bilateral economic objectives, the Chinese wished to discourage the *Keidanren*'s deepening involvement in the Siberian development projects and to encourage it to influence the LDP government to end the stalemate in the treaty of peace and friendship negotiations.

Inayama organized the Japanese Association for Promotion of the Japan-China Long-Term Trade Agreement; he became its chairman and Dokō Toshio and Fujiyama Aiichirō were made advisers. After extensive negotiations with Inayama in Tokyo in September 1977, Liu Xiwen organized the Chinese Association for Promotion of the China-Japan Long-Term Trade Agreement. It was through the efforts of these two associations and frequent Liu-Inayama negotiations that the Long-Term Trade Agreement was smoothly and successfully negotiated.[37] This process contrasted sharply with the intense political discussions that had accompanied the Sino-Japanese trade negotiations in the late 1960s. In January 1978 the Japanese association was reorganized into the Japan-China Long-Term Trade Committee (JCLTC), chaired by Inayama; Dokō was its "supreme adviser" and the other advisers were Fujiyama Aiichirō, Okazaki Kaheita (adviser to the JCEA), and Kamieda Kazuo (president of the Kansai Headquarters of the Japanese Council for Promotion of International Trade).[38] The Board of Directors enlisted 91 prominent leaders of Japan's economic, commercial, and financial circles, but no government officials or LDP dietmen were included. Its Chinese counterpart, the China-Japan Long-Term Trade Committee (CJLTC), was chaired by Vice-Minister of Foreign Trade Liu Xiwen; 19 other Chinese members represented a variety of economic bureaucracies, such as the Ministries of Foreign Trade, Metallurgical Industry, Petroleum Industry, Railways, and Coal Industry, the SPC, the Bank of China, and the China Council for Promotion of International Trade. Conspicuously absent was a representative of the Chinese Ministry of Foreign Affairs.[39]

On February 16, 1978, Liu Xiwen and Inayama signed the Long-Term Trade Agreement (1978–1985) in Beijing's Great Hall of the People.[40] In terms of its underlying principles and format, this agreement was a successor to the old memorandum trade agreement (1963–1967) concluded by LDP Dietmen Matsumura Kenzō and Takasaki Tatsunosuke. The two sides shortened this new agreement's duration from ten to eight years in order to make it coincide with the concluding year of China's Ten-Year Plan (1976–1985) and Sixth Five-Year Plan (1981–1985). The Chinese recognized the close relationship between the Ten-Year Plan and the Long-Term Trade Agreement. The principle of balanced trade was adopted; each side was expected to export about $10 billion to the other during the entire period (Article One). In the initial five years (1978–1982), Japan planned to sell to China $7–8 billion in industrial technology and plants and $2–3 billion in construction machinery and materials, and to apply the method of low-interest deferred payment (Eximbank funds and commercial bank loans) to these exports (Articles Two and Three). Table 4 shows the amounts of crude oil and coal (coking and steam) that China was obligated to supply to Japan in this five-year period. In addition, both sides agreed to establish the specific plans for the last three years (1983–1985) in 1981. They also promised not to abrogate this agreement or any contract signed under it without mutual consent (Article Ten).

The underlying economic formula for this agreement was relatively simple and straightforward: to fulfill the goals of its rapid industrialization plans, China would import Japan's advanced modern technology early in the eight-year period and would pay Japan back with increased exports of natural energy resources. Japanese capital was also expected to be used to finance some of China's natural resource development projects so that Japanese needs would be satisfied. Much of the Inayama-Liu economic diplomacy therefore focused on the assessment of Japan's projected domestic energy requirements and China's export capabilities. The Chinese tended to make overly optimistic predictions of their future oil and coal production and to offer a greater amount of this estimated production for export than Japan was prepared to pur-

TABLE 4
LONG-TERM TRADE AGREEMENT:
CHINESE EXPORTS TO JAPAN, 1978–1982
(in thousands of metric tons)

YEAR	CRUDE OIL	COKING COAL	STEAM COAL
1978	7,000	150–300	150–200
1979	7,600	500	150–200
1980	8,000	1,000	500–600
1981	9,500	1,500	1,000–1,200
1982	15,000	2,000	1,500–1,700
Total	47,100	5,150–5,300	3,300–3,900

SOURCE: *Ekonomisuto*, October 3, 1978, p. 13.

chase. As Table 5 shows, the Japanese functional subcommittee on Chinese oil imports surveyed Japan's future need for heavyweight Daqing crude oil and recommended importing a total volume of 43.1 million metric tons over the five-year period (1978–1982). This recommendation was a compromise of the policy differences existing between the petroleum refining industry and the steel industry in Japan; whereas the refiners, who were concerned about the new capital investment required for handling the waxy Daqing crude, resisted any significant oil imports from China, the steelmakers wanted to increase Japan's oil imports so they could sell China more steel.[41] Since the Chinese proposed to export as much as 50.5 million metric tons by 1982 and were willing to sell up to 15 million metric tons during 1982 alone, Inayama made a "political" decision to accommodate China's strong export desire by increasing the amount of Japan's 1982 oil import to 15 million metric tons. For the first four years (1978–1981) both sides made equal concessions. Inayama was confident that Japan's annual oil importation from China would easily reach 30 million metric tons by 1985.[42]

At this time the Chinese leaders and foreign oil experts reinforced each other's gross, unscientific overestimation of China's oil productivity. In his Ten-Year Plan, formally adopted by the First Session of the Fifth National People's Congress (NPC) in March 1978, Premier Hua Guofeng promised that China would construct ten Daqing-type oil and gas fields and produce 250 million metric tons of crude oil a year by 1985.[43] Based on the figure of 104 million metric tons of oil produced in 1978, Hua's plan called for an increase of almost 20 percent per year through 1985. Many Japanese and other foreign observers did not anticipate any serious difficulty in fulfilling the plan and even predicted that China would emerge as one of the world's largest oil exporters by 1990.[44]

The Chinese negotiators were much less successful in increasing their steam coal exports to Japan. A functional subcommittee on steam coal imports was established comprising representatives from thermal electric companies, cement makers, and coal industries. However, not all these Japanese consumers of steam coal were enthusiastic about the Chinese proposal. They expected to have a surplus stockpile of steam coal and wanted to protect Japan's growing domestic coal industry. For the first four years the Japanese negotiators were simply unable to meet China's obviously inflated expectations, but they grudgingly agreed to increase Japan's 1982 imports by 500,000 tons (see Table 6).

Even though the Long-Term Agreement was not an intergovernmental accord, both sides made it clear that it was based upon the spirit of the 1972 Zhou-Tanaka Joint Statement and the 1974 Trade Agreement and was signed with "support from each government." The

TABLE 5
NEGOTIATIONS ON CHINESE OIL EXPORTS TO JAPAN, 1978–1982
(in thousands of metric tons)

STAGE	1978	1979	1980	1981	1982	TOTAL
Chinese proposal	6,800–7,000	7,600–8,000	8,500–9,500	9,500–11,000	15,000	47,400–50,500
Japanese subcommittee recommendation	6,830	7,651	7,960	9,385	11,320	43,150
Japanese proposal	6,800	7,600	8,000	9,400	15,000	46,800
Final agreement	7,000	7,600	8,000	9,500	15,000	47,100

SOURCE: Japan-China Economic Association.

NEGOTIATIONS ON CHINESE STEAM COAL EXPORTS TO JAPAN, 1978–1982
(in thousands of metric tons)

STAGE	1978	1979	1980	1981	1982	TOTAL
Chinese proposal	500	500	1,000	1,500	2,000	5,500
Japanese proposal	150–200	150–200	500–600	1,000–1,200	1,000–1,200	2,800–3,400
Final agreement	150–200	150–200	500–600	1,000–1,200	1,500–1,700	3,300–3,900

SOURCE: Japan-China Economic Association.

Japanese practice of intimate business-government cooperation was unmistakably evident in the Long-Term Trade Agreement negotiations, particularly because Dokō Toshio and Inayama Yoshihiro obtained the commitments from Prime Minister Fukuda Takeo and Minister of International Trade and Industry Kōmoto Toshio that they would accommodate China's projected oil exports and solve the technical problems associated with importing heavyweight Daqing oil.[45] Minister Kōmoto supported the use of Eximbank funds to finance Japanese plant exports to China despite the pressure exerted by the United States and other Organization for Economic Cooperation and Development (OECD) member-states. He specifically instructed Yano Takahiko (director of the Bureau of International Trade Policy) and three other government officials to accompany Inayama's "private" business delegation to Beijing in February 1978. As *Keidanren* President Dokō explained in Beijing, the Long-Term Trade Agreement was viewed as a welcome step to stimulate Japan's sagging economy and to achieve a 7 percent real economic growth rate per annum in Japan.[46]

The Long-Term Trade Agreement created a positive climate for accelerating the four-year-long negotiations to conclude a treaty of peace and friendship between China and Japan. The Chinese demanded that an anti-hegemony clause be incorporated in the main text of the treaty just as it had been in the Zhou-Tanaka Joint Statement, but the Japanese were reluctant to accept it, mainly because of the strong objection raised by the Soviet Union. They also argued that the treaty, as a legally binding document, should not include an ill-defined and highly controversial concept like hegemony (*haken* in Japanese, or *baquan* in Chinese). On August 12, 1978, however, Foreign Ministers Huang Hua and Sonoda Sunao reached a compromise on the issue and signed the five-article Treaty of Peace and Friendship in Beijing.[47] The Chinese had every reason to rejoice over the treaty because although the principle of antihegemonism was somewhat qualified, it was nonetheless prominently asserted in an intergovernmental legal document for the first time. The Japanese were pleased with a long-term legal framework that would be useful both for smooth expansion of trade and for establishing other types of stable relationships with China. In particular, Article Three stated:

> The Contracting Parties shall, in a good-neighborly and friendly spirit and in conformity with the principles of equality and mutual benefit and non-interference in each other's internal affairs, endeavor to further develop economic and cultural relations between the two countries and to promote exchanges between the people of the two countries.

Encouraged by the euphoria of friendship and cooperation, Vice-Premier Li Xiannian and Minister of International Trade and Industry Kōmoto Toshio agreed in September 1978 to extend the Long-Term Trade Agreement from 1985 to 1990 and to increase more than threefold the planned volume of two-way trade.[48]

When Vice-Premier Deng Xiaoping visited Japan in October 1978 to attend the ratification ceremony of the Treaty of Peace and Friendship, he discussed the specific steps for implementing the Li-Kōmoto agreement in his meetings with Prime Minister Fukuda Takeo and other Japanese government and business leaders. At his Tokyo press conference, Deng declared:

> We have signed a long-term trade agreement between the two countries. But just one such agreement is not enough. The total business turnover involved in this agreement is 20 billion U.S. dollars. It will be doubled or trebled. The road will be even broader when our country is developed. We have much to learn from Japan. There are many fields in which we can make use of Japanese scientific and technological achievements and even funds . . . It is only natural that with the conclusion and implementation of the China-Japan Peace and Friendship Treaty, cooperation between the two peoples will be strengthened. Cooperation between the two countries in political, economic, cultural and scientific fields will all be increased.[49]

The Japanese were prepared to reciprocate China's enthusiasm. In March 1979 Liu Xiwen and Inayama Yoshihiro signed the five-article memorandum on the Long-Term Trade Agreement in Tokyo.[50] They agreed to extend the Long-Term Trade Agreement until 1990 and to double or triple the total amount of bilateral trade during that period—an increase up to between $40 and $60 billion.

Although the Chinese were embroiled in policy debates over economic readjustment and its international implications, the Japanese leaders, both government officials and top businessmen, were optimistic about the prospect of achieving the long-range trade targets. In addition to the obvious primacy of reaping their projected profits in the China market, many Japanese businessmen revealed a generally favorable inclination toward China and felt a sense of guilt about Japan's past aggression against and exploitation of China. This favorable tendency was well illustrated by Ikeda Yoshizō, chairman of Mitsui and Company, the first Japanese company to set up a branch office in Beijing. He visited China five times during the 1970s and surprised the Chinese delegation by delivering his speech in Chinese. In 1979, when asked about China, he responded:

TABLE 7
CHINA'S NATIONAL ECONOMY, 1949–1981
(in millions of yuan)

VARIABLE	1949	1952	1957	1965	1975	1978	1979	1980	1981
Population (in millions)	(541.7)	(574.8)	(646.5)	(725.4)	(919.7)	(958.1)	(970.9)	(982.6)	(996.2)
Agricultural output value	32,600	48,400	53,700	59,000	128,500	145,900	158,400	162,700	172,000
Industrial output value	14,000	34,300	70,400	139,400	321,900	423,100	459,100	499,200	519,900
National income	35,800	58,900	90,800	138,700	250,500	301,000	335,000	366,000	388,000
Revenue	6,520[a]	18,370	31,020	47,330	81,560	112,110	110,330	108,520	106,430
Expenditure	6,810[a]	17,600	30,420	46,630	82,090	111,100	127,390	121,270	108,970
Volume of retail sales	14,050	27,680	47,420	67,030	127,110	155,860	180,000	214,000	235,000
Total imports	2,130[a]	3,750	5,000	5,530	14,740	18,740	24,390	29,140	36,770
Total exports	2,020[a]	2,710	5,450	6,310	14,300	16,760	21,170	27,240	36,760

SOURCE: *Beijing Review*, August 10, 1981, and November 29, 1982.

[a]1950 figures.

Here is a land with enormous potential. The people there have a complexion that is similar to ours. We may not speak the same language, but we can communicate because we use the same script. We are thus more relaxed in each other's company than with Westerners. Also, we have long historical ties . . . We can understand their sentiments because of the similarities of the people. So I think we should be able to help each other both spiritually and materially.[51]

Ikeda was not a unique Sinophile among Japanese businessmen. The Japan-China Long-Term Trade Committee, for example, included a number of prominent leaders who had experienced direct personal association with China prior to the end of the Pacific War. They ranged from a bank official (Okazaki Kaheita) and a capital investor (Fujiyama Aiichirō) to a trade representative (Mizukami Tatsuzō) and a prisoner of war (Kimura Ichizō).[52] All shared a romantic and sympathetic view of China and had made a significant contribution to the promotion of economic and diplomatic relations between Tokyo and Beijing. However, it took only a couple of years for them to realize that inherent in the Long-Term Trade Agreement was a set of substantial difficulties that their goodwill and honest efforts alone were not sufficient to overcome. For Sino-Japanese economic diplomacy did not always move in the direction envisaged by treaties and agreements; at times a fundamental structural as well as psychological readjustment between the two neighbors was required. This readjustment usually reflected the limits of China's overall economic performance (see Table 7).

Steel Industry: The Baoshan Complex

TWO

After the purge of the Gang of Four, Premier (and CCP Chairman) Hua Guofeng and his associates in the State Council resurrected and refined the Outline of the Ten-Year Plan for the Development of the National Economy (1976–1985). In August 1977, under Hua's guidance, the Eleventh National Congress of the CCP adopted a new party Constitution, which promised to make China a "powerful socialist country with a modern agriculture, industry, national defense, and science and technology by the end of the century."[1] It emphasized the principle of "building socialism by going all out, aiming high and achieving greater, faster, better and more economical results." Similar phrases, first articulated by the late Chairman Mao Zedong during the Great Leap Forward Movement, were invoked to rationalize Hua's new "all-round leap forward" policy. In his Political Report to the Congress, Hua declared: "we must bring the country's entire economy into the orbit of planned, proportionate, and high-speed socialist development."[2]

Hua's goal of high-speed economic development generated a great deal of excitement and expectation in China, which were in marked contrast to the stagnation and frustration caused by the ten years of Cultural Revolution. The 1978 New Year's Day editorial in *Renmin Ribao* [People's daily], for example, stated:

> A higher speed is not only necessary but possible. We are fully confident of our ability to accelerate the development of our national economy because we have Chairman Mao's proletarian

revolutionary line and the strong leadership of the Party Central Committee headed by Chairman Hua, we have the superior socialist system and hundreds of millions of industrious, courageous and ingenious workers, peasants and intellectuals who have heightened their consciousness through education by positive and negative examples during the Cultural Revolution and in the 11th two-line struggle in particular, and we have rich natural resources and the material foundation built up in the past 28 years. A higher speed in 1978 will make things easier in 1979.[3]

As a specific target of the Ten-Year Plan endorsed by the First Session of the Fifth National People's Congress in March 1978 (see Table 8), Hua pledged an increase in industrial output of approximately 10 percent a year and production of 60 million metric tons of steel (as well as 400 million metric tons of grain) a year by 1985. His commitment to a doubling of domestic steel output in eight years was central to his economic development philosophy: "we must take steel as the key link [*yigang weimang*]" in high-speed industrialization programs.[4] Hua clearly recognized the urgent need to modernize China's weak steel industry.

TABLE 8
CHINA'S TEN-YEAR PLAN, 1976–1985

OUTPUT, BY SECTOR	PROJECTED GROWTH
Agriculture	
Average annual growth rate	4–5 percent
Grain output in 1985	400 million metric tons (285 million metric tons in 1977)
Industry	
Average annual growth rate	10 percent
Coal production in 1985	1,000 million metric tons (537 million metric tons in 1977)
Steel production in 1985	60 million metric tons (26 million metric tons in 1977)
Oil production in 1985	200–300 million metric tons (90 million metric tons in 1977)
Electricity output in 1985	500 billion kwh (223 billion kwh in 1977)

SOURCE: Tagawa Gorō, *Chūgoku no keizai* [China's economy] (Tokyo: Kyōikusha, 1982), p. 40.

NOTE: Total investment required: 1,000 billion yuan (about $600 billion).

The average annual growth rate of China's aggregate steel output between 1952 and 1977 (12 percent) exceeded that of China's aggregate industrial output (10.3 percent). China was the fifth largest steel producer in the world in 1977. However, the Chinese steel industry suffered from a number of serious shortcomings. The per capita amount (25 kg) of China's 1977 steel production was woefully inadequate in view of its ambitious economic plans, especially in comparison with the per capita steel production of the United States (524 kg), the Soviet Union (577 kg), and Japan (899 kg).[5] Chinese steel plants were small-scale, outdated facilities that produced steel of poor quality, and they were widely scattered in remote locations. China had rich deposits of iron ore, but its low quality required importation of 3 million metric tons of iron ore annually from Australia and other countries. Moreover, the combination of political instability and economic disruption caused a sharp decline in China's steel production during 1976 (see Table 9). Steel imports, mostly finished items, totaled 4.5 million metric tons in 1976 and 4.8 million metric tons in 1977 (see Table 10); the $1.5 billion cost

TABLE 9
CHINA'S STEEL PRODUCTION, 1949–1981
(in millions of metric tons)

YEAR	AMOUNT
1949	0.16
1952	1.35
1953	1.77
1955	2.85
1957	5.35
1958	11.08
1959	13.35
1960	18.45
1965	12.23
1966	16.00
1967	10.00
1968	12.00
1969	17.80
1971	21.00
1972	23.00
1975	23.90
1976	20.46
1977	23.74
1978	31.78
1979	34.48
1980	37.12
1981	35.60

SOURCES: *Zhongguo Jingji Nianjian* [China's economic yearbook], 1981; Chinese government; and Japan-China Economic Association.

CHINA'S STEEL IMPORTS, 1965–1980
(in millions of metric tons)

YEAR	TOTAL IMPORTS	FROM JAPAN		FROM EEC NATIONS		FROM USSR/ EASTERN EUROPE	
		Amount	Percentage	Amount	Percentage	Amount	Percentage
1965	723	221	30.6	229	31.6	235	32.5
1966	1,299	647	49.8	433	33.3	115	8.9
1967	1,608	603	37.5	745	46.3	62	3.9
1968	1,691	997	59.0	460	46.3	110	6.5
1969	1,808	1,252	69.2	414	23.0	89	4.9
1970	2,282	1,580	69.2	373	16.4	155	6.8
1971	2,193	1,634	74.5	310	14.1	123	5.6
1972	2,270	1,430	63.0	501	22.0	140	6.2
1973	3,665	2,604	71.1	833	22.7	120	3.3
1974	3,586	2,873	80.1	507	14.2	127	3.5
1975	3,902	2,830	72.5	730	18.8	181	4.6
1976	4,518	3,481	77.1	707	15.6	160	3.5
1977	4,845	3,981	82.2	637	13.2	132	2.7
1978	8,843	5,534	62.6	2,515	28.4	139	1.6
1979	7,500	4,373	58.2	2,235	29.7	124	1.7
1980	4,709	3,202	68.0	683	14.5	166	3.5

SOURCE: *Nitchū Keizai Kōryū* [Japan-China economic exchange], 1981, p. 256.

in 1977 (a dramatic fourfold increase since 1970) constituted the largest single category in China's growing list of imports.[6] It was ironic that while steel imports increased, the stockpiles of China's unused domestic steel products also increased (by 12 million metric tons in 1977) due to low quality.[7]

Baoshan Decisions

○   To solve this problem, the Ten-Year Plan called for the modernization and expansion of China's seven major existing steel plants (Anshan, Benxi, Shoudou, Baotou, Taiyuan, Wuhan, and Maanshan) and construction of three new large-scale integrated steel complexes: Baoshan (with an annual production capacity of 6 million metric tons) in a suburb of Shanghai, Jidong (capacity of 10 million metric tons) in Hebei Province, and the second Anshan complex (capacity of 5 million metric tons) in Liaoning Province. The Chinese chose to locate the Baoshan iron and steel complex (*Baoshan Gangtie Zongchang—Baogang* as commonly referred to in Chinese, or *Hōzanseitetsujo* in Japanese) in Shanghai rather than at other possible seashore sites (such as Lianyungang in Jiangsu Province and Zhenhai in Zhejiang Province) because Shanghai had the necessary industrial infrastructure, which included a high level of scientific and technological development and a reservoir of trained technicians and other workers. Moreover, Shanghai contributed 12 percent of China's total industrial output, it was a major consumer of steel products, and it enjoyed a strong local financial base. They also determined that *Baogang*'s location along the Changjiang (Yangzi) River (leading to the Yellow Sea) would result in an economical transportation system, because 85 percent of *Baogang*'s materials were expected to use waterborne transport. Even though the Chinese were aware of the hazards of Baoshan's unstable geological structure and the Changjiang's shallow estuary and shifting channels, they were confident that those problems would be solved. It is also conceivable that Hua hoped that locating a major industrial project in Shanghai—the power base of the Gang of Four—would allow him to woo Shanghai's population.[8]

In 1977 the Chinese decided to seek the Nippon Steel Corporation's cooperation for *Baogang*'s construction and operation. There were several reasons for this decision. The Chinese had neither the advanced modern technology nor the experience required for building an integrated steel mill along a river or coast. They believed that compared with the United States, West Germany, and other possible foreign partners for the Baoshan project, Japan presented a few distinct advantages. Since China imported most of its steel from Japan (77.1 percent in

1976 and 82.2 percent in 1977), the Chinese were thoroughly familiar with the technology, management, and personnel of the Japanese steel industry. The geographic proximity between China and Japan meant a comparative advantage in terms of transportation costs. (As a result of the West German involvement in the building and operation of the Wuhan iron and steel complex, China had incurred enormous expenses for shipping equipment back to West Germany for repair, and for inviting West German technicians to China.) In addition, the cultural and linguistic similarities between the two Asian neighbors would facilitate extensive daily contacts between Chinese and Japanese personnel at Baoshan and the training of thousands of Chinese technicians and managers in Japan. The Chinese thought of this relationship as a concrete and positive manifestation of the new Sino-Japanese cooperation in economic as well as political areas.

When asked why China selected Nippon Steel from among several major Japanese steelmakers, Huang Jinfa (*Baogang*'s deputy general manager and chief engineer) cited its efficient operation of large-scale, technologically advanced plants, particularly in Kimitsu (on the Bōsō peninsula, along Tokyo Bay in Chiba Prefecture) and Ōita (on Kyūshū Island, at Beppu Bay).[9] He also admitted that the Chinese favored Nippon Steel because of its earlier participation in the construction of the Wuhan steel project and its record of constructing steel mills in Brazil, Argentina, Mexico, Malaysia, Egypt, and Algeria. The Chinese were particularly impressed by Nippon Steel's technical assistance to South Korea's Pohang Iron and Steel Corporation, one of the most successful steel plants in any of the developing nations. That Nippon Steel contributed a large portion (about 35 percent) of Japanese steel exports to China and had both the necessary organizational framework (China Projects Cooperation Division, or *Chūgoku kyōryoku honbu*) and personnel who had worked in and were knowledgeable about China was also a factor. Most important was Nippon Steel Chairman Inayama Yoshihiro's long-standing personal rapport with Chinese government officials, coupled with his influential status in Japan. In 1958 Inayama (then executive director of the Yahata Steel Corporation) had led the Japanese business delegation that concluded a major steel agreement with China. He also made a contribution to the Tokyo-Beijing diplomatic rapprochement and headed the Japan-China Economic Association established in 1972. As *Keidanren* vice-president (and an heir apparent to its president, Dokō Toshio), he exercised enormous clout in Japanese economic and political circles and demonstrated superb skill in putting together a package of economic and financial arrangements on China's behalf. As discussed in Chapter 1, he assumed an important leadership role in the negotiation of the Long-Term Trade Agreement between China and Japan, of which the Baoshan project was a principal (though implicit) component.

The Japanese economic interest in Baoshan was obvious. Nippon Steel, as well as the Ministry of International Trade and Industry, was determined not to lose this tremendous opportunity to Japan's two steel rivals—West Germany and the United States. Inayama and other Nippon Steel leaders were prepared to offer the most advanced steel production technology to China as long as they were assured of a large share of Baoshan's contracts and some control over its operations. Other Japanese steelmakers anticipated the adverse effect that Baoshan's projected productivity would have on their own future exports to China, but, as a MITI official put it, they probably felt "shiyōganai" ("there was no other way").[10] They hoped that they would be able to take part in Baogang's construction and that despite China's plan to double its aggregate steel production by 1985, it would continue to import high-quality steel products from Japan.

China and Japan exchanged a number of steel delegations and proposals for technical programs prior to formal conclusion of the agreements with Nippon Steel concerning Baoshan. The sixteen-member Chinese Metals Society delegation headed by Ye Zhiqiang (society president and vice-minister of metallurgical industry), which included top-level leaders from the Anshan, Shoudou, Maanshan, and Baotou steel complexes, spent almost a month in Japan between September and October 1977 and conducted thorough investigations of Nippon Steel and other Japanese steel producers that included inspection of facilities. The Chinese visitors focused on one major theme (The Processes of Rapid Development of Japanese Steel Industries in the Postwar Era) and studied specific methods for implementing China's steel-doubling plan. Ye was designated general director of the Baoshan Steel Construction Headquarters. Another nine-member Chinese steel delegation headed by Xu Anchang (general manager of the Anshan iron and steel complex) visited Japan in November 1977. These visitors observed Japanese seamless steel production for one month, during which they visited Nippon Steel plants. At the same time Vice-Premier Li Xiannian and Nippon Steel Chairman Inayama agreed in principle to cooperate on the Baoshan project.[11]

Soon thereafter (December 13–23, 1977), Nippon Steel dispatched a 5-member survey team to China. The Chinese hosts told the survey team that the Ministry of Metallurgical Industry had already chosen Baoshan as the site for China's new steel mill and had decided to build two 4,000 m^3 blast furnaces to produce a total of 5 to 6 million metric tons of steel a year.[12] The Japanese survey team held a series of in-depth technical discussions in Beijing and conducted a preliminary study at Baoshan, and then submitted its report to the Chinese. Although the Japanese had some reservations about the geological conditions of Baoshan and the advanced technological requirements of the proposed blast furnaces, they were reluctant to question or criticize the Chinese decisions. A couple of months later, another Japanese steel delegation, consisting of 21 engineers and scientists from Nippon Steel and other steel companies, visited China to conduct studies on the feasibility of modernizing China's old steel mills, particularly those in Anshan, Ben-xi, Shoudou, and Wuhan. At the same time, the 20-member Shanghai steel delegation led by Chen Jinhua (Shanghai vice-mayor and vice-president of the Chinese Metals Society) investigated the specific technical and managerial aspects of the Nippon Steel plants at Kimitsu, Oita, and Yawata; the first two plants subsequently served as a model for *Baogang*. Chen Jinhua was appointed deputy general director of the Baoshan Steel Construction Headquarters.

Baoshan Agreements and Contracts

○   Shortly after the Long-Term Trade Agreement between China and Japan was signed, the China National Technical Import Corporation (CNTIC), an agency established under the Ministry of Foreign Trade to negotiate and administer importation of complete plants and new technical know-how and to conclude licensing agreements with foreign companies, accelerated its negotiations with Nippon Steel officials. On May 23, 1978, CNTIC Deputy General Manager Yang Youde and Nippon Steel President Saitō Eishirō signed the Protocol Concerning the Construction of the Shanghai Baoshan Iron and Steel Complex in Beijing. It was the first major implementation of the Long-Term Trade Agreement. The signing ceremony was attended by Duan Yun (vice-chairman of the State Planning Commission), Cui Jun (vice-minister of foreign trade), Liu Xiwen, Xu Yun (general director of the *Baogang* Engineering Headquarters), Nippon Steel Vice-President Harada Kanae, and its managing director, Ōgaki Makoto.[13] The next day Vice-Premier Kang Shien (chairman of the State Economic Commission), who was in charge of China's policy on oil and other energy resources, received the Nippon Steel delegation.[14]

This thirteen-article protocol (*xieyishu* in Chinese or *giteisho* in Japanese) contained the following agreements:

1. Nippon Steel will make the utmost effort to assist the construction of an integrated steel complex (with an annual production capacity

of 6 million metric tons of steel and 6 million metric tons of pig iron) in the "shortest period of time." The first of the two blast furnaces, with a volume of 4,000 m³, should be built and operating by 1980.

2. Nippon Steel will offer the "most advanced facilities and sophisticated technology," which must not lag behind the present levels at the Oita and Kimitsu steel complexes.

3. Nippon Steel assumes the responsibility to develop a comprehensive construction plan and to assure the "consistency" and "coordination" of construction, management, operation, and training.

4. Foreign equipment will be supplied to *Baogang* in accordance with "rational international prices and foreign trade customs."

This protocol was unprecedented in that it indicated China's willingness to accept Nippon Steel's involvement in every aspect of the planning, construction, and management of a major industrial project. The increased Sino-Japanese cooperation symbolized by conclusion of the Peace and Friendship Treaty in August 1978 ensured a political climate that would allow the protocol to be translated into a more concrete operational agreement. When Vice-Premier Deng Xiaoping visited Japan in October 1978 to attend the treaty ratification ceremony, he visited the Kimitsu works and expressed his support for the Nippon Steel–*Baogang* connection. As one who had worked at the Le Creusot steel mill in France as a work-study student during 1921 and 1922, Deng must have been impressed by Kimitsu's advanced equipment.[15] At a Tokyo press conference he expressed China's hope to learn from Japanese scientific and technological achievements.[16] On December 22, 1978, the Basic Agreement (*zongxieyishu* in Chinese or *kihongōgisho* in Japanese) concerning *Baogang* was signed in Beijing by CNTIC General Manager Peng Runming and Nippon Steel President Saito; in addition, CNTIC Deputy General Manager Liu Xinghua and Nippon Steel Vice-President Harada signed three separate agreements on the blast furnaces, the coking oven, and the steelmaking plant.[17] A number of Chinese and Japanese dignitaries were present at the occasion—such as Vice-Minister of Metallurgical Industry Ye Zhiqiang (who was also general director of the Baoshan Steel Construction Headquarters), Vice-Minister of Foreign Trade Liu Xiwen, Shanghai's Vice-Mayor Chen Jinhua, Japanese Ambassador to China Satō Shōji, and Nippon Steel Chairman Inayama. The protocol served as a "spiritual guideline," establishing the general framework for cooperative effort; the basic agreement spelled out the details of such cooperation: production capacities, contractual procedures, and the total price paid for Nippon Steel's assistance (400 billion yen for soft and hard supplies). It was agreed that the first phase of Baoshan's construction would be completed by October 1, 1981, and that the second phase would be completed by January 1983. The Chinese had decided to divide the project into two phases; Nippon Steel went along with this decision but did not generally endorse the concept of dual division (because the project required an integrated "two-lung" system—a system based upon two blast furnaces working together).

The following day about 20,000 people took part in elaborate ground-breaking ceremonies at Baoshan amidst great fanfare; colorful flags, balloons, bands, and parades aroused a celebratory mood in the crowd that gathered along the banks of the serene Changjiang River. A huge placard proclaimed Premier Hua Guofeng's message: "The Chinese working class has the spirit, competence, trust, and determination to build a modernized, strong, and socialist country within this century."[18] Nippon Steel Chairman Inayama spoke of the opening of a "new era" in Sino-Japanese economic relations, and Vice-Premier Gu Mu (chairman of the SCCC) noted "great significance" in the building of China's most modern steel plant by Sino-Japanese cooperation. He confidently stated that *Baogang's* "high speed, high quality, and high standards" would promote the "high-speed" development of the Chinese national economy and would further friendship between the Chinese and Japanese peoples. Shanghai's Vice-Mayor Peng Chong (member of the CCP Political Bureau) and Minister of Metallurgical Industry Tang Ke also spoke. Japanese Minister of International Trade and Industry Ezaki Masumi and his predecessor, Kōmoto Toshio, who supported the Long-Term Trade Agreement, sent congratulatory telegrams. That evening, more than 400 people attended the gala banquet in Shanghai and enjoyed programs of Chinese music and dance. The distinguished Japanese participants included Ambassador Satō Shōji and Shanghai Consul-General Asada Taizō and representatives of eighteen companies, seven banks, and twelve trading firms directly involved in the Baoshan project. The guest list was a brief "Who's Who" of Japan's economic leaders—among them were Ikeda Yoshizō (president of Mitsui and Company), Yamada Toshisaburō (Mitsubishi Shōji Company vice-president), Kanamori Masao (Mitsubishi Heavy Industries president), Nagata Toshio (Hitachi Shipbuilding Company president), Shindo Sadakazu (Mitsubishi Electric Company president), Kashiwagi Yūsuke (Bank of Tokyo president), and Ikeura Kisaburō (Nihon Kōgyō Bank president). The titles of the Chinese participants were equally impressive. Gu Mu, Peng Chong, and Tang Ke were joined by Chai Shufan (minister of sixth machine building), Gu Ming (vice-chairman of the SPC), Song Yangchu (vice-chairman of the SCCC), and vice-ministers Liu Xiwen and Ye Zhiqiang.

The most ambitious and expensive industrial project ever undertaken in China was also a symbol of Premier Hua's four modernizations
campaign and of the promise of Sino-Japanese economic cooperation.
The Chinese proudly stated: "Its completion is of key importance to
achieving the goal of producing 60 million tons of steel a year in 1985,
and will provide valuable experience for building more large and modern projects in the coming years."[19] Reviewing *Baogang*'s salient fea-
tures, they pointed to new production techniques, high efficiency,
scientific management, and low consumption of energy resources
combined with effective measures to protect the environment.[20]
Moreover, they maintained that (1) all operational processes would be
controlled by computers, (2) labor productivity would be several times
higher than in other iron and steel industries in China, and (3) coal
consumption per metric ton of steel would be one-third lower than in
other Chinese steel plants.

The Chinese had made initial preparations in 1977, and construction work began in early 1978 at the Baoshan site—11 km^2 (7 km by 1.6
km) of old airfields and farmland along the Changjiang River. By the
time of the ground-breaking ceremonies, they had brought about 20,000
administrators, engineers, and technicians from all over the country to
Baoshan. In addition, a group of experienced workers had been recruited
from eight or nine construction corporations; like migratory birds, they
moved from one steel construction site to another. They built main
roads, high-tension electrical lines, a water supply system, 140 apart-
ment buildings, and shipping berths. The Chinese initially had a high
degree of genuine enthusiasm for their top-priority project. A young
Nippon Steel technician at Baoshan observed: "The Chinese personnel
lag behind in technology, but, thanks to their high intelligence, they
catch up quickly once they are taught."[21]

In the summer of 1978, the CNTIC started the negotiations for
plant importation under Nippon Steel's technical supervision and guidance. About two years were required to sign all contracts for *Baogang*'s
first-phase construction projects. The contracts were negotiated and
concluded regarding: (1) sale of soft and hard supplies by Nippon Steel,
(2) agreement with other specialized Japanese suppliers recommended
by Nippon Steel, and (3) importation of other plants (such as a seamless
steel pipe plant, a cold rolling mill, and a hot strip mill) that were not
mentioned in the Nippon Steel protocol and that therefore had to be
negotiated independently of Nippon Steel's responsibilities (see Table
11).

Nippon Steel's soft supply (27.3 billion yen) was divided into four
distinct categories.[22]

1. Cooperation in drafting basic construction plans—preliminary project outlines, plant layout, and procedures for technical collaboration (1.7 billion yen)
2. Cooperation in procuring equipment and supplies—preparation and analysis of purchase order forms, technical evaluation of manufacturers' estimates, and advice for the approval of delivered plants (2.1 billion yen)
3. Cooperation in supervision and guidance of construction and construction processes—the equipment production process, the equipment-unloading process, and equipment test operations (2 billion yen)
4. Cooperation to ensure smooth operation—preparation of technical materials for production, training, and other preparatory programs, and guidance of on-site plant operations (21.5 billion yen)

Contracts covering the sales of hard supplies by Nippon Steel were negotiated in four equipment packages, ranging from the first package (the number one blast furnace, coking oven, and steelmaking plant) to the fourth package (the number two blast furnace and other related items). The first and second packages were agreed upon by the end of 1978 and the third was approved a year later; the costs of Nippon Steel's contracts (excluding the fourth package, which has not yet been approved), totaled 290 billion yen. When the negotiations regarding the third package (chemical treatment facility, power distribution and communications, power-piping facility, water supply and exhaust facility, laboratory, and casting plant) began, the Chinese, in view of the drastic economic readjustment policy adopted in December 1978 to reduce Chinese importation of expensive foreign plants, showed a strong desire to use their own equipment and material as much as possible. During negotiation of the fourth package (which marked the beginning of second-phase construction) in 1980, they insisted on 50 percent self-supply and thus saved 40 billion yen.[23] They mentioned China's economic retrenchment guidelines and cited dwindling reserves of foreign exchange. They also stated that they hoped they would learn much from the first-phase construction and would be able to develop China's technical competence.

In other protocol-related contract negotiations, Nippon Steel selected a few appropriate Japanese suppliers for each plant, who in turn submitted their blueprints and cost estimates to the Chinese. The CNTIC, with Nippon Steel's technical advice, processed and finalized the contracts. All Japanese contracts for the first-phase construction projects had been signed by April 1980. In the same month, Nippon Sharyō Seizōgaisha (NSSG), a manufacturer for the Japanese national railway system, outbid its rival, Hitachi, and concluded a contract in the amount of 15.7 billion yen for building the Baoshan transportation

TABLE 11
BAOSHAN PROJECT CONTRACTS, JUNE 1981
(in billions of yen)

FIRST-PHASE PROJECTS	AMOUNT	SECOND-PHASE PROJECTS	AMOUNT	PRIMARY CONTRACTORS
Soft projects[a][b]	27.3			Nippon Steel
Quaywall structure	4.3			Nippon Steel
Raw material processing facility 1	27.9	Raw material processing facility 2	2.4	Nippon Steel
Coking oven 1	53.6	(Coking oven 2)		Nippon Steel
Chemical treatment facility 1	23.4	(Chemical treatment facility 2)	87.9	Nippon Steel
Blast furnace 1	35.9	(Blast furnace 2)		Nippon Steel
Steelmaking plant[b]	45.6			Nippon Steel
Blooming mill	51.6			Nippon Steel
Casting plant	2.1			Nippon Steel
Power piping facility[b]	8.8			Nippon Steel
Power distribution and communications[b]	16.2			Nippon Steel
Water supply and exhaust facility[b]	10.9			Nippon Steel
Test and analysis laboratory[b]	7.0			Nippon Steel

Project		Contractor
Blast furnace blower system 1	5.1	Mitsui Shipbuilding
Lime calcining plant 1	4.2	Mitsubishi Heavy Industries
Port cargo loading facility 1	6.2	Ishikawajima-Harima Heavy Industries
Maintenance shops and warehouses[b]	8.9	Mitsubishi Heavy Industries
Energy facilities—boilers, tanks, etc.[b]	8.6	Mitsubishi Heavy Industries
Baoshan transportation system[b]	15.7	Nippon Sharyō Seizōgaisha
(Continuous casting plant)	37.0	Hitachi Shipbuilding, Sumitomo Heavy Industries, West German Group
Seamless steel pipe mill	60.0	Mannesmann-Demag-Maer AG
		Schloemann-Siemag consortium
Cold rolling mill	130.0	Mitsubishi group
Hot strip mill	85.0	Mitsubishi group
Baoshan thermal power plant[b]	38.0	Hitachi Manufactory
Beilun trans-shipment port[b]	7.0	Kurozaki Refractories, Shinagawa Refractories, British Group
(Refractory material production plant)	25.0	
Blast furnace blower system 2	2.8	
(Lime calcining plant 2)	2.0	
Port cargo loading facility 2	4.4	

SOURCE: Nippon Steel Corporation.

NOTE: Parentheses indicate projects with no contracts.

[a] Contracts were signed only for the 3.8 billion yen portions.

[b] Projects extended into the second phase of the construction period.

system.[24] The contract included 73 diesel locomotives and railway freight cars, 220 tractors, dump trucks, trailers, and tank cars, steel-scrap stockyards, electrical equipment, and roadway engineering, as well as technical assistance. The two sides agreed to use dollars and yen each for one-half of the contracted value and to adopt the following financing terms:

> 10 percent down payment
>
> 10 percent payable after all supplies had been delivered
>
> 10 percent payable at commencement of plant operations
>
> 70 percent five-year deferred payment of balance at the Eximbank's interest rate of 7.25 percent per annum

NSSG was pleased to obtain its largest foreign sale and planned to start its Baoshan shipments from Nagoya in late 1981.

For the remaining contracts, which were not protocol related, the CNTIC invited international tenders and chose its partners without Nippon Steel's technical or supervisory involvement.[25] Coordinated by a 28-unit organization of its top leaders, or Friday Council (Kinyōkai), the Mitsubishi group—Mitsubishi Shōji, Mitsubishi Heavy Industries, and Mitsubishi Electric—won a contract amounting to 38 billion yen for the building of a thermal power plant complex and a contract totaling 85 billion yen to build a hot strip mill, which was expected to produce 4 million metric tons of strip steel (2,050-mm wide) in Baogang's second phase of construction. Mitsubishi's earlier participation in Nippon Steel's Wuhan rolling mill project gave it an advantage in the intense bidding competition against U.S. Steel, West Germany's Mannesmann-Demag-Maer AG and Schloemann-Siemag (SMS), and Japan's Ishikawajima-Harima Heavy Industries.

Mannesmann-Demag-Maer AG defeated the Sumitomo Metals Company and received a contract totaling 60 billion yen to build a mill that would produce 140-mm seamless steel pipe, which the Chinese needed for their oil pipelines. West German manufacturers were also successful in winning another hotly contested bid for a contract in the amount of 130 billion yen to build Baogang's most expensive single plant—a cold rolling mill whose annual production capacity would reach 2.1 million metric tons of steel strip (2,030-mm wide) in coils and sheets. Led by SMS, this sixteen-company consortium outbid three other consortia: a Japanese group (Nippon Steel, Hitachi, Mitsubishi Heavy Industries, Mitsubishi Electric), a West German group (Mannesmann-Demag, Japan Steel Tubes), and a U.S. Steel group. SMS had an inside track because it had played a major part in the construction of Wuhan's cold strip mill and continuous casting plant. The contract was signed in June 1980 after seventeen months of negotiations; SMS agreed to start delivery in 1982, to complete it by mid-1984, and to begin operating the plant in 1985 after a year of tests. The SMS consortium was one of the first West German–Japanese–U.S. cooperative programs in China; it included West Germany's Siemans AEG and Man, Nippon Steel, and Wean United of Pittsburgh. Nippon Steel shared 10 percent (13 billion yen) of the contracted cost for *Baogang's* cold rolling mill; Wean United assumed a larger responsibility (16 percent). For this reason Wean's Senior Vice-President Jeremy C. T. Thomas spent a total of twelve weeks in China during 1980; at one point there were 80 representatives of the consortium's member-companies in China.[26] As a result of President Jimmy Carter's determination (in April 1980) that it was in the U.S. national interest for the U.S. Eximbank to do business with China, the Eximbank authorized an $80 million credit for Wean. Unlike the Japanese financing arrangements for *Baogang*, the U.S. Eximbank provided credit up to 75 percent of the U.S. contract price at a fixed interest rate of 8.75 percent per annum; the Chinese were required to pay cash for 15 percent and Wean agreed to finance 10 percent with its own funds at an annual interest rate of 8.25 percent.

The patterns of China's Boashan contract negotiations suggested that Nippon Steel exercised a pre-eminent advisory influence, but the Chinese made all final decisions. They sought the most advanced technology regardless of price, but they definitely favored those companies with which they had previous mutually beneficial cooperation. The Japanese involvement in Boashan was extensive: 7 primary contractors (Nippon Steel, Hitachi Shipbuilding, Kōbe Steel, Mitsui Shipbuilding, Mitsubishi Heavy Industries, Ishikawajima-Harima Heavy Industries, and NSSG), about 200 equipment suppliers and 10 trading firms involved in the Nippon Steel–contracted portions alone, and Eximbank and approximately 30 commercial banks. Japanese contracts totaled about 500 billion yen. Even though the Japanese government was not directly engaged in the initial discussions or feasibility studies, it was keenly attentive to the development of the Baoshan complex because of its size and its economic ramifications. The government remained supportive of Japanese business interests at Baoshan. More specifically, the MITI and other Japanese agencies permitted the use of Eximbank funds, issued special export licenses, relaxed COCOM regulations regarding computer sales, and underwrote plant export insurance.

Nippon Steel estimated the cost of the foreign soft and hard supplies for the entire two-phase *Baogang* project to be 886 billion yen ($4.4

billion). The Chinese cited a total construction cost (domestic plus foreign) of 21.4–22.7 billion yuan ($13.4–14.2 billion) for all aspects of Baoshan's construction, from the cost of importing foreign plants and the cost of domestic supplies to labor costs, operational expenses, and sums spent for infrastructure, housing projects, and energy and material resources.[27] The enormity of this amount in view of China's modest economic capabilities is easily seen; it is almost equal to China's total exports (21.2 billion yuan) and a little less than half of China's total capital construction budget (50 billion yuan) during 1979. Nippon Steel's more realistic calculation, however, put *Baogang*'s total construction cost, both foreign and domestic, at about 1,300 billion yen ($6.5 billion).[28]

The target date for completing *Baogang*'s first-phase construction was set as "within 1980" in the May 1978 protocol but was readjusted to October 1981 in December 1978, August 1982 in December 1979, and January 1983 in June 1981.

Readjustment Policy and Public Debates

O   From its conception the scope, goals, and procedures of the Baoshan project were potential subjects of policy controversies. The project was also caught in the dynamic crosscurrents of China's post-Mao power struggles and economic policy shifts. When the Baoshan basic agreement was being negotiated and signed in late 1978, the Eleventh CCP Central Committee, at its Third Plenary Session, was in the process of making a fundamental reappraisal of Premier Hua's Ten-Year Plan (1976–1985). Influenced by Deng Xiaoping's growing political power, the committee reinstated Chen Yun as vice-chairman of the Central Committee and member of the Standing Committee of the Political Bureau (the positions he had held before the Cultural Revolution), elected three other new members to the Political Bureau (Hu Yaobang, Deng Yingchao, and Wang Zhen), and rehabilitated Bo Yibo and other Cultural Revolution victims. Chen Yun was made the first secretary of the powerful new Central Commission for Inspecting Discipline in the Chinese Communist Party. A former typesetter for Shanghai's Commerce Press and a Long March veteran, Chen Yun (born in 1905) was elected a member of the Political Bureau in 1940, was vice-premier from 1949 to 1966, and had held several important economic positions: chairman of the Financial and Economic Commission (1949), minister of heavy industry (1949), minister of commerce (1956), and chairman of the State Capital Construction Commission (1958). At this Third Plenary Session, Chen Yun led the harsh criticism of the

Ten-Year Plan, which had been the basis for the China-Japan Long-Term Trade Agreement and the origin of the Baoshan project.

The committee decided that China's main economic efforts should be concentrated on advancing agricultural development as fast as possible and that a higher priority should be given to light industry than to heavy industry. (The Ten-Year Plan, in contrast, emphasized the high-speed development of heavy industries such as steel.) The CCP communiqué declared that "our country's economic construction is bound to advance rapidly and steadily once again"; however it also stated:

> Due to sabotage by Lin Biao and the "Gang of Four" over a long period there are still quite a few problems in the national economy, some major imbalances have not been completely changed and some disorder in production, construction, circulation and distribution has not been fully eliminated. A series of problems left hanging for years as regards the people's livelihood in town and country must be appropriately solved. We must conscientiously solve these problems step by step in the next few years and effectively achieve a comprehensive balance, so as to lay a solid foundation for rapid development. We must make concentrated efforts within the limits of our capabilities to carry out capital construction actively and steadily and not rush things, wasting manpower and material.[29]

The Chinese leaders, under Chen's influence, criticized "leftist" economic thinking and adopted a new policy of economic readjustment (*diaozheng*) that was to extend over the three-year period 1979–1981.

Because of his previous experience, it was probably quite clear to Chen by the end of 1978 that Hua's new "Great Leap Forward Movement" had all the ingredients for another economic disaster. Basic capital construction expenditures drastically increased to 47.9 billion yuan in 1978 (a 50.2 percent increase over the preceding year), with emphasis on heavy industry, and foreign trade deficits reached almost 2 billion yuan in 1978. As Table 12 demonstrates, during 1978 there was a frenzied spree of foreign plant purchasing (almost $7 billion), including the plants purchased under the Baoshan contracts, while China's foreign currency reserves were less than $2 billion. Chen saw an urgent need to reverse Chinese economic policy and to save China from potentially traumatic consequences, as he had done in the early 1960s following Mao's disastrous Great Leap Forward Movement. Therefore, the number of planned construction projects was substantially reduced and stringent economy measures were introduced to curb the importation of expensive foreign plants.

TABLE 12
CHINA'S CONTRACTS FOR PLANT IMPORTS, 1972–1979
(in millions of dollars)

CATEGORY	1972	1973	1974	1975	1976	1977	1978	1979
Petrochemicals	0	698	114	90	136	39	3,325	29
Iron and steel	0	0	551	0	40	0	2,978	312
Fertilizer	0	392	120	0	8	0	0	15
Coal and electric power	23	161	46	0	0	0	202	736
Transport	0	0	0	200	0	0	79	66
Communications and electronics	0	0	0	0	0	0	217	125
Nonferrous metals	0	0	0	0	0	0	127	3
Manufacturing	0	8	0	74	1	21	6	279
Petroleum and gas	0	0	0	0	0	20	0	31
Other	35	0	0	0	0	1	0	110
Total	58	1,259	831	364	185	81	6,934	1,706

SOURCE: U.S., Congress, Joint Economic Committee, *China Under the Four Modernizations*, pt. 1 (Washington, D.C.: Government Printing Office, 1982), p. 523.

The first symptom of this new readjustment policy, though it was not yet fully formulated, appeared in February 1979 when China abruptly decided to freeze many contracts for plant imports, including all such Baoshan contracts, and to suspend all major trade negotiations with Japan, including those concerning the Bohai oil development. This decision was made immediately after the Sixth Meeting of the Fifth National People's Congress Standing Committee and in the middle of the Sino-Vietnamese border war. The 22 contracts with Japan that were frozen amounted to $2.7 billion by March 10, 1979.[30] A principal reason given for this about-face was Japan's unwillingness to offer suitable financial terms to China, but it may have reflected an intensified policy debate among China's top decision-makers.

While Chen Yun assailed the high-speed growth policy of the Ten-Year Plan and attempted to reduce the number of major construction projects, other top Chinese leaders continued to publicly defend the plan. Han Guang (vice-chairman of the SCCC and former governor of Heilongjiang Province), for example, promised in March 1979 to "speed up the pace of construction" and to undertake 120 major construction projects announced by Premier Hua in 1978. He unequivocally declared: "If Japan, West Germany and some other countries have been able to develop their national economies at high speed after World War II, there is no reason why socialist China, with a superior social system, with a correct line as it has now, with policies, principles and organizational machines geared to the line, cannot do the same . . . We Chinese people are confident of fulfilling our ten-year and 23-year plans."[31]

However, a *Renmin Ribao* editorial (March 24, 1979) criticized the tendency to build too many projects at the same time, thus widely dispersing financial and material resources; it also suggested the importance of stopping or postponing a number of projects. Likewise, Li Chengrui and Zhang Zhuoyuan supported the notion of "proportionate development" and praised what was viewed as Chen Yun's correct policy of "three major balances" as enunciated in the late 1950s—the balance of the state budget, the balance between foreign currency receipts and payments for foreign goods, and the balance of supply of and demand for materials.[32] The balance between receipts and payments of foreign exchange was added in the early 1960s.

The delegates to the CCP's Central Working Conference, which met in April 1979, discussed the direction of China's economic policy, criticized the influence of "leftist" economic philosophy, and adopted the Chen Yun–inspired "eight-character" principles of "readjusting, restructuring, consolidating, and improving" the national economy. These eight Chinese characters descriptive of the economic readjustment were reminiscent of the similar "eight-character" policy adopted under Chen Yun's influence in January 1961 for the purpose of correcting the "leftist" economic policy following Mao's Great Leap Forward Movement.[33] The conference's 1979 decision was later explained as follows:

> The Party indicated that economic construction must be carried out in the light of China's conditions and in conformity with economic and natural laws; that it must be carried out within the limits of our own resources, step by step, after due deliberation and with emphasis on practical results, so that the development of production will be closely connected with the improvement of the people's livelihood; and that active efforts must be made to promote economic and technical cooperation with other countries on the basis of independence and self-reliance.[34]

Now that the conference delegates had clarified Chen Yun's initial readjustment policy, Vice-Premier Gu Mu, Han Guang's immediate superior, attempted to rationalize it: "Our industry has developed at a high speed in the two years since the downfall of the 'Gang of Four' and there has been a slight improvement in the people's livelihood, which remained on the same level for quite a long time. However, serious disruption by Lin Biao and the 'Gang of Four' in the past decade has thrown our economy out of balance and this situation has not yet been completely changed. Hence the need for readjustment."[35] Yet Premier Hua Guofeng, in his report to the Second Session of the Fifth National People's Congress in June 1979, still described a "jubilant mood" prevailing throughout the countryside and painted a rosy picture of his two-year economic achievements, namely, a 55.3 percent increase in steel output during the 1977–78 period. He maintained: "In the past two years we have made a good start at importing advanced technology and using funds from abroad and the results have been positive. Never in the past decade have we witnessed such a flourishing and gratifying situation in the economic front as a whole."[36]

Notwithstanding Premier Hua's optimistic economic assessment, a few deputies attending the Second Session of the Fifth National People's Congress raised some doubts and questions about the Baoshan project. Tang Ke, minister of metallurgical industry (a veteran technocrat in the oil and steel industries), and other Chinese government leaders refused to recognize the existence of any problem, actual or potential, at Baoshan, and maintained that the project was "economically profitable" and that its completion would improve the technological level, quality, and management of China's steel industry.[37] The incipient challenge was thus effectively thwarted and it was not reported in China's controlled media at that time.

Implementation of the economic readjustment policy resulted in reduction of the target for China's steel production in 1985 from 60 million metric tons to 45 million metric tons and cancellation of all other projects for new steel plants. It did not stop resumption of *Baogang*'s plant contracts with Japan in the summer of 1979 because Japan made concessions in financial arrangements. (With regard to the Baoshan-related plant sales, the Japanese government agreed to provide Eximbank funds in a five-year deferred payment plan at the annual interest rate of 7.25 percent permitted by OECD guidelines.) As discussed earlier, the Baoshan contract negotiations and construction operations went ahead during 1979 despite China's internal policy debates and drastic readjustment measures, perhaps because the Baoshan project was still an unchallengeable, sacrosanct, top-priority item.

However, the delegates to the NPC session of June 1979 ratified a very important organizational change in China's economic policymaking apparatus. Chen Yun, Bo Yibo, and Yao Yilin were appointed vice-premiers of the State Council and were made members of the newly created Financial and Economic Commission. Chen Yun was appointed chairman of the commission and Yao became its secretary-general. As part of the supercabinet machinery, the commission was empowered to coordinate all economic and financial agencies and programs and to formulate a basic national economic policy. The commission served as the instrument by which Chen Yun aggressively and systematically carried out his bold readjustment plans with the cooperation of his able and experienced protégés. Yao (born in 1917), a former radical and articulate leader of anti-Japanese demonstrations at Beijing's Qinghua University in 1935, had served as vice-minister of commerce under Minister Chen Yun in the mid-1950s and had accumulated a wide range of economic knowledge and administrative experience; he had been vice-minister of trade in 1949, vice-minister of commerce in 1954, minister of commerce in 1960, vice-minister of foreign trade in 1974, and minister of commerce in 1978.[38] Bo Yibo (born in 1908), a radical student leader at Peking University and in Taiyuan during the 1930s, was elected to the Seventh CCP Central Committee in 1945 and was made an alternate member of the Political Bureau in 1956; his important administrative positions included appointment as minister of finance in 1949, director of the SCCC in 1954, chairman of the State Economic Commission and vice-chairman of the Scientific Planning Commission in 1956, vice-premier in 1956, and vice-chairman of the

SPC in 1962. In 1949 Bo had served as vice-chairman of the Financial and Economic Commission headed by Chen Yun; both had been members of the Central Administrative Council. Like Deng Xiaoping, Chen, Yao, and Bo all fell from their influential positions during the Cultural Revolution; in particular, Bo was attacked as a "fat old man," was abused on the Qinghua University campus in 1967,[39] and was the last major leader to be rehabilitated in 1978.

With Deng Xiaoping's support, the Chen-Bo-Yao trio, commonly referred to as the "new economic group," gradually gained the upper hand in economic debates with the so-called petroleum group. The latter consisted of Vice-Premiers Li Xiannian (CCP vice-chairman and ex–finance minister), Yu Qiuli (chairman of the SPC, member of the Political Bureau, and ex–minister of petroleum industry), Gu Mu (chairman of the SCCC, the State Administrative Commission on Foreign Investment, and the State Administrative Commission on Import and Export Affairs), and Kang Shien (chairman of the State Economic Commission and ex–minister of petroleum and chemical industries). It also included Minister of Metallurgical Industry Tang Ke (who had served as vice-minister of petroleum and chemical industries in 1975–1977 under Minister Kang) and Minister of Petroleum Industry Song Zhenming (former Daqing CCP committee secretary and former vice-minister of petroleum and chemical industries under Minister Kang). Li was vice-chairman of the Financial and Economic Commission under Chen, and Yu, Gu, and Kang were among its members. It was widely assumed that the members of petroleum group, with Premier Hua's support, were the chief advocates of the Ten-Year Plan of high growth rates and of the grandiose scheme of expensive foreign plant purchases and heavy construction investments. They expected to finance the plan by dramatically increasing China's petroleum output and exports. Vice-Premier Gu Mu and Minister Tang Ke were particularly influential in launching the Baoshan project and in ensuring its Japanese connection. The economic debates in the State Council were probably not a hostile confrontation, in view of Chen Yun's acknowledged leadership positions, but were rather an effort to strike a reasonable policy compromise between two economic viewpoints.

Chen Yun's economic philosophy was characterized by a belief in fiscal conservatism, balanced growth, realistic economic planning, a de-emphasis on heavy industry, and a deep concern with people's daily welfare. An intelligent, tough, and straightforward economic old hand, he exhibited a desire to repeat the achievements of the First Five-Year Economic Plan (1953–1957) and the gains resulting from the retrenchment policy (1963–1965) that followed the Great Leap Forward Movement—the two moderate and successful programs that he had promoted. His philosophy was supported and elaborated upon by Hu Qiaomu (president of the Academy of Social Sciences), Xue Muqiao (adviser to the SPC and director of its Economic Research Institute), Sun Yefang (adviser to the Economics Institute), and other moderate researchers and scientists. Chen Yun and Xue had been close associates since 1949, when Xue was secretary-general of the Financial and Economic Commission headed by Chen. It has been suggested that both Chen and Xue emphasized indirect planning, pricing policy, material incentives, and profit retention by enterprises.[40]

More specifically, the economic guidelines of Chen Yun's philosophy were as follows:

1. Reduce the ratio of capital accumulation to consumption to a reasonable level—preferably about 25 percent.[41] The ratio of 36.5 percent in 1978 was too high, just as it was in 1959 (43.8 percent) and in 1960 (39.6 percent)—see Table 13.

2. Correct the imbalance in capital investments between heavy and light industry (57.3 percent versus 42.7 percent in 1978). Whereas heavy industry is capital-intensive, has a long production cycle, and yields low profits, light industry is labor-intensive, has a short production cycle, requires small investments, yields high profits, and generates sound revenue. Therefore, light industry also helps to improve people's living standards and increases China's competitiveness in the international market.[42]

3. Stop the government's deficit spending and eliminate the foreign trade imbalance. Drastically reduce capital construction investment and importation of expensive foreign plants to a level commensurate with China's limited financial and material capabilities.

4. Make production levels responsive to demands from the proper quarters. It was a mistake that "the enterprise managers were answerable only to their higher-ups in many cases, not to the customers or consumers."[43]

5. Rectify the erroneous "leftist" economic policy of "taking steel as the key link [*yigang weimang*]" in industrial modernization programs.[44] A serious mistake was committed in 1958–1960 and 1971–72 and again in 1977–78 when a rapid increase in steel production was excessively emphasized; this policy led to the deterioration of light industry and agriculture, an unbalanced economy, unemployment, contradictions among different segments of heavy industry, and sacrifices by consumers.

6. Put technically competent experts and managers, not political leaders, in charge of the steel industry. "Since most of the secretaries

TABLE 13
CHINA'S NATIONAL INCOME GROWTH
AND ACCUMULATION, 1950–1979
(percentages)

PERIOD	ANNUAL ACCUMU- LATION	ANNUAL NATIONAL INCOME GROWTH	ANNUAL AGRICUL- TURAL GROWTH	ANNUAL INDUS- TRIAL GROWTH
Economic recovery (1950–1952)	15.8	19.3	14.1	34.8
First Five-Year Plan (1953–1957)	24.2	8.9	4.5	18.0
Second Five-Year Plan (1958–1962)	30.8	−3.1	−4.3	3.8
1958	33.9	—	—	—
1959	43.8	—	—	—
1960	39.6	—	—	—
1961	19.2	—	—	—
1962	10.4	—	—	—
Economic readjustment (1963–1965)	22.7	14.5	11.1	17.9
Third Five-Year Plan (1966–1970)	26.3	8.4	3.9	11.7
Fourth Five-Year Plan (1971–1975)	33.0	5.6	4.0	9.1
Fifth Five-Year Plan (1976–1980)				
1976	31.1	−2.3	2.5	1.3
1977	32.3	8.3	1.7	14.3
1978	36.5	12.3	9.0	15.6
1979	33.6	6.9	8.6	7.7

SOURCE: *Wuhandaxue Xuebao* [Wuhan University journal], no. 1 (1981), p. 52.

NOTE: "Accumulation" refers to the accumulation of reinvestment funds out of the total national income.

(CCP) and directors do not know much about technology, they always hesitate to make decisions. This is a sort of man-made hindrance which greatly interferes with the efficiency and speed of advance."[45]

Chen's (and Deng's) political position was appreciably strengthened in February 1980 when the Eleventh Central Committee, at its Fifth Plenary Session, removed four of Hua's close allies and powerful supporters from the Political Bureau (Wang Dongxing, Ji Dengkui, Wu De, and Chen Xilian) and set up a new eleven-member CCP Secretariat under General Secretary Hu Yaobang. Chen's close political associates (Yao Yilin, Wan Li, Wang Renzhong, and Hu Qiaomu) were included in the Secretariat, which was responsible for the CCP's day-to-day decisions and operations.[46] The official communiqué reaffirmed the correctness of the economic readjustment policy.[47] Deng's decisive political victory allowed Chen's group to concentrate its efforts on the pressing economic issues. Deng and Chen, who had shared similar experiences during their long revolutionary and administrative careers (although Chen had occupied a higher CCP position than Deng in the 1940s and 1950s), may have agreed to a division of labor by making themselves respectively responsible for political and economic matters.

The first public criticism against the Baoshan complex was made by Vice-Premier Bo (who was also chairman of the Machine Building Industry Commission, which supervised and coordinated eight machine building ministries) in July 1980. He told a group of visiting Japanese economic analysts that although *Baogang*'s technology and equipment were among the best in the world, the technology was not necessarily the most appropriate for China and that *Baogang* was not a desirable example for China's modernization to follow but was rather a "burden" to the Chinese people.[48] Significantly, this remark was made only a month after Premier Hua Guofeng and Vice-Premier Gu Mu had inspected the Baoshan construction sites on their return from a state visit to Japan and had exhorted the Baoshan workers—both Chinese and Japanese—to increase their efforts. Accompanied by Shanghai's top leaders, Premier Hua, after having been briefed by Vice-Minister of Metallurgical Industry Ye Zhiqiang, expressed his satisfaction over the progress made in Baoshan.[49] Seen in this context, Bo's statement signaled the beginning of the open attacks against the Baoshan-Japan connection. Zhou Chuandian (deputy director of the Office of Science and Technology in the Ministry of Metallurgical Industry), in an article in *Gongren Ribao* [Worker's daily] dated July 7, 1980, argued that the Japanese model of building expensive new steel plants was not suitable to China; he asked the government to adopt the U.S., West German, and Soviet models (which emphasized the modernization of old steel mills), for new facilities had supplied only 5–10 percent of the total steel output of those countries during the 1970s. *Renmin Ribao* [People's daily], on July 28, 1980, candidly admitted that the massive purchases of big foreign plants in 1978 required excessive consumption of energy resources, thus undermining China's economic readjustment efforts. Moreover, in private, some Chinese charged that Japan delivered used equipment to Baoshan and even cheated China.[50] When confronted with these charges, Nippon Steel officials calmly said that the best response was to complete a fine steel plant at Baoshan. Nippon Steel Vice-President Ōgaki Makoto (subsequently general manager of the China

Projects Cooperation Division) expressed no anxiety in 1980 and predicted that *Baogang* would not be a Chinese burden in ten years.[51] Nippon Steel officials received Vice-Premier Gu Mu's repeated assurances that the Baoshan criticism was China's internal matter and would have no effect on Japan's connection with *Baogang.*

The growing debate over Baoshan climaxed in the unprecedented open and extensive interpellation of Minister of Metallurgical Industry Tang Ke, his Vice-Ministers Ye Zhiqiang and Zhou Chuandian, and other Chinese officials at the Third Session of the Fifth National People's Congress in August–September 1980. Before about 70 Beijing deputies, Qinghua University President Liu Da asked Tang Ke a set of sharply critical questions about Baoshan. Tang responded with a lengthy explanation, stating the following points in justification of Baoshan.[52]

1. Since 1949, China has imported 65 million metric tons of steel at a cost of $17.2 billion; in the 1970s alone, 46 million metric tons were imported, costing $13.9 billion. It has been estimated that China will import 55 million metric tons at a cost of $22 billion in the 1980s. Hence it is more economical in the long run to build two or three major steel complexes in China than to continue steel imports.

2. Once completed, *Baogang* can produce 6.7 million metric tons of steel, 6.5 million metric tons of pig iron, and 4.2 million metric tons of urgently needed high-quality plate steel and steel tubes each year. Some of these products are not being produced by China's existing plants.

3. *Baogang* can produce goods worth 4.95 billion yuan and can generate profits of 1.63 billion yuan annually; therefore, *Baogang*'s original construction cost can be recovered in thirteen years.

Tang admitted that the Ministry of Metallurgical Industry had failed to conduct detailed feasibility studies or to consult specialists and had frequently exceeded its financial limits.

However, Tang's admission could not stop the unrestrained barrage of criticisms and questions from NPC deputies and from members of the Chinese People's Political Consultative Conference (CPPCC) over the next several days.[53] They charged that the *Baogang* project was a "bottomless pit" (*wudidong*) requiring endless expenditures and high interest payments and asked why the Ministry of Metallurgical Industry had not decided to modernize old steel plants and to use the abundant labor force from these plants, and how the profits from *Baogang* could be sufficient to repay 1.71 billion yuan in interest per year (calculated at an 8 percent interest rate). They pointed out that Baoshan was the wrong place for a big steel mill because it had to be built on soft and sandy ground, was far from coal mines, and faced the Changjiang estuaries, which were too shallow for large ships. They also asked: Why did the government agree to use expensive iron ore imported from Australia? What happens if foreign countries refuse to ship iron ore and other materials needed by *Baogang*?

Environmental issues were also raised: cancer-causing pollutants, industrial wastes, and contaminated water would harm 10 million Shanghai citizens and would poison rice paddies, vegetable fields, and the fishing and poultry industries. As *Baogang* was expected to create 200 tons of sulfur dioxide per day, it would create acid rain (*suanyu*) over Shanghai. An especially harsh attack referred to the ministry's "irresponsible," "arrogant," and "unsatisfactory" bureaucratic behavior. Hang Huilan (deputy from Henan Province) determined that the root cause of *Baogang*'s dilemna was an erroneous, blind bureaucratic tendency to "have a tiger by the tail" (*qihu nanxia*). A few deputies expressed thinly veiled anti-Japanese sentiments when they accused the ministry of having "too generous" an attitude toward Japan and clearly implied that whereas China had given up its war reparations from Japan, Japanese capitalists were eager to reap profit from Baoshan. The lingering resentment of Japan's past aggression against China was evident in their remarks.

CPPCC Deputy Fei Xiaotong (British-educated president of the Chinese Sociological Research Association) proposed that a special joint NPC-CPPCC committee be constituted to investigate the Baoshan project. Although Vice-Premier Deng had initially been enthusiastic about the Baoshan project, this unusual parliamentary maneuver had probably been orchestrated by the Deng-Chen coalition to (1) demonstrate Premier Hua's inept leadership in launching a high-speed, steel-centered modernization program, (2) convince the petroleum group how widespread *Baogang*'s unpopularity was, and (3) vent public frustrations against Hua's broken economic promises, the high rate of inflation, and rising urban unemployment. Subsequently, Hua was publicly blamed for "his share of responsibility for impetuously seeking quick results in economic work and for continuing certain other 'Left' policies."[54] Moreover, one purpose of the NPC debates had been to eliminate the Ministry of Metallurgical Industry's traditional dominance over the economic ministries. As Yu Guangyuan (vice-president of the Chinese Academy of Social Sciences and vice-chairman of the State Scientific and Technological Commission) pointed out during his 1981 visit to Japan, the ministry had bypassed the Chinese Academy of Social Sciences, the Ministry of First Machine Building, and other bureaucracies concerned with Baoshan.[55] *Renmin Ribao* (September 10,

1980) suggested that Deng may have used the occasion to experiment with a degree of institutional checks and balances. Most important, the NPC debates were meant as a warning to the well-entrenched, complacent, and unresponsive bureaucrats who were careless and inefficient in the management of public funds. In this context it is interesting to note that in an award-winning short story, *Sanqianwan* [30 million yuan], a relatively unknown 33-year-old factory worker vividly depicted the rampant manifestations of China's chronic bureaucratism in a construction project totaling 30 million yuan: corruption, nepotism, waste, injustice, cadre privileges, and bad party leadership.[56]

Baoshan Renegotiations

○   During the NPC debates, Minister Tang Ke maintained that the number one blast furnace at Baoshan would be completed by the end of 1982 and that the cold rolling plant, the hot strip mill, and the number two blast furnace would be operational by the end of 1984. Vice-Premier Gu Mu reassured Nippon Steel officials that the NPC debates would have no effect on Japan's connection with Baoshan, and Vice-Minister Ye Zhiqiang repeated the same assurance to Okubo Shizuo (general manager of Nippon Steel's Shanghai Baoshan office) as late as September 23, 1980.[57] The second-phase contract negotiations were soon resumed. Yet the Japanese, bewildered by the unusual continuous public uproar in China, wondered whether the debates were an exercise intended to teach a lesson to Chinese bureaucrats or a prelude to a drastic policy change regarding Baoshan. Indeed, the NPC debates did effectively remove *Baogang's* shield of unassailability and made it impossible to treat the Baoshan case as an exception to China's comprehensive readjustment policy. It seemed just a matter of time before the ax would fall on Baoshan.

In November 1980 the State Council decided to *postpone Baogang's* second-phase construction as well as construction of some unrelated petrochemical plants and to freeze all ongoing contract negotiations. Vice-Premier Gu Mu frankly admitted to a visiting Japanese economic delegation that although the Chinese government was seriously concerned about its international credibility, it had a more urgent problem of restoring the credibility of the Chinese people, for without economic readjustment their livelihood would be in jeopardy.[58] Nippon Steel Vice-President Ōgaki Makoto still believed (or perhaps hoped) that the second-phase construction would not be canceled because it would be difficult to operate *Baogang* with one blast furnace for more than three or four years. At the first annual Sino-Japanese ministerial conference in early December 1980, Vice-Premier Yao Yilin (who had replaced Yu Qiuli as chairman of the SPC in August 1980) told Director-General of the Economic Planning Agency Kōmoto Toshio that in view of China's continuous economic difficulties, the readjustment period would be extended through 1983.[59] He also explained that because of the decline in China's oil production, China would limit its oil exports to Japan to only 8.3 million metric tons a year in both 1981 and 1982, not 9.5 million metric tons (1981) and 15 million metric tons (1982) as promised in the Long-Term Trade Agreement.[60] The reduction in China's exports to Japan meant a net loss of almost $2 billion of foreign earnings over the two years ($290 million in 1981 and $1,620 million in 1982).

Continuing economic hardship was a top agenda item at the CCP's ten-day (December 16–25, 1980) Central Working Conference.[61] Chen Yun, who retained his cabinet-level chairmanship of the Financial and Economic Commission (even after he had resigned from the vice-premiership in September 1980), played a dominant role in the adoption of a series of drastic economic measures. He admitted the inadequacy of his readjustment policy (perhaps blaming the lack of cooperation among his colleagues) and identified the persistent problems of budget deficit, high rate of inflation, and excessive money supply. The resultant decisions were to (1) extend the period of economic readjustment through 1983 and perhaps until 1985, (2) eliminate budget deficits completely in 1981, (3) reduce capital construction expenditures by 45 percent (from 55 billion yuan in 1980 to 30 billion yuan in 1981), (4) stop all construction projects that would not have immediate benefits, (5) issue 5 billion yuan in treasury bonds and borrow 8 billion yuan from local governments, and (6) conduct all economic activities in accordance with China's reality.

China's economic difficulties in 1980 were indeed alarming. Government budget deficits amounted to approximately 12.7 billion yuan (about 10 percent of the total budget—see Table 14), 35 billion yuan was in circulation (compared with 27 billion yuan in 1979), the inflation rate in urban areas had soared to 15 percent, and the number of unemployed persons had reached 10 million. Moreover, 800–900 large and medium-sized projects under construction required a total of 100 billion yuan, but the availability of major construction materials remained low (steel, 85 percent; lumber, 60–70 percent; cement, 60 percent; and energy sources, 70 percent).[62]

The impact of these belt-tightening decisions upon *Baogang* was immediate and negative. Vice-Premier Yao told an Australian press delegation on December 22, 1980, that China had decided to cancel

TABLE 14
CHINA'S NATIONAL BUDGET, 1977–1983
(in millions of yuan)

YEAR	REVENUE	EXPENDITURE	BALANCE	TOTAL CAPITAL CONSTRUCTION INVESTMENT	CAPITAL CONSTRUCTION INVESTMENT IN BUDGET	DEFENSE COST
1977						
Final	87,450	84,353	3,097	36,400	29,200	14,910
1978						
Final	112,110	111,100	1,010	47,900	39,500	16,784
1979						
Budgeted	112,000	112,000	0	50,000	39,000	20,230
Final	110,330	127,390	− 17,060	55,000	44,380	22,270
1980						
Budgeted	106,290	114,290	− 8,000	37,350	24,150	19,330
Final	108,520	121,270	− 12,750	53,900	34,640	19,384
1981						
Budgeted	107,400	112,400	− 5,000	55,000	24,150	20,170
Revised	97,600	97,600	0	30,000	17,000	—
Final	106,430	108,970	− 2,540	42,790	25,840	16,797
1982						
Budgeted	110,450	113,450	− 3,000	38,000	18,630	17,870
Revised	110,690	113,690	− 3,000	30,270	—	17,870
Final						
1983						
Budgeted	123,200	126,200	− 3,000	36,180	19,630	17,870

SOURCE: Chinese government.

Baogang's second-phase construction altogether.[63] On January 19, 1981, Vice-Premier Gu and Vice-Minister Ye Zhiqiang formally informed Nippon Steel Vice-President Ōgaki of the same decision.[64] Ōgaki urged Gu to complete the project on the ground that it was uneconomic not to do so. A week later the CNTIC delivered to the Beijing office of Mitsubishi Shōji a simple Chinese letter dated January 13, 1981, stating that due to its national economic readjustment, China had decided to (1) stop the construction of the hot strip mill (contracted for 85 billion yen), (2) immediately terminate that contract, and (3) have further discussions about the financial settlement.[65] The same message was sent to SMS to cancel construction of the cold rolling plant (contracted for 130 billion yen) and to four Japanese companies (Nippon Steel, Mitsui Shipbuilding, Kōbe Steel, and Ishikawajima-Harima Heavy Industries) that had already signed the contracts (totaling 13.9 billion yen) for *Baogang*'s second-phase construction projects (see Table 15). A few days later a similar cancellation notification was delivered to each of the Japanese industrial and trading firms that had the contracts for plant sales for three petrochemical complexes (Nanjing in Jiangsu Province, 5 projects totaling 82.5 billion yen; Shengli in Shandong Province, 9 projects totaling 84.5 billion yen; and Yansan in Beijing, 1 project amounting to 6.3 billion yen) and one chemical complex (Dongfang in Beijing, 2 projects totaling 6.5 billion yen).

Once a celebrated symbol of Sino-Japanese economic collaboration, the Baoshan project had now become a source of embarrassment, frustration, and friction between China and Japan. The Soviet Union as well as Taiwan promptly publicized the failure of Sino-Japanese joint economic endeavors. The Japanese, both at Nippon Steel and in the

TABLE 15
STATUS OF BAOSHAN CONTRACTS, JUNE 1981
(in billions of yen)

CATEGORY	AMOUNT
Continued projects	
Soft projects	27.3
First-phase projects	462.9
Total	490.2
Suspended projects	
Second-phase projects with contracts	228.9
Second-phase projects without contracts	166.9
Total	395.8
Grand total	886.0

SOURCE: Nippon Steel Corporation.

Mitsubishi group, were immensely disappointed not only with the substance of China's contract abrogation, but also with the manner in which the Chinese made and announced their decisions. Neither Nippon Steel nor Mitsubishi was consulted prior to China's unilateral, secret decision to break the contracts. Both believed that it was part of a clever Chinese maneuver—to initially reveal their decision to a third party (Australia) and in China's Japanese-language publication *Pekin Shūhō* [Beijing weekly] and then to impose it on Japanese industries as a fait accompli. Even *Keidanren* President Inayama, a pro-Beijing architect of the Long-Term Trade Agreement, suggested that the Chinese must learn international commercial ethics. Nippon Steel Vice-President Ōgaki complained that the Chinese had a weak notion of what constituted a business contract duly signed.[66] The entire Nippon Steel establishment found itself in an awkward, "face-losing" dilemma. The Mitsubishi group, with a large amount of business at stake, first protested China's unilateral decision and then requested adequate compensation. However, it did not follow SMS's example and threaten to go to the international court.[67] Some of Nippon Steel's own units and many of the several hundred subcontractors that had already started their work were forced to stop. However, some equipment had already been loaded on ships bound for China; the Mitsubishi group had also received and trained about 170 Chinese technicians.

Gravely concerned with the adverse long-range effects of the Chinese cancellations, the Japanese government stepped into the matter, asked China to respect international business customs, and sent former Foreign Minister Ōkita Saburō to Beijing as a special representative. Ōkita had had a lifelong personal tie with China. He was a native of China's Dalian who, as a wartime electrical engineer, had assisted China's steel and aluminum industries under the Japanese Ministry of Greater East Asia Coprosperity; more recently he had been an economic adviser to the PRC government. He was relieved to obtain a firm promise from CCP Vice-Chairman Deng Xiaoping and Vice-Premier Gu Mu that China would compensate Japanese companies in accordance with internationally accepted customs.[68] The promise was prominently reported in *Renmin Ribao* (February 12 and 13, 1981). The Japanese government was worried that because the Baoshan contracts had no cancellation provision, any legal challenge to China's contractual noncompliance would have to be contested in a Chinese court. It preferred not to use its export insurance funds (100 billion yen in 1981) and thought that if China failed to compensate the Japanese companies, no government insurance coverage would be available for future plant exports to China. On their part, of course, Deng and Gu were aware of the far-reaching adverse international consequences of their failure to compensate the companies for the canceled contracts. In his discussions with Ōkita, Deng explored the possibilities of Japanese government loans (*zhengfu daikuan*) for China's troubled construction projects and Chinese joint ventures (*hezi jingying*) with Japanese companies.[69] Gu Mu emphasized the importance of the common strategic and economic interests of Japan and China and said he hoped that the problems caused by China's current readjustment policy would not undermine their friendly relations. (Other possible options that China considered were reselling contracted equipment to a third country, postponing the contracts, and renegotiating their terms.)

As for China's economic readjustment policy, Chen Yun (then still CCP vice-chairman) continued to reign effectively as an economic czar even after the NPC's Standing Committee, at its Seventeenth Session, abolished the cumbersome, top-heavy Financial and Economic Commission headed by him in March 1981.[70] He disagreed subtly with Premier Zhao Ziyang's celebrated "Sichuan model," which emphasized the reform principles of enterprise autonomy, free market mechanisms, and private plots. It was apparently Deng's decision to seek Chen's continuing supervisory role in economic policy. A collection of Chen's economic reports and commentaries, written between 1956 and 1962, was issued as an internal publication (*neibu wenjian*) and was made a required text for China's top economic managers. However, the power to implement Chen's retrenchment policy was now centralized in the State Council's new Office of Economic Readjustment headed by Vice-Premiers Wan Li (chairman) and Yao Yilin (vice-chairman); each provincial and municipal people's government also set up its own readjustment office. Wan Li had long been Deng's protégé and Zhao's close political ally. Like Deng, Wan (born in 1916) was educated in France; he was appointed vice-minister of building construction in 1953, vice-minister of urban construction in 1955, and Beijing vice-mayor in 1958. He fell with Deng during the Cultural Revolution and resurfaced as minister of railways in 1975. Once again he followed Deng in disgrace in April 1976 after the Tiananmen Square incident. In 1977 Wan was appointed Anhui provincial governor (and first party secretary); he and then Sichuan Provincial Governor (and First Party Secretary) Zhao Ziyang were pragmatic and efficient local political twins. In 1980, Wan became a member of the new CCP Secretariat, senior vice-premier, and chairman of the State Agricultural Commission. Vice-Premier Yao Yilin's powerful State Planning Commission, not the State Capital Construction Commission, was empowered to determine and supervise all new central and local construction projects. The SPC included Vice-

Premiers Gu Mu and Kang Shien as its vice-chairmen. Vice-Premier Gu Mu relinquished the chairmanship of the SCCC to Han Guang in December 1980, but, with his other three cabinet-level positions intact, he continued to assume primary responsibility for economic relations with Japan. To renegotiate the Japanese plant contracts, the State Council established an interagency working-level council to reduce the chronic bureaucratic problems of vertical organization and to coordinate all aspects of Sino-Japanese economic relations. Gu did not take the suggestion of Ōkita and Foreign Minister Itō Masayoshi that he visit Tokyo for comprehensive policy discussions; however, Liu Xinghua (CNTIC deputy general manager) went to Japan in February 1981 to offer a profuse apology and to conduct a wide range of preliminary negotiations with the Japanese companies involved in the Baogang project. His visit was followed in April by that of Gu's deputy, Zhou Jiannan (vice-chairman of the State Administrative Commission on Import and Export Affairs and of the State Administrative Commission on Foreign Investment). Japan, too, sent various business and governmental delegations to China in an attempt to ascertain the direction of China's future economic policy toward Japan. Deng Xiaoping, Li Xiannian, Zhao Ziyang, and Gu Mu attempted to reassure the Japanese visitors, especially 85-year-old Dokō Toshio (the ex-Keidanren president who replaced Inayama as president of the Japan-China Economic Association), Okazaki Kaheita (permanent adviser to the JCEA), and Fujiyama Aiichirō (president of the Japanese Council for Promotion of International Trade), that despite China's recent contract cancellations, the future of Sino-Japanese economic cooperation was bright and that China's potentially successful readjustment policy would pave the road to a sound future.[71]

The dramatic reduction of national construction expenditures (by 45 percent), coupled with the second-phase construction cancellation and fundamental policy reassessment, was felt immediately in Baoshan. Local construction funds (which were 8–9 billion yuan by the end of 1980) were cut substantially and salary payments were delayed. Part of the 50,000-member labor force was reportedly transferred elsewhere or was on vacation in early 1981, and the bonus system (a monthly average of 9 yuan per worker) was made less generous.[72] The Chinese stopped work on the extension of the thirteen-story Baoshan Binguan (hotel), which housed foreign technicians and visitors, and cranes and other expensive foreign equipment were left idle. The first-phase construction was slow, disorderly, and uncertain. During my two-hour visit to Baogang's various construction sites on a hot Friday morning (July 3, 1981), I counted fewer than 50 Chinese at work on the huge Baoshan construction field; it was almost deserted. While some Chinese women workers were repairing roads, a group of Nippon Steel technicians in brown uniforms and helmets was conducting "Safety Week" inspections of plants under construction. A Nippon Steel representative mentioned that the differences in social customs and business practices between Japan and China often hindered collaborative efforts at Baoshan.[73] He said that all Nippon Steel technicians and consultants lived in the Baoshan Binguan without their families; their average tour at Baoshan was half a year although a few stayed for two years. On Saturdays they went to Shanghai for recreation, but they felt socially isolated because they had few personal contacts with their Chinese co-workers.

I saw a large sign hung on a blast furnace under construction that read: *tongxin tongde jianshe baoshan, bainian daji zhiliang diyi.* [Let us build Baoshan with the same mind and same virtue, Quality is number-one priority for one-hundred-year great plan.] No quotation from Chairman Mao's writings was visible; nor did I see the common slogan "In industry, learn from Daqing." *Baogang's* Deputy General Manager Huang Jinfa was not prepared to predict when the first-phase construction would be completed.[74] He did say he would like to see the second-phase construction eventually undertaken—even by the Chinese themselves, if necessary. When asked about public criticism of *Baogang*, he admitted with a broad smile that there was some truth in the criticism, but he quickly added that the public did not fully comprehend *Baogang's* positive aspects, such as the antipollution measures that would be introduced.

In fact, Nippon Steel officials vigorously attempted to convince their Chinese counterparts that China must complete the first-phase construction quickly and resurrect the second-phase plans in due time. They contended that the estimated total cost for Baoshan's first- and second-phase construction (1,300 billion yen) was quite reasonable (in comparison with the 2,000 billion yen required for a comparable project in Japan), that China's per capita annual steel production of 42 kg in 1981 (in comparison with the worldwide average of 170 kg in 1981) was too low to sustain healthy economic growth, and that the economic losses that would be caused by any further delay in *Baogang's* construction would be extremely high for both countries. Nippon Steel prepared a long specific list of these losses.[75]

Losses by Chinese side:

1. Interest on unused equipment (loss of 50 billion yen a year)
2. Cost of storage and transportation of equipment

3. Cost of maintenance, prevention of deterioration, and coating process for some machinery
4. Cost increase caused by inflation (loss of 10 billion yen a year)
5. Cost of keeping skilled and trained personnel idle (8 billion yen a year)
6. Waste caused by equipment imbalance

Losses by Japanese side:

1. Salaries of Japanese technical supervisors (2.5 billion yen a year for Nippon Steel alone; an amount several times higher for all Japanese companies)
2. Cost of technical cooperation for storage and maintenance of equipment
3. Warranty losses
4. Interest increase caused by delayed equipment delivery (10 billion yen a year for equipment worth 100 billion yen)
5. Cost for storage and maintenance of equipment in Japan (4 billion yen a year per 100,000 tons)
6. Costs resulting from delayed projects
7. Losses by subcontractors

The Chinese were impressed by Nippon Steel's detailed persuasive arguments, but because of their severe funding constraints, they proposed to form a joint venture with Nippon Steel or to seek a low-interest loan of $800 million (1.5 billion yuan) for Baoshan's remaining first-phase local construction expenses (including wages, infrastructure, materials, and training programs). The loan request was part of a $2.68 billion package submitted by Zhou Jiannan to Japan in 1981. In addition to Baoshan's portion, it included $1,350 million for Nanjing petrochemical projects and $530 million for Daqing petrochemical complexes. The Chinese said that if either proposal was not accepted, *Baogang*'s first-phase construction might be delayed for four or five years because China's economic readjustment period would be extended that long.[76] Nippon Steel flatly rejected the idea of a joint venture as unrealistic and risky but urged the Japanese government to accommodate China's credit requests.

In an attempt to provide a political solution to the problem of deteriorating Sino-Japanese economic relations, the Japanese government (mainly, the Ministries of Foreign Affairs and International Trade and Industry as well as the Economic Planning Agency) put together a five-year, mixed credit formula for China in April 1981. The loan, totaling 400 billion yen, included commodity loans (up to 140 billion yen), commercial bank syndicate loans (up to 250 billion yen), and Eximbank loans. The amount reflected a reduction of China's credit request for the Nanjing petrochemical complexes because West Germany's contracts accounted for about 50 percent of the contracts in Nanjing. Since the Chinese were reluctant to use commercial bank loans because of their high interest rates, the Japanese government came up with a new 300 billion yen formula in June 1981 that completely eliminated any credit for the Nanjing project.[77] The loan, earmarked for Baoshan and Daqing only, included: commodity loans (100 billion yen at 3 percent interest rate to be repaid over 30 years), Eximbank loans (100 billion yen at 6.25 percent interest to be repaid over 20 years), and commercial bank loans (100 billion yen at higher interest rates). The Japanese proposed to transfer to commodity loans those parts of the government's yen-denominated Official Development Assistance (ODA) loans that China had not used in 1979–80 and did not expect to use in 1981–82 because of the postponement of two major projects: the Wuqiangxi hydroelectric power plant in Hunan Province and the Hengyang-Guangzhou Railway expansion project (mainly, construction of the Dayaoshan Tunnel). The initial reaction of the Chinese to this loan transfer was unfavorable because they, particularly the Ministries of Railways and Electric Power, hoped to resume both projects in the near future, but they eventually accepted Japan's revised formula.

On the Japanese side, however, the dynamics of bureaucratic politics complicated the situation. The Foreign Ministry, the MITI, and the Economic Planning Agency joined in pushing the revised formula, but they encountered stiff bureaucratic resistance to the use of additional Eximbank funds for China. The Ministry of Finance was concerned about Japan's budgetary deficits and did not want to upset other nations (notably, West Germany and the United States) by making pro-Beijing financial offers.[78] Moreover, the Japanese Eximbank balked because it had already committed $2 billion in bank loans (6.25 percent interest, ten-year repayment) for China's resource development (mainly oil and coal) and it anticipated making a further commitment of $1 billion for China's coal production after 1985. A typical and often effective tactic used by the Chinese to pressure Japan was to flirt with Western Europe. While the Japanese government was engaged in internal debates over China, Vice-Premier Gu Mu, who had deliberately snubbed Japan's invitation to visit Tokyo, led a 99-member delegation to Brussels to open the "China Week" sponsored by the European Economic Community in March 1981.[79] China established a formal relationship with the EEC in 1975, and signed a long-term trade agreement with it in 1978; China's trade with the EEC totaled $5 billion during 1980. The MITI was uneasy about China-EEC developments, but Foreign Ministry officials argued that Japan's active economic support for Deng Xiaoping's moderate political leadership was in its own best interests and was also consistent with the Washington-Tokyo agreement to help China.[80] Asked about the decline of China's credibility in Japan, Wu Shudong, a Japan-educated veteran trade official who was then a Chinese commercial counselor in Tokyo, suggested that the Japanese press sensationalized the issue of contract cancellations and did not adequately report China's willingness to compensate for the canceled contracts.[81] An official in the MITI agreed with Wu's suggestion and said that the Japanese mass communications media, because they had been preoccupied with the automobile disputes with the United States, had not paid much attention to the development of Sino-Japanese economic negotiations in the spring of 1981.[82] He added that the Ministry of Foreign Affairs was not fully aware of specific economic issues and had released misleading news items on China.

Under Prime Minister Suzuki Zenkō's leadership, the Japanese government bureaucracy ironed out its policy differences and formulated a final version of the 300 billion yen funding package for China in September 1981. Its decisions were as follows:[83]

1. To keep the ceiling of 300 billion yen for *Baogang*'s first-phase construction and for the Daqing petrochemical project
2. To transfer the unused portions (the postponed Wuqiangxi hydroelectric power plant and Hengyang-Guangzhou Railway expansion) of yen-denominated, low-interest, long-term government loans to commodity loans totaling 130 billion yen
3. To avoid the use of Eximbank funds (thus accommodating objections raised by the bank and by the Ministry of Finance), but to offer suppliers' credits of 100 billion yen for deferred payments provided by the Eximbank
4. To provide 70 billion yen in syndicated loans, which would be generated by a consortium of Japanese private financial institutions

In September 1981, Vice-Premier Gu Mu, in his discussions with Dietman Nikaidō Susumu (chairman of the LDP Executive Council and a participant in the Tokyo-Beijing diplomatic normalization negotiations in 1972), accepted the Japanese funding formula. Shortly thereafter, in accordance with the Advisory Committee's recommendation and as a result of Premier Zhao Ziyang's inspection tour of Baoshan, the Chinese State Council decided to resume *Baogang*'s first-phase construction projects on a full scale, but to make some adjustments in its completion schedule.[84]

Earlier that year the Chinese had expressed their wish either to form a joint venture with the Mitsubishi group or to freeze the contract for the canceled hot strip mill (85 billion yen) for five years (presumably until the conclusion of China's economic readjustment programs) because they recognized that a new contract would be more expensive.[85] In March 1981, the three Mitsubishi firms (Mitsubishi Heavy Industries, Mitsubishi Electric, and Mitsubishi Shōji) rejected both proposals as uneconomical and prepared a detailed conceptual memorandum to explain the principles of international commercial transactions to China. The Mitsubishi officials made it clear that they simply could not afford to lose money because they were accountable to their shareholders. In April 1981, in consultation with SMS, they developed a compensation proposal by "cumulative methods," which estimated the amounts for equipment under construction, supply of technology, operation of factories, and anticipated profits. They explained that the proposed amount (18.2 billion yen, or about 20 percent of total contractual value) was much less than SMS's compensation request (60 billion yen, or 50 percent of total contractual value) because they wanted to maintain "friendly relations" (yūkō kankei) with China.[86] In fact, the Mitsubishi group had a variety of other ongoing business operations in China, including Baogang's lime calcining plant, thermal power plant, maintenance shops, and energy facilities, the contracts for which totaled about 60 billion yen. However, the Chinese regarded the 8 billion yen down payment as fair compensation, and they entered into negotiations with Mitsubishi over the difference. In August 1981 both sides reached a final compensation figure of 9,315 million yen—11 percent of the original contract. Since the Mitsubishi group had already received the 8 billion yen down payment, the Chinese agreed to pay 1.3 billion yen within a year and promised to buy a hot strip mill from Mitsubishi if a decision were made to build one at Baogang at a later date.[87] The Mitsubishi formula was used as a model to settle China's compensation obligations to four other Japanese companies that had signed Baogang's second-phase construction contracts: Nippon Steel for a raw materials processing facility (2.4 billion yen), Mitsui Shipbuilding for a blast furnace blower system (2.8 billion yen), Kōbe Steel for an oxygen generation plant (4.3 billion yen), and Ishikawajima-Harima Heavy Industries for a port cargo loading facility (4.4 billion yen). The Chinese agreed in September 1981 to provide an 8.5 percent compensation package (1,186 million yen) for these four projects.[88] Subsequently, the Chinese reluctantly accepted SMS's sixteen-company consortium's request to effect an initial three-year freeze of the cold rolling plant (contracted at 130 billion yen).[89] They also decided in 1981 to reactivate, on a cash basis, the unilaterally abrogated contracts for the Nanjing, Shengli, Yansan, and Dongfang chemical projects.[90]

The State Council's decision to resume Baogang's first-phase reconstruction brought many workers and technicians back to Baoshan and gave their activities a new momentum in the fall of 1981. *Beijing Review* reported:

> About 40 per cent of the installation work for the first stage have [sic] now been completed. Construction of a 113-metre-high blast furnace is nearing completion, and the building of auxiliary projects are [sic] in full swing. One of the two 350,000-kilowatt thermal power generating units has been installed and is scheduled to go into operation next spring, while the other unit is being installed. Thanks to the joint efforts of responsible members of the engineering headquarters, technicians and workers, all the work done is up to the required standard.[91]

In addition, port facilities at Beilun (in Zhenhai, Zhejiang Province) were operating smoothly. This trans-shipment harbor, completed by Hitachi in July 1981 at a cost of 7 billion yen, was designed to handle 100,000-ton vessels importing iron ore from Australia and other countries. Their cargo was delivered to Baoshan (200 km away) via smaller carriers because the mouth of the Changjiang River was shallow.[92]

During 1982 construction momentum was further accelerated because China gradually re-emphasized heavy industry. By April 1982 about 99 percent of foreign equipment and material (mostly from Nippon Steel) had been delivered to Baoshan; 75 percent of it had received open-package inspection.[93] In April the coal-unloading berth along the Changjiang River was completed; it was capable of handling four cargo vessels (5,000-ton class) and one oil tanker at any given time. On the eve of May Day one of the two thermal power plants was finished; this plant (with a capacity of 350,000 kw), built by Mitsubishi, was intended to supply electricity to *Baogang* as well as to Shanghai. (The second plant was expected to be completed by early 1983). When revisiting *Baogang* at the end of May 1982, I was immediately struck by the way the overall atmosphere had changed since my visit a year before. The almost deserted site I saw in July 1981 was now a scene of noisy activity. Groups of Chinese workers were busy at each project, and trucks, cranes, and bulldozers were in full operation. The blast furnace (113 m high) was almost completed. A vessel unloaded coal at the berth in the Changjiang River and it was transported to the power plant by a conveyer-belt system. The power plant smokestack (200 m high) belched pale blue smoke. In response to my question, Jian Wensheng, deputy director of *Baogang*'s Foreign Affairs Office, said that about 70,000 Chinese and 400 foreigners (mostly Japanese) were involved in the *Baogang* project.[94]

Jian's staff included about 300 persons competent in the Japanese language and 10 English-language interpreters. He maintained that the quality of Japanese equipment delivered to *Baogang* was generally good but that not all Japanese equipment was necessarily of high quality. He implied that some Japanese equipment was of 1978 vintage—the year when the protocol and basic agreement were signed. At the Ministry of Foreign Affairs, Deputy Director of the First Department of Asian Affairs Ding Min explained that there had been disputes over some outmoded or deficient Japanese equipment at *Baogang*, but all had been resolved to China's satisfaction.[95]

Like China's other central bureaucracies, the administrative leadership concerned with making *Baogang* decisions underwent a significant change in May 1982. Vice-Premiers Gu Mu and Kang Shien were stripped of their vice-premierships as well as their specialized cabinet-level functions and were appointed state councillors in the streamlined State Council; therefore, their direct roles with regard to *Baogang* were considerably diminished. Bo Yibo, too, moved from vice-premiership to state councillorship; at the Twelfth CCP National Congress in September 1982, he was elected senior vice-chairman of the new Advisory Commission chaired by Deng Xiaoping.

However, Premier Zhao Ziyang and his two remaining vice-premiers, Wan Li and Yao Yilin, strengthened their relative political and administrative positions; at the Twelfth CCP National Congress both were elected to the 28-member Political Bureau and re-elected to the 11-member Party Secretariat chaired by General Secretary Hu Yaobang.[96] Wan gave up his chairmanship of the State Agricultural Commission (abolished in May 1982), but Yao retained his chairmanship of the powerful State Planning Commission. Chen Yun's continuing influence on China's economic policy was assured, and Chen Muhua (state councillor, minister of the reorganized Ministry of Foreign Economic Relations and Trade, and alternate member of the Political Bureau) and Zhang Jingfu (state councillor, chairman of the expanded State Economic Commission, and member of the Central Committee) emerged as important new voices in the conduct of China's economic diplomacy. The Ministry of Foreign Economic Relations and Trade absorbed the State Administrative Commission on Import and Export Affairs and the State Administrative Commission on Foreign Investment; the State Capital Construction Commission was incorporated into the new Ministry of Urban and Rural Construction and Environmental Protection.

Minister of Metallurgical Industry Tang Ke, who played a major policy role in the *Baogang* affair, replaced Kang Shien as minister of petroleum industry and was succeeded by Vice-Minister Li Dongye; Li had been a CCP secretary at the Anshan iron and steel complex. The number of vice-ministers in the Ministry of Metallurgical Industry was dramatically reduced from twenty to four; Zhou Chuandian, who had argued against the Japanese model of steel modernization for China, was one of the two surviving vice-ministers. Vice-Minister Ye Zhiqiang, who had concurrently been general director of the Baoshan Steel Construction Headquarters since 1978, was transferred to the China National Metals and Minerals Import and Export Corporation. Ye was replaced by Li Feiping, who resigned as vice-minister and became an adviser to the Ministry of Metallurgical Industry. This team of two former vice-ministers, Li Dongye and Li Feiping, was henceforth directly in charge of *Baogang*'s steel construction projects.

Although much progress was being made in *Baogang*'s construction, in May 1982 the Chinese State Council decided to extend the projected date of commencement of its first blast furnace operation from the end of 1983 to the fall of 1985.[97] This decision was based upon three major considerations. First, the plans for development and transportation of coal were not being effectively carried out. The *Baogang* operation required a proper mix of coal from seven different mines scattered in three Chinese provinces: 40 percent from Anhui, 50 percent from Shandong, and 10 percent from Jiangsu. Second, the industrial water supply system presented a very difficult problem. Since salty water from the Changjiang River was unsuitable for industrial usage, especially in the winter, the original *Baogang* plan called for the installation of a double pipeline to bring water from Dingshanhu Lake 50 km away. As the work progressed, however, it became clear that this plan was simply too expensive. In July 1982 the State Economic Commission, the Ministry of Urban and Rural Construction and Environmental Protection, and the Shanghai Municipal Government jointly decided to scrap the Dingshanhu plan altogether and to build a new reservoir near the Changjiang River.[98] Third, despite Japan's generous loans, *Baogang*'s first-phase construction projects still suffered from chronic fund shortages.

Added to these three considerations was the persistence of two fundamental problems: policy inconsistency and pervasive bureaucratic inefficiency. The direction of policy decisions regarding *Baogang* was often determined not only by a shift in China's economic policies, but also by the outcome of its domestic power struggles. In spite of the drastic reorganization of Beijing's central economic organizations and the change in *Baogang*'s top leadership, the Chinese found it difficult to resolve the problem of huge and top-heavy central bureaucracies and vertical organization at Baoshan. There was no easy way to coordinate mutually reinforcing policies among the multitude of organizations involved in the *Baogang* project;[99] interbureaucratic jurisdictional disputes and policy differences were indeed detrimental to *Baogang's* overall progress.

Yet, prior to the opening of the Twelfth CCP National Congress in September 1982, the Chinese attempted to demonstrate that the Baoshan iron and steel complex was a successful project after all; they pointed out that its large facilities, including seventeen computers, ultilized the most advanced modern technology and had already begun to produce economic benefits for China.[100] In the subsequent months *Renmin Ribao* prominently reported the completion of some construction projects at *Baogang*.[101] *Baogang* was no longer Hua Guofeng's pet program; its tangible achievements or failures were now to be attributed to the Deng Xiaoping–Hu Yaobang leadership. Even if *Baogang's* first-phase construction was completed by 1985, the Chinese were still confronted by the task of deciding when and how they should embark upon its second-phase construction. They were in full agreement with Nippon Steel's position that *Baogang's* "one-lung" operation, without the second blast furnace, would be highly risky and unprofitable. *Baogang's* CCP Secretary Zhu Erpei contended that the completion of *Baogang's* first-phase construction would consume two-thirds of the total cost including the cost of the second-phase construction, but that the first-phase plants could produce no more than one-third of what the totally integrated complex, including the second-phase plants, could produce.[102] Asked about the future of *Baogang's* second-phase construction projects, Deputy Director Ding Min said only that they were under active consideration.[103] In the summer of 1982, the Chinese seemed to be interested in reopening negotiations for construction of the cold rolling plant and the hot strip mill, but it was quite clear that for the second-phase construction they would insist upon the maximum utilization of China's domestic resources, both human and material.[104] In the Sixth Five-Year Plan (1981–1985) submitted to the National People's Congress in December 1982, Premier Zhao Ziyang set a modest target (39 million metric tons) of annual steel production by 1985 (see Table 16), which sharply contrasted with Hua Guofeng's promise of 60 million metric tons.[105] Although the premier emphasized the importance of *Baogang's* first-phase construction programs, he made no reference to its second-phase construction in the Sixth Five-Year Plan. Hence it was expected that the Chinese would undertake *Baogang's* second-phase construction in the latter half of the 1980s.

The short record of Sino-Japanese economic diplomacy concerning the *Baogang* project shows a drastic fluctuation of negotiating patterns—from exaggerated expectations to great frustrations and then to a

TABLE 16
CHINA'S SIXTH FIVE-YEAR PLAN, 1981–1985

OUTPUT, BY SECTOR	PROJECTED GROWTH
Agriculture	
Average annual growth rate	4–5 percent
Grain output in 1985	360 million tons (12.3 percent over 1980)
Industry	
Average annual growth rate	4–5 percent
Coal production in 1985	700 million tons (12.9 percent over 1980)
Steel production in 1985	39 million tons (5.1 percent over 1980)
Oil production in 1985	100 million tons (5.7 percent under 1980)
Electricity output in 1985	362 billion kwh (20.4 percent over 1980)

SOURCE: *Renmin Ribao*, December 14, 1982.

NOTE: Total investment required: 360 billion yuan (about $210 billion).

search for a realistic adjustment of the economic relationship of the two nations. It also suggests that whereas the Chinese are capable of making an important economic decision without sufficient scientific investigation and with a misplaced political motive, the Japanese are, at times, inclined to uncritically accept and accommodate China's expressed preferences and economic requests. Finally, it demonstrates the continuing importance of the interbureaucratic dynamics that constrain the range of policy options open to both China and Japan. No one in either country disputed the fact that China required an increasing amount of high-quality steel products to meet the goals of its four modernizations program and that Japan was in an advantageous position to provide a package of modern technology and funding for China. However, the *Baogang* episode has taught both China and Japan how difficult it is for them to consummate an agreement promising mutual economic benefit, even in the most harmonious political atmosphere. Although traditional friendship, cultural affinity, and geographical proximity constitute a positive factor for their understanding and cooperation, China and Japan are equally vulnerable to the vagaries of their recent historical experiences. The Chinese are extremely sensitive to any appearance of dishonesty or arrogance on Japan's part; China's anti-Japanese feeling has been quite widespread even among its top economists.[106] Similarly, the Japanese are not completely free of a tendency to be overly critical of any sign of Chinese inconsistency or inefficiency; as a result of *Baogang's* contract cancellations, Chinese credibility declined sharply in the eyes of Japanese businessmen during 1981. In a way the record of the *Baogang* project, whether it succeeds or fails, will reflect the complexity of the economic, political, and historical relations between China and Japan. Given the enormous economic and political stakes of both nations in the Baoshan iron and steel complex, they will continue to pay a great deal of attention to its progress and to regard it as an important barometer of Sino-Japanese relations.

Oil Development at Bohai and Oil Exports

THREE

The history of oil production in China can be traced to the Western Han period (106–232 B.C.), but large-scale oil exploration efforts started only in the 1950s, with technical and financial assistance from the Soviet Union.[1] The most successful case of Sino-Soviet cooperation was the famous Daqing oilfield in the northeastern (or Manchurian) region, test-drilled in September 1959. Even after the withdrawal of Soviet technical assistance in 1960, the Chinese were able to continue production and reached the level of oil self-sufficiency in 1965. The slogan "In industry, learn from Daqing" was invoked to hasten China's industrial development. In the early 1970s, China exported oil to Japan. However, the bulk of China's oil production (over 100 million metric tons in 1978; see Table 17) was onshore; limited technology and capital shortages left offshore oil exploration in a rueful state of underdevelopment. The only successful offshore oil drilling was in three small areas (Chengbei, Haixi, and Shijiutuo) in the Bohai Sea. France and other noncommunist countries provided technical advice and equipment for China's offshore oil development in the 1970s.

Bohai Negotiations and Agreements

O   Direct Japanese involvement in the Bohai Sea oil projects did not occur suddenly but resulted from a series of extensive technical exchanges and prolonged negotiations between China and Japan. The principal Chinese delegations that visited Japan to study Japan's

TABLE 17
CHINA'S CRUDE OIL AND NATURAL GAS
PRODUCTION, 1950–1981

PERIOD	AVERAGE ANNUAL OUTPUT OF CRUDE OIL (in millions of metric tons)	AVERAGE ANNUAL OUTPUT OF NATURAL GAS (in 100 million m³)
Economic recovery (1950–1952)	0.32	0.06
First Five-Year Plan (1953–1957)	1.00	0.28
1957	1.46	—
Second Five-Year Plan (1958–1962)	4.45	8.24
Economic readjustment (1963–1965)	8.76	10.60
1965	11.31	—
Third Five-Year Plan (1966–1970)	19.36	18.06
1970	28.50	—
Fourth Five-Year Plan (1971–1975)	56.12	61.88
1971	36.70	—
1972	43.00	—
1973	54.50	—
1974	65.30	—
1975	77.06	—
Fifth Five-Year Plan (1976–1980)		
1976	87.16	101.00
1977	93.64	121.23
1978	104.05	137.34
1979	106.15	145.15
1980	105.95	142.76
Sixth Five-Year Plan (1981–1985)		
1981	101.22	127.40

SOURCES: *Zhongguo Jingji Nianjian* [China's economic yearbook], 1981; Chinese government; and Japan-China Economic Association.

offshore oil development technology and related facilities included a ten-member oceanic geological survey team from the Chinese Geological Association in March 1976, a ten-member oil facility study group from the China National Machinery Import and Export Corporation (CNMIEC) in July and August 1977, and a nineteen-member delegation from the Petroleum Company of China (PCC) headed by Sun Jingwen

(PCC general manager and vice-minister of petroleum and chemical industries) in February 1978.[2] The CNMIEC and PCC visitors were in Japan on their return from the United States. The high-level leaders of China's oil production and development bureaucracies spent two to three weeks in Japan, during which they inspected all major Japanese oil companies and petroleum refineries, observed offshore oil exploration sites and facilities, and held a variety of technical and policy discussions with their Japanese hosts.

After these carefully arranged firsthand investigations, the Chinese reached a tentative decision to collaborate with Japan in the Bohai Sea projects by early 1978—at about the time that the Long-Term Trade Agreement between China and Japan was signed (February) and Premier Hua Guofeng publicly unveiled the ambitious Outline of the Ten-Year Plan for the Development of the National Economy (March). The trade agreement made oil exports to Japan the centerpiece of the projected commercial transactions between the two nations (totaling $20 billion in the eight-year period); Premier Hua pledged to develop crude oil, along with iron and steel, coal, and electricity, to place China in "the world's front ranks in terms of output," and to build or complete ten "Daqing-type" oil and gas fields by 1985.[3] The Chinese regarded Japan as a suitable partner for their Bohai oil development programs because the two countries enjoyed cultural and geographical proximity and because Japan, unlike the United States, did not pose a potential threat of intruding into the politically sensitive Bohai Sea so close to Beijing.[4] Moreover, they wished to provide a concrete economic impetus for the opening of new diplomatic and commercial relations with Japan.

Japanese leaders in both the government and private sectors were profoundly concerned about the uncertainty of future oil supplies and expressed their strong desire to participate in the Bohai Sea oil exploration programs. They estimated that the Bohai Sea contained several billion metric tons of recoverable oil deposits.[5] In his meeting with Sasaki Tadashi, chairman of *Keizai Dōyūkai* (Japan Committee for Economic Development), in May 1978, Vice-Premier Kang Shien (chairman of the State Economic Commission and ex–minister of petroleum and chemical industries) agreed to accept Japan's assistance in China's planned surveys of the continental shelf.[6] At about the same time, the Chinese Embassy in Tokyo informed Ōkubo Tadaharu (managing director of the Japan-China Economic Association) that it would welcome a delegation sent by the Japan National Oil Development Corporation (JNODC) to visit the Chinese oilfields and to hold technical discussions with Chinese specialists. The Chinese decided to establish their direct cooperative relations with the JNODC, rather than with numerous other Japanese oil companies, because it was a government-financed public agency with extensive experience in foreign oil exploration and development and because it had strong support from Japan's leading economic organizations, including *Keidanren, Keizai Dōyūkai,* and Inayama's JCEA. The JNODC officials had consciously cultivated their close technical and personal relationships with visiting Chinese oil delegations and had already prepared for an anticipated oil adventure in China.

At the formal invitation issued by the Chinese Geological Association (which in fact belonged to the State Geological Bureau under the State Council), the Japan National Oil Corporation (or JNOC, the new name given to the JNODC) organized a thirteen-member delegation to visit China toward the end of June 1978. Led by JNOC Vice-President Miyazaki Jin (former bureau director in the Economic Planning Agency) and Director Matsuzawa Akira, and with JCEA's Ōkubo as an adviser, it included specialists in a wide range of technical subjects: geophysical prospecting, geology, geochemistry, drilling, facilities, production, refining, finance, and law. The delegation's Chinese hosts represented the State Geological Bureau (SGB), the Ministry of Petroleum Industry (which, along with the Ministry of Chemical Industry, replaced the Ministry of Petroleum and Chemical Industries in March 1978), and the ministry's subsidiary agencies—the Petroleum Company of China and the China National Oil and Gas Exploration and Development Corporation (CNOGEDC). For almost one month the Japanese visitors had many useful technical discussions with Chinese personnel, traveled through China, visited petroleum and geological research institutes, and inspected oilfields at Daqing, Shengli, and the Zhujiang (Pearl River) estuary in Guangdong Province. They were unexpectedly taken to Shijiutuo, a newly drilled offshore oilfield in the northern Bohai Sea. (The Chinese also successfully drilled the Chengbei and Haixi oilfields in the western Bohai Sea.) In the process they learned a great deal about Bohai's geological structure and recoverable oil reserves, and China's exploratory efforts and technological levels.

At the outset of the discussions the Chinese, notably Vice-Minister of Petroleum Industry Zhang Wenbin (who was also general manager of the PCC and the CNOGEDC), made it clear that they needed Japan's cooperation to explore and develop Bohai's substantial oil reserves. They also indicated that the expenses incurred might be repaid by the production-sharing method—whereby the host country (China) and the foreign participant (Japan) share the oil output produced by their cooperative efforts—as distinguished from traditional concession contracts. The Japanese responded enthusiastically and agreed to prepare a comprehensive plan for Bohai's joint oil development by September 1978. On the eve of their departure from China, the members of the Japanese delegation met with Vice-Premier Kang Shien for two hours in Beijing's Great Hall of the People. He said that although a number of Japan's private companies had made various proposals for Sino-Japanese joint oil development, China preferred to collaborate with a consortium of Japanese companies organized by the JNOC. Miyazaki explained that just as the JNOC had done in other cases of foreign oil exploration (in Indonesia and the Soviet Union), it planned a new consortium-established company for China. The meeting was prominently reported, accompanied by a group photograph, in China's *Renmin Ribao* (July 24, 1978); this signified China's anticipated approval of the Bohai-Japan connection. Having obtained Kang's explicit, wholehearted blessing, the Japanese fully expected to conclude a contract for Bohai's joint exploration and development in several months. No one on the Japanese side could foresee that the JNOC delegation's visit would be only the first of ten negotiation meetings and that almost two years of intermittent, complicated, and frustrating discussions would be required for China and Japan finally to conclude a contract in May 1980.

These negotiations had three distinct phases. As Table 18 shows, phase I consisted of the first three meetings, from June 1978 to February 1979. Using JNOC-prepared documents as well as draft contractual forms, both sides discussed such important issues as the geographical boundaries of joint development projects, the financial risks involved, the methods of capital investment and production-sharing compensation, and the financing arrangements. At the end of the third meeting in February 1979, almost all substantive issues had been settled and both parties agreed to initial a basic agreement on February 24, 1979. However, one week prior to that date, the visiting Chinese delegation abruptly left without any explanation. As discussed in Chapter 2, it was at this time that the Chinese decided to freeze $2.7 billion worth of plant importation contracts with Japan for the ostensible reason that they were unhappy about the financing terms. More important, the Chinese leaders were then engaged in intense debates over Vice-Premier Chen Yun's suggested downward readjustment of Hua's Ten-Year Plan, especially in regard to the imports of expensive foreign plants and technology.

No doubt the Japanese negotiators were frustrated by China's mysterious and seemingly irresponsible behavior. The only viable option available to them was to wait patiently for the Chinese to resume the negotiations. Meanwhile, the Sino-Vietnamese border war ended

TABLE 16
BOHAI NEGOTIATIONS, 1978–1980

PHASE	MEETING	YEAR	FROM	TO	SITE	JAPANESE LEADER	SIZE OF DELEGATION	CHINESE LEADER	SIZE OF DELEGATION
I	1	1978	6/28	7/25	Beijing	Miyazaki	13	Li Xuan	—
I	2	1978	10/9	10/25	Beijing	Matsuzawa	13	Li Jingxin	14
I	3	1979	1/16	2/17	Tokyo	Matsuzawa	18	Li Jingxin	14
II	4	1979	7/30	8/14	Beijing	Matsuzawa	4	Li Jingxin	10
II	5	1979	9/26	10/18	Beijing	Matsuzawa	8	Li Jingxin	18
II	6	1979	11/22	12/7	Beijing	Miyazaki	9	Li Jingxin	14
II	7	1980	1/28	2/6	Beijing	Matsuzawa	9	Zhong Yiming	10
III	8	1980	3/27	4/12	Beijing	Matsuzawa	11	Zhong Yiming	16
III	9	1980	5/1	5/10	Beijing	Matsuzawa	11	Zhong Yiming	12
III	10	1980	5/17	5/28	Tokyo	Matsuzawa	11	Zhong Yiming	8

SOURCE: Japan-China Oil Development Corporation.

inconclusively. The CCP's Central Working Conference in April 1979 adopted the "eight-character" policy of readjusting and reforming the national economy for three years (1979–1981) and drastically reduced the amount invested for capital construction. The Japanese were particularly concerned because although there had been no breakthrough in the Bohai situation in the summer of 1979, the Chinese had assigned exploration rights to eight blocks of the Yellow Sea and South China Sea to U.S., French, and British oil companies. And the Japanese Eximbank had agreed to provide the Bank of China with $2 billion in bank loans for oil and coal development.

When Vice-Premier Kang Shien and Minister of Petroleum Industry Song Zhenming visited Tokyo on their way back from the United States and Brazil in June 1979, they met with Minister of International Trade and Industry Ezaki Masumi (and Foreign Minister Sonoda Sunao) and may have discussed the possibility of resuming the Bohai oil negotiations. One month thereafter, the JNOC received notification of the reopening of the Bohai negotiations and thus phase II began, lasting from July 1979 to February 1980. These discussions focused upon the specific conditions and terms of basic agreements and contracts. On October 17, 1979, JNOC Director Matsuzawa and CNOGEDC Deputy General Manager Li Jingxin (who was also a member of the China-Japan Long-Term Trade Committee) signed a contract for joint geophysical surveys of the southern Bohai Sea. The contract enabled the JNOC to purchase, computer-analyze, and interpret the seismic prospecting data that the Chinese themselves collected along the 11,000 km surveyed in 1978–79. Although it was a small step toward Sino-Japanese joint oil development in Bohai, the contract had a symbolic, psychological significance for the two negotiating teams.

A significant event in Sino-Japanese resource diplomacy took place on December 6, 1979, when Matsuzawa and Li Jingxin signed the Agreement on the Joint Exploration and Exploitation of Petroleum and Natural Gas in the Southern and Western Parts of the Bohai Sea. This was accomplished despite the tragic accident that occurred in the northern Bohai Sea on November 25, 1979: a Chinese oil-drilling rig capsized while being towed during a gale, and 72 of the 74 persons on board died.[7] The Chinese negotiators had been under intense political pressure, presumably from Premier Hua Guofeng, to complete the agreement so that it could be signed during Prime Minister Ōhira Masayoshi's state visit to China. Hua probably wished to demonstrate this achievement in anticipation of Ōhira's substantial yen-loan offers to China. The signing ceremony in the Beijing Hotel was witnessed by Chinese and Japanese dignitaries, such as Vice-Minister of Petroleum Industry Zhang Wenbin, JNOC Vice-President Miyazaki Jin, Takahashi Kiyoshi (deputy director of MITI's Bureau of International Trade Policy), and Hiroumi Masamitsu (director, North Asian Division in Takahashi's MITI bureau).[8] The agreement (*xieyishu* in Chinese and *gōgisho* in Japanese) provided a general framework for the joint offshore oil exploration and development of 25,500 km^2 of the Bohai Sea; this was China's first such venture with a foreign country. The pace of subsequent negotiations quickened and in February 1980 the two nations concluded an agreement to cooperate in the development of the Chengbei (or Teihoku in Japanese) oilfield in the western Bohai Sea, which the Chinese had independently test-produced in December 1977.[9] Since the Chinese had already invested heavily in prospecting and drilling Chengbei, the Japanese deliberately decided not to include it in the main Bohai negotiations. However, the Chengbei agreement was modeled after the December 1979 agreement on Bohai.

Three agreements were thus successfully concluded during the second phase of negotiations. In phase III, from March to May 1980, the Chinese examined the Japanese-drafted contracts, which dealt with the rights and obligations of both sides in the southern and western Bohai Sea, including the Chengbei oilfield, as well as logistics, accounting, and rental, legal, operational, and other procedural issues. On May 29, 1980, during Premier Hua's first state visit to Japan, both sides signed these contracts. Vice-Minister of Petroleum Industry Zhang Wenbin, CNOGEDC Deputy General Manager Li Jingxin, JNOC President Tokunaga Hisatsugu (ex–MITI vice-minister), Eximbank President Takeuchi Michio, JCEA President Inayama, and Moriyama Shingo (director-general of MITI's Agency of Natural Resources and Energy) were present at the signing ceremony in Tokyo's Hotel New Otani.[10] Both sides were obviously pleased with this result; the joint press communiqué issued in Tokyo by Premier Hua and Prime Minister Ōhira stated:

> Both believed that, particularly in view of the critical situation
> in natural resources, energy resources included, it was desirable
> for the two countries to establish long-term and stable ties of
> co-operation in this domain, including the joint exploitation of
> petroleum and coal, in accordance with the agreements reached
> by the parties concerned of the two countries. They acclaimed
> the fact that the Chinese and Japanese parties concerned would
> soon conclude a contract on the prospecting and exploitation of
> oil in the Bohai Sea and that similar projects of co-operation are
> being undertaken in other parts of China.[11]

In the course of their two-year negotiations, the two sides had addressed and resolved a number of substantive issues concerning Bohai's joint exploitation. The most important ones were as follows.

Geographical Boundaries   At the first meeting in June 1978, the Japanese expressed their strong wish to collaborate with China in development of the entire exploitable area (60,000 km^2 of the Bohai Sea's total area of 70,000 km^2). This was the area referred to in the JNOC's initial comprehensive Bohai plan submitted to China in October 1978. When they discovered that China intended to parcel out the northern portion of the Bohai Sea to the French state-owned Société Nationale Elf Aquitaine, they stated that they preferred to concentrate their primary cooperative efforts on the southern Bohai Sea (20,000 km^2) for several reasons: (1) the available geological data made them confident of this zone's potential profitability, (2) this was largely "virgin" territory (the Chinese had already surveyed and drilled oil wells in the western and central zones, and a long time would be required to resolve the complicated issue of reimbursing China's investments), and (3) the area had milder winter weather than the northern zone. The Japanese proposed that for other areas of Bohai, China should assume a primary operational and therefore financial responsibility and should purchase Japan's advanced equipment and technology. This proposal was not attractive to the Chinese negotiators, who were severely constrained by China's drastic economic retrenchment policy. At the fourth meeting (August 1979), Vice-Minister of Petroleum Industry Qin Wencai (who had visited Japan in early 1978 as deputy head of the PCC delegation) asked the JNOC to expand its proposed operational area in the Bohai Sea. As a result, the Japanese agreed to reduce the scope of their cooperation in the southern Bohai Sea to 14,100 km^2 but to pick up an additional area of 11,400 km^2 in the western Bohai Sea. (The Chengbei oilfield in the western Bohai Sea covered a small area of 24 km^2.) The French company was assigned to develop the northern zone (9,400 km^2), which included the Shijiutuo oilfield.[12]

Nature of Contracts   Although the Japanese were fully prepared, from the outset, to adopt a "risk contract" method so that Japan, not China, would bear the financial risk if oil exploration failed, it was China's unmistakable preference to offer a "nonrisk contract" to Japan. Vice-Premier Kang Shien clearly stated in July 1978 that whereas he would accept only risk contracts with foreign companies for exploration of the Yellow Sea and South China Sea, he favored a nonrisk contract formula for the Bohai Sea. This position probably reflected China's initial assessment that there was no risk whatsoever in the Bohai Sea and that a nonrisk contract would yield a more favorable financial arrangement for China. The Japanese, still unsure of China's true intentions, included a risk contract formula in the proposed comprehensive plan but were persuaded by the Chinese to change it to a nonrisk contract formula. In phase II, however, Vice-Minister Qin, perhaps in view of the CCP Central Working Conference's "eight-character" economic readjustment policy, proposed to conclude a risk contract after all. Since it had been their original plan, the Japanese promptly and graciously accepted Qin's proposal. The nonrisk formula was also used in the JNOC's joint offshore oil projects with Indonesia (Indonesia Nippon Oil Corporation) and the Soviet Union (Sakhalin Oil Development Corporation). The issue of contractual format did not arise with regard to Chengbei because there was no risk in developing a previously verified oilfield.

The Japanese negotiators were completely surprised by Vice-Minister Qin's new position in August 1979 that once Japan had completed geophysical surveys of the Bohai Sea, China would open international bidding to select a foreign partner for Bohai's oil exploitation. Qin explained that the Chinese government had just adopted such a general policy for the Pearl River estuary area and other areas in China's continental shelf. The Japanese negotiators, who had been led to believe throughout phase I that they would be directly involved in both exploration and exploitation of the Bohai Sea, were clearly disappointed. The Japanese asked that a final decision on this issue be delayed for two months so that they could formulate a proposal for China that would avoid an international bidding procedure. In December 1979, the Chinese accepted a basic agreement with Japan and never again raised the question of international bidding in the Bohai Sea. It was unclear whether Vice-Minister Qin had raised this issue as a clever negotiating tactic to extract the best possible terms from Japan or whether this apparent turnabout indicated the uncertainty or inconsistency of China's oil diplomacy.

Financial Arrangements   Needless to say, the crux of the negotiations in all three phases was the extent to which each side would invest in and benefit from Bohai's oil and gas production. Although the details of specific financial proposals and counterproposals are still shrouded in secrecy, it appears that the two sides did not encounter too much difficulty in agreeing on three guiding principles: (1) Japan should assume all the exploration costs, estimated at $210 million over five to seven years; (2) China and Japan would share the development expenses, estimated at $1,020 million over four to five years, in proportions of 51 percent and 49 percent, respectively; and (3) China alone would bear the cost of the fifteen-year commercial production (see Table 19). It was understood that if the development (or exploitation) cost exceeded the projected amount, Japan would provide additional funds.

The Japanese assumed that China's share ($520 million) of the

TABLE 19
ORIGINAL PLANS FOR BOHAI AND CHENGBEI OIL PROJECTS

	BOHAI	CHENGBEI
Chinese organization	Offshore branch	Offshore branch
Japanese organization	Japan-China Oil Development Corporation	Chengbei Oil Development Corporation
Scope	25,500 km²	24 km²
Exploration period	5–7 years	Duration of feasibility study in 1980
Cost	China: none Japan: $3 million for data purchase; $210 million for prospecting and data analysis	China: none Japan: $3 million
Development period	4–5 years	2–3 years
Cost	Total cost: $1,020 million China: 51 percent Japan: 49 percent	Total cost: $250 million China: 51 percent Japan: 49 percent
Production period	15 years	15 years
Cost	China: pays all Japan: pays none	China: pays all Japan: pays none
Total production	110 million kl	3.2 million kl
Production share	China: 42.5 percent Japan: 42.5 percent (China: 15.0 percent for production cost)	China: 42.5 percent Japan: 42.5 percent (China: 15.0 percent for production cost)

SOURCE: Japan-China Oil Development Corporation.

development expenditures would be financed by the $2 billion in bank loans that the Japanese Eximbank had already earmarked for China's coal and oil development projects under the OECD guidelines (6.25 percent interest rate per year up to the maximum period of fifteen years). Once again they were surprised to learn from Vice-Minister Qin in August 1979 that the JNOC should obtain a new low-interest, dollar-denominated bank loan for the Chinese share. He contended that the $2 billion yen-denominated loans were not specifically intended for Bohai's oil development and that yen-denominated financing was unfavorable to China because of the yen's inflated international value.[13] The issues of loans—amounts, interest rates, and denomination—proved to be the most difficult and hotly debated problem throughout the negotiations. Because the Japanese negotiators and the MITI were unable to accommodate the Chinese request for a new loan from the Eximbank, the Chinese exerted political pressure upon the Japanese government and business community. Vice-Chairman of the State Capital Construction Commission Xie Beiyi stressed the "special relations" existing between China and Japan, citing the fact that 25 percent of China's total imports and 60 percent of China's total purchases of foreign plants came from Japan.[14] Moreover, in an attempt to demonstrate the close relation between economic and political matters, Vice-Premier Gu Mu, in a September 1979 Tokyo press conference, declared: "An economically developed and technologically advanced Japan and a gradually prospering and modernized China working in close cooperation with other friendly nations in the Asia-Pacific region would in a very large measure ensure stability in the East."[15]

At the crucial sixth meeting, in November–December 1979, the Chinese made a significant concession in agreeing to use part of the Eximbank's $2 billion loans (denominated in yen) for most of their exploitation costs (up to $500 million) and to allocate yuan-denominated local funds for the balance ($20 million). This rare concession was made because the Chinese, in light of the substantially reduced number of economic projects, did not urgently need the entire $2 billion loan for other resource development programs and also because they expected to receive Japanese "gifts" of low-interest, multibillion-dollar ODA loans (at a 3 percent annual interest rate with ten-year grace and twenty-year repayment) over the next five years. Yet they insisted that the dollar-denominated Japanese share ($500 million) of the development costs should have low interest, roughly equal to the Eximbank rate. They were afraid that the higher Japan's total investment (including interest) was, the larger would be the compensation demand. A final compromise was struck to set aside 15 percent of Bohai's total fifteen-year oil output as compensation for China's entire production expense and to divide the remaining portion equally between China and Japan (42.5 percent each). Another sticky but relatively minor issue concerned Japan's agreement to purchase the survey data compiled by the Chinese in the Bohai Sea. The Japanese negotiators wished to incorporate this purchase price in their estimated exploration cost, but they eventually conceded to China's request that they pay about $3 million for the Chinese data but not include this expense in the calculations of their total investment.

In making the Chengbei financial arrangements, both sides largely followed the Bohai model to determine the ratios for dividing exploitation costs (51 percent for China versus 49 percent for Japan) and for distributing oil output (42.5 percent for each, provided that percentage exceeded Japan's total Chengbei investment). The Japanese assumed all exploration costs (mainly for feasibility studies, estimated at $3 million); they estimated the total exploitation costs at $250 million.

The two sides discussed the possibility of negotiating their joint oil development in the area around the disputed Diaoyu (or Senkaku in Japanese) Islands in the South China Sea, and the Chinese appeared to be agreeable at first. Vice-Premier Gu Mu suggested in September 1979: "The Diaoyu and other islands have always been part of Chinese territory. In consideration of the joint exploitation of oil, the issue of sovereignty could be left to be settled by our coming generations. It is to the advantage of both parties to undertake now the joint exploitation of the oil resources there."[16] The Japanese leaders were also anxious to start negotiations on the matter. However, the continuing territorial dispute prevented the two teams from conducting any further substantive discussions on oil development of the Diaoyu area. They also agreed that they would do so once their respective governments had reached a settlement or understanding on this highly sensitive political issue.

The JNOC conducted its long Bohai negotiations with China in close consultation with the MITI and its specialized subsidiary organization, the Agency of Natural Resources and Energy, Eximbank, the JCEA, and private oil companies and other related industries in Japan. The MITI, through the Agency of Natural Resources and Energy, broadly outlined Japan's energy policy and issued general instructions to the JNOC. The JNOC negotiating delegation included representatives from the Agency of Natural Resources and Energy, the JCEA, Eximbank, and some commercial oil companies as advisers or bona fide members. The JCEA was particularly helpful to the JNOC in sharing its business expertise and in giving advice on logistical arrangements and communications with China. The Japanese negotiating team was especially well served by a Japanese staff member of the JCEA office in Beijing; born and educated in China, he proved to be an indispensable interpreter and local aide. JCEA President Inayama was instrumental in promoting an atmosphere conducive to Sino-Japanese cooperation and in mobilizing Japanese governmental and business support for the Bohai negotiations. Matsuzawa Akira, a ubiquitous participant in all phases of the negotiations, played a vital role in the successful Bohai outcome. He was a geology and geophysics specialist and former Teikoku Oil Company employee who had gained wide experience as a result of his participation in Japan's war reparations program for Burma (particularly oil development projects) and in Japan's foreign oil activities from Saudi Arabia to Indonesia. He was consistently supported by JNOC Vice-President Miyazaki and ably assisted by his dedicated and experienced staff. The JNOC set up a special eighteen-member China project office under Matsuzawa in January 1979 and in April 1980 organized two new companies—the Japan-China Oil Development Corporation (JCODC) and the Chengbei (or Teihoku in Japanese) Oil Development Corporation (CODC), because the JNOC was not authorized to be directly involved in the operational aspects of overseas oil exploration and exploitation.[17] The two separate companies were required to keep separate accounting records, although they shared offices, personnel, and actual operations. Nippon Steel Chairman Inayama Yoshihiro (who was JCEA president) became the JCODC board chairman, and Inoue Makoto (Tokyo Gas Company auditor and former director of MITI's Bureau of Public Works) and Matsuzawa Akira were appointed president and executive vice-president, respectively, of both companies. President Inoue signed the final two contracts with China in May 1980; the JNOC's direct participation in the Bohai project, in form at least, was terminated at that time. (Functionally equivalent organizations of China and Japan are shown in Table 20.)

The organizational network of Chinese negotiators was rather complicated. At the first meeting of negotiators in Beijing during June and July 1978, the State Geological Bureau served as institutional host for the JNOC delegation. Bureau Deputy Director Li Xuan headed the Chinese negotiating team, which included Vice-Minister of Petroleum Industry and head of the PCC Zhang Wenbin and Deputy General Managers of the CNOGEDC Li Jingxin and Zhao Shengzhen (who had visited Japan in July 1977). When the Japanese visited the Bohai Sea in the summer of 1978, they met Deputy General Manager Zhong Yiming and other officials of the PCC's offshore branch (*haiyang fengongsi*) based at Tanggu, a port city on the outskirts of Tianjin.

TABLE 20
OIL DEVELOPMENT IN CHINA AND JAPAN:
ORGANIZATIONS OF FUNCTIONAL EQUIVALENCE, 1980

CHINA	JAPAN
State Council	Cabinet
Ministry of Petroleum Industry	Ministry of International Trade and Industry
Petroleum Company of China	Agency of Natural Resources and Energy
China National Oil and Gas Exploration and Development Corporation	Japan National Oil Corporation
Offshore branch of the Petroleum Company of China	Japan-China Oil Development Corporation
	Chengbei Oil Development Corporation

The Japanese negotiators initially understood that the SGB (which was to be elevated to the Ministry of Geology in 1979) was responsible for oil exploration in the Yellow Sea, East China Sea, and Pearl River Basin, whereas the Ministry of Petroleum Industry (MPI) was responsible for exploration in the Bohai Sea, and that they would negotiate exploratory issues with the SGB and exploitative issues with the MPI. However, between the first and second meetings in 1978, the Chinese State Council apparently decided to resolve the inherent problem of administrative dualism and designated the MPI as the primary agency to deal with foreign oil companies. The SGB (and later the Ministry of Geology) was primarily assigned to conduct research of China's oil resources, both onshore and offshore. Hence SGB representatives were absent from the subsequent negotiations and the offshore branch was heavily represented in the Chinese delegation. Representatives from the Bank of China, the Ministry of Finance, and the CNTIC took part in various stages of the negotiations with Japan. Guided by Vice-Premier Kang Shien and Vice-Ministers Zhang Wenbin and Qin Wencai (who was also PCC deputy general manager), CNOGEDC Deputy General Managers Li Jingxin and Zhao Shengzhen and offshore branch Deputy General Manager Zhong Yiming effectively protected China's oil interests. The fourteen-member Chinese negotiating team that came to Tokyo in January 1979 was headed by Li Jingxin; Zhao and Zhong served as its deputy leaders. On behalf of the offshore branch, which was an operational agency for oil development in the Bohai Sea (as well as

Yellow Sea, the East China Sea, and Korea Bay), Zhong affixed his signature to the final contracts in May 1980 (see Chart 1).

The Bohai negotiations served as a useful learning experience for the Chinese oil specialists, who had had limited exposure to the practices of international oil diplomacy. In addition to their relative inexperience, the dynamic shifts in China's national economic policy, particularly its readjustment guidelines, made their policy inconsistent, detracted from their authority, and also frustrated their Japanese counterparts. U.N. advisers and consultants hired from Norway's state-owned oil company (Statoil) assisted the Chinese negotiators in the legal, technical, and financial aspects of international oil diplomacy. Statoil set up a China cooperation department at its headquarters and a liaison office in Beijing, and emerged as an influential policy adviser to China in the Bohai Sea project as well as other offshore oil projects. As Saitō Takashi, a geologist who was a key member of the JNOC negotiating team, put it, at first the Japanese were negotiating with their Chinese colleagues, while teaching them about technical matters and

CHART 1
CHINA'S OIL DEVELOPMENT, 1980

Ministry of Petroleum Industry
|
Petroleum Company of China ....   China National Oil and Gas Exploration and Development Corporation

    .... Daqing oilfield
    .... Shengli oilfield
    .... Offshore branch (Bohai Sea, Yellow Sea, East China Sea, Korea Bay)
    .... South China Sea branch (South China Sea, Beibu Gulf)
    .... Northeast branch (Heilongjiang, Jilin, and Liaoning provinces except Daqing)
    .... North China branch (Dagang oilfield, Renqiu oilfield, North China Plains except Shengli)
    .... Northwest branch (Karamai oilfield, Yumen oilfield, Lenghu oilfield)
    .... Southwest branch (Chuanzhong oilfield, Chuannan gas field, Sichuan Basin)

SOURCES: Japan-China Oil Development Corporation and Japan External Trade Organization.

international practices. "Unfortunately," he quickly added, "they learned the intricacies of oil negotiations much too soon."[18] He also observed that unlike the Japanese, with their *tanki* (quick temper or impatience), the Chinese negotiators were extremely patient and tough and did not tire easily, either physically or mentally. However, he observed, unlike the Japanese, who made every effort to adhere to a contract, the Chinese were tenacious in their attempt to change an agreement or a contract as soon as it proved to be unfavorable to them. Matsuzawa Akira pointed out that in addition to this behavioral contrast, differences in business customs, banking practices, legal systems, and even ways of handling press releases presented some difficulties for the Bohai negotiations. Most ironically, he noted a frustrating problem caused by the language barrier (*kotoba no kabe*) between the Japanese and Chinese negotiators, because all the agreements were written in both languages and both texts had equal legal authority. He concluded:

> There are many people who speak of the "common script" between Japan and China because Japanese and Chinese languages belong to the same cultural sphere of Chinese characters. However, the two languages are not only different in pronunciations and grammatical structures, but also, strictly speaking, there is a considerable difference between Japan and China in regard to the ways of thought and perceptions on which the languages are built. The Chinese did not understand the documents written in Japanese as they were and for the same reason the Japanese were uncomfortable with a straightforward translation of Chinese languages; hence we avoided straightforward translations and emphasized the meanings of the phrases written in Japanese and Chinese languages. It was up to our interpreters to determine whether the documents written in Japanese and Chinese had the identical meanings or not, and we, negotiators on both sides, had no way to know this process. If Japanese and Chinese languages used the different vocabularies in describing the same thing, there was no real problem. If, however, both languages used the vocabularies which appeared to be identical, but in fact were slightly different in meanings and nuances, we paid a great deal of attention to avert a problem. In retrospect, I feel that the contracts should have been written in English if both sides so agreed.[19]

Two Chinese participants in the Bohai negotiations, Deputy General Manager Wu Xunze and Chief Geologist Li Bingquan of the offshore branch—both of whom were Qinghua University graduates—expressed their high regard for the Japanese negotiators' competence and dedication.[20] Asked to compare the participation of the Japanese and the French in the Bohai negotiations and operations, Wu observed that whereas the French had more overseas oil business experience and a higher degree of competence in seismic surveying techniques, the Japanese were more economy-minded, more sensitive to the details of a plan, and less willing to hire foreign co-workers. (He explained that there was no difference between Japanese and French Bohai contracts regarding the ratios of shared exploitation costs and oil distribution, but the French, unlike the Japanese, assumed only 49 percent of the estimated exploration cost.) However, he said that the Chinese learned much from both countries about advanced technology, managerial and organizational innovation, preoperation preparedness, and safety measures. Perhaps in an attempt to reduce the language barrier, Wu himself was studying Japanese a couple of hours a week.

The interest of the Chinese leaders in the Bohai project was demonstrated by the visits of CCP General Secretary Hu Yaobang and Vice-Premier Kang Shien to the offshore branch at Tanggu. Although the State Council in August 1980 had formally handed down a "demerit of the first degree" to Vice-Premier Kang in connection with the Bohai No. 2 accident, he was appointed Minister of Petroleum Industry in February 1981 to succeed Song Zhenming, who had resigned in August 1980. Under Kang and Vice-Premier Yu Qiuli, chairman of the newly created State Energy Commission, the MPI and its subsidiary organizations, such as the PCC and its offshore branch and South China Sea branch, pursued a deliberate, cautious, long-range policy even at the cost of a decrease in oil output. For the Bohai incident had a sobering effect on Chinese oil administrators; Wu Xunze said that as a result of it they paid more serious attention to operational and managerial procedures and scientific methods and avoided the past tendency to let one high official make all important decisions. The MPI assumed the increasingly complex task of cooperating with foreign countries, in exploring and developing not only the Bohai Sea, but also other continental shelf areas—the East China Sea, South China Sea, Yellow Sea, the Beibu (Tonkin) Gulf, and the Pearl River basin.

Bohai Operations

○   The JNOC established and partially funded (60 percent) the JCODC and the CODC; the remaining 40 percent of corporate stock was shared by 47 private companies: 13 oil development companies (67.5 percent), 17 oil refineries (22.5 percent), 9 electric power companies (6.0 percent), and 8 steel companies (4.0 percent). Sixteen Japanese banks were also involved in the project. As majority stock-

holder, the state-owned JNOC, under the guidance of the MITI, retained
the dominant decision-making power regarding Japan's Bohai operations. In fact, the JCODC and the CODC were set up in the same
building used by the JNOC. The relatively small initial investments
(4,280 million yen for the JCODC and 230 million yen for the CODC)
were expected eventually to grow to 43,500 million yen and 550 million
yen, respectively. About 100 people were employed by both companies
by the end of 1980; the number increased as the Bohai operations
progressed. Approximately 90 percent of them took a leave of absence
from JNOC and other affiliated companies; most newly recruited persons were placed in secretarial positions. In addition, the two corporations set up a shared field office at Tanggu (*Tenshin Kōgyōjo*—Tianjin
mining station or field office) and liaison offices at Beijing and Tokyo in
July 1980. Vice-President Matsuzawa himself headed the field office at
Tanggu during its formative months. The two-person Beijing office
negotiated with China's central government agencies and served as a
transmission belt for Tokyo-Tanggu communications. In May 1981 the
Tianjin field office consisted of 30 resident Japanese and 48 local
Chinese staff members, including interpreters of Japanese. This field
office, along with the French Elf office and various foreign subcontrac-
tors (such as Geoservices, Geomex, Western Geophysical, Schlumber-
ger, and Japex), rented a five-story research institute building from the
Chinese offshore branch in an area bordering the Bohai Gulf. Japanese
staff members were temporarily boarded in the nearby International
Seaman's club (a hotel with a restaurant and recreational facilities) at
Tianjin's New Port (Xingang).[21]

The offshore branch, consisting of 14,000 persons, also opened its
own support offices for Japanese and French operations: the China-
Japan Cooperation Department (*Zhongri hezuobu*) and the China-
France Cooperation Department (*Zhongfa hezuobu*). The former, with
about 25 members, including interpreters, coordinated Chinese and
Japanese activities in Bohai. The Chinese and Japanese decided to set up
a Joint Committee consisting of three representatives from each side. At
first it was cochaired by Vice-President Matsuzawa and Deputy General
Manager Zhong Yiming. The Joint Committee, which met regularly
twice a year and held special sessions in Tanggu or Tokyo, was empow-
ered to draft master plans, discuss joint operational projects, select
drilling locations, and approve financial and technical arrangements.
The Joint Committee also set up a Joint Technical Subcommittee in
Tanggu and a Joint Procurement Subcommittee in Tokyo. Deputy
General Manager Wu Xunze explained to me in July 1981 that the Joint
Committee's operational and financial decisions required approval by

the Ministry of Petroleum Industry within fifteen days. Matsuzawa reported to the Board of Directors of both Japanese corporations and indirectly to the JNOC and the MITI. In this sense, the Bohai operations were intergovernmental in nature.

According to a master plan, the Japanese decided to conduct a geophysical survey of a 16,450-km area in the southern and western zones of the Bohai Sea, analyze the data generated, test-drill about 48 wells, and select sites for about eight offshore oilfields. All these exploratory operations would take five to seven years. In the next stage of oil development, for four to five years, they planned to drill 610 wells and to construct 56 production platforms. It was estimated that these wells would produce 100 million kl out of 114 million kl of recoverable oil reserves over fifteen years; as of 1979, only three Chinese oilfields—Daqing, Shengli, and Huabei—produced more crude oil than the Bohai Sea's projected peak-year output. The Japanese planned to complete feasibility studies in the Chengbei oilfield in 1980 and to drill 46 wells with two to three platforms in two to three years (by 1983 or 1984). They were confident that they could extract all of the 3.2 million kl of recoverable oil reserves at Chengbei. At the peak of production, Japan's total oil share in Bohai and Chengbei was expected to reach 4.08 million kl a year (3.8 million kl from Bohai and 0.28 million kl from Chengbei). Even this maximum annual volume constituted only 1.5 percent of Japan's total oil imports (277 million metric tons) during 1979 or one-half of China's total oil sales to Japan during the same year, but it was seven times Japan's own 1979 oil production. The Chinese and the Japanese did not think of their Bohai collaboration as an isolated experience; they hoped that this experiment would open a door to other and perhaps more substantial oil projects elsewhere in China's rich continental shelf, perhaps near the Diaoyu Islands and the Pearl River. Moreover, the Chinese wished to benefit from the potentially wide-ranging technical spillover from the Bohai experience.

On the basis of the JNOC's earlier analysis of the Chinese data collected in the southern Bohai Sea during 1979, the Joint Committee in September 1980 selected four possible locations for oil prospecting. It took several months for both sides to prepare for the first drilling operation and to negotiate and conclude seventeen subcontracts. For the Bohai project the Japanese agreed to use Chinese machinery and workers, mostly from the offshore branch; they rented a jack-up type of offshore drilling rig, Bohai No. 6 (produced by Bethlehem Steel in Singapore, purchased in 1975, and delivered to China in March 1979), with its 75-member Chinese work force, supply boats (Binhai No. 211 and Binhai No. 207), tugboats, helicopters, trucks, cranes, and other necessary equipment. On December 13, 1980, the first joint exploratory drilling started at a location (BZ28-1-Loc. A) 24 m deep at a central point in the southern Bohai Sea; it was about 180 km from Tanggu (and 100 km from Longkou on the Shandong peninsula), requiring a one-hour flight by helicopter or a ten-hour navigation by supply boat from Tanggu. The Japanese were somewhat reluctant to start during the cold, icy, and windy winter weather, but the Chinese insisted on an early undertaking. The Chinese workers on the rig, plus two Japanese technical supervisors and two interpreters, were divided into two teams; in order that drilling could proceed continuously, each team worked twelve hours a day, seven days a week.

The unexpectedly mild weather allowed them to drill 30–40 m a day. After an uninterrupted four weeks of work, they returned to the land for a three-week rest.[22] The Japanese reserved rooms in the Tianjin Guest House and rented Beidaihe's seaside resort facilities. On March 6, 1981, the drilling stopped at the depth of 3,334.5 m. The core samples extracted from this well were promptly flown to Japan. A series of laboratory tests conducted there pleased both sides immensely because they showed this to be a high-yield oil well that would produce 1,000 metric tons (7,500 barrels) of crude oil, 600,000 m^3 of natural gas, and 50 tons of condensate a day.[23] Moreover, this high-quality, low-sulfur, and lightweight crude oil (39° API, 0.06 percent sulfur content, and 30° pour point) was superior to Daqing oil (33° API, 0.1 percent sulfur content, and 32.5° pour point) and resembled the Arabian-light Middle Eastern crude.

Although drilling of this well cost 2 billion yen, the Japanese and Chinese were very happy with the success of their first collaborative effort and were also hopeful for comparable achievements in the future. The success was particularly welcome news to the Chinese, who were in the embarrassing process of renegotiating the cancellations of plant imports, including Baoshan equipment, from Japan. *Renmin Ribao* (May 14, 1981) proudly reported this news of Sino-Japanese cooperation on its front page with a photograph of the Bohai No. 6 rig showing burning oil in the Bohai Sea. If Baoshan was a source of widespread disappointment and frustration in the new era of Sino-Japanese economic cooperation, Bohai symbolized a promise of interdependence and mutually beneficial relations between the two Asian neighbors. A comparison of Bohai with Baoshan shows that the Chinese were more deliberate and patient in their Bohai negotiations and more modest and realistic in their financial and technological commitments to its projects. The intense Baoshan debates in China, especially the anti-Japanese sentiments that were expressed, did not seem to have any negative effect upon the Sino-Japanese cooperative efforts in Bohai. Conversely, both sides wished to demonstrate that despite the Baoshan setback they had tangible proof of productive economic cooperation. The Japanese, who had a kind of inferiority complex in oil development technology because of the advancements of their more experienced U.S. and West European competitors, regarded the Bohai experiment as an opportunity to confirm their international status. In fact, JCODC President Inoue called the Bohai experiment a "victory of Japanese science and technology."[24] Whereas the Chinese, perhaps due to their immediate economic difficulties, preferred to start oil production promptly from a successfully tested well, the Japanese wished to have a comprehensive and technologically feasible picture prior to any production attempt.

In late May 1981 the two sides moved Bohai No. 6 50 km west and started drilling the second test well (BZ25-1-Loc. A) in the southern Bohai Sea. When I visited Bohai (July 10, 1981), drilling had reached 3,100 m at the rate of 30 m a day and the core deposits from this well clearly showed a trace of black oil. Drilling stopped at 4,000 m on September 12, 1981. The test of this second well indicated that it would produce 360 metric tons of crude oil and 28,000 m^3 of natural gas a day.[25] Although the estimated output was less than that of the first test well, the quality of the second well's oil was equally good—33° API, 0.13 percent sulfur content, and 22.5° pour point (see Table 21).

With regard to the western Bohai Sea, the Japanese had concluded a contract to use the offshore branch's seismic surveying resources and had started their survey in July 1980 by using Binhai No. 511 (built by Mitsui Shipbuilding in 1979) and Binhai No. 504 (a remodeled ferry purchased from France in 1976). Based on the data analysis by Japanese and Western subcontractors, the Joint Committee, in April 1981, chose two drilling locations. The Japanese chartered another Chinese jack-up type rig, Bohai No. 8 (produced by Marathon Le Tourneau, purchased in 1978, and delivered to China in January 1980), for their drilling in an area 12 m deep (CFD13-1-Loc. A) in the western Bohai Sea, 50 km from Tanggu, in July 1981. When the drilling stopped in October 1981, this third test well, too, was found to be a successful one; it was expected to produce 272 metric tons per day of good crude oil (35° API, 0.19 percent sulfur content, and 27° pour point) and 36,000 m^3 of natural gas a day.[26] The promising offshore oil explorations in the Bohai Sea (and in the Beibu Gulf) enabled Premier Zhao Ziyang to make an optimistic report on China's energy policy at the National People's Congress in December 1981, which received prolonged applause from its delegates.[27] Moreover, the first appraisal well drilled in a location 2 km north of the first test well confirmed a daily output of 390 metric tons of high-

TABLE 21
RESULTS OF TEST AND APPRAISAL WELLS

	FIRST TEST WELL	SECOND TEST WELL	THIRD TEST WELL	FIRST APPRAISAL WELL	SECOND APPRAISAL WELL	DAQING OIL
Date of completion	Mar. 1981	Sept. 1981	Oct. 1981	Apr. 1982	Aug. 1982	—
Depth (m)	3,334	4,000	3,000	3,990	3,200	—
Crude output (tons/day)	1,000	360	272	390	32	—
Weight API (°)	39.0	33.0	35.0	40.7	—	33.1
Sulfur content (percent of wt.)	0.06	0.13	0.19	—	—	0.11
Pour point (°C)	30.0	22.5	27.0	—	—	32.5
Gas output (m³/day)	600,000	28,000	36,000	70,800	620,000	—
Gas condensate (tons/day)	50	—	—	—	238	—

SOURCES: International Oil Trading Corporation, Japan-China Economic Association, and *Renmin Ribao* (May 14, October 12, and November 14, 1981; and June 15 and October 3, 1982).

quality crude oil and 70,800 m³ of natural gas in May 1982.[28] A nearby appraisal well completed in August 1982 did not yield a high daily output of crude oil (only 32 metric tons) but showed a large natural gas deposit (620,000 m³ per day).[29]

The Chengbei operation was also moving smoothly. The Japanese completed their feasibility studies in Tokyo with the participation of Chinese technicians and decided to begin their development efforts, using two platforms, in the spring of 1982. Nippon Steel had a $1.5 million contract to manufacture a production platform (B) and delivered it to China in November 1981; another platform (A) was built by the Chinese with Nippon Steel's software assistance. The two platforms (A and B) are 1.6 km apart in the Bohai Sea and are linked by a pipeline that is intended to move oil from platform A to platform B so that the accumulated oil can be transported by tanker.[30] The production of oil by Sino-Japanese joint efforts at Chengbei is expected to start in late 1984 at platform B and a year later at platform A. The Chinese, who had discovered the Chengbei oilfield in November 1972 and had test-produced oil there beginning in December 1977, produced a modest amount of crude oil (6,933 metric tons per month as of February 1981) from eight wells and exported it to Japan through Dalian. However, the quality of Chengbei oil was not good and Japanese customers were reluctant to buy it.

The close daily contacts between Chinese and Japanese personnel at Bohai revealed that language differences still presented a barrier to effective communication and joint operations. In 1981, in an attempt to overcome this persistent problem, the Japanese selected 37 Chinese students who had studied Japanese at Lushun (or Port Arthur, near Dalian) and brought Japanese language teachers to China to train them for three months; the best eight Chinese students were then sent to Japan's Takushoku University for a six-month intensive Japanese program. The Chinese returnees assumed an important role in facilitating communications at Bohai; I was impressed by their ability to converse in Japanese.

Although the Chinese had plenty of available manpower for the Bohai project and the offshore branch had no difficulty in choosing the most qualified persons from its work force of 14,000, the Japanese were confronted by a potentially serious shortage of technically competent and experienced supervisory staff members. The operations in the Bohai Sea required physical rigor, the ability to co-operate with foreigners, and above all the willingness to work continuously in a distant, lonely, and alien environment. The Japanese had a difficult task; the lofty principles or rhetoric of friendship and cooperation did not help much at

Tanggu or in the middle of the Bohai Sea. On a hot, humid, and dusty summer day in 1981, I saw young Japanese technicians and managers working hard in rented Chinese offices without air conditioners; some were busy preparing for Japanese Ambassador Yoshida Kenzo's impending inspection of Bohai. Yet they showed a sense of pride in their technological achievements. In the field office director's room were displayed a blown-up color photograph of Bohai No. 6, a few elaborately labeled bottles of sample crude oil and liquid natural gas extracted from the first test well, and a large wall chart showing daily drilling progress.

Because the numbers of drilling rigs, production platforms, survey ships, and other required facilities were expected to increase every year, the problem of a manpower shortage was bound to loom large for the Japanese oil executives. Although they were reluctant to imitate the French, who had widely advertised the Bohai jobs in Hong Kong and elsewhere in Southeast Asia, they knew this might become an unavoidable option. Another option might be to hire Chinese personnel and to provide them with the necessary technical and managerial training. But the Japanese were uneasy about China's lack of a clear legal framework for international economic relations, including the employment of Chinese personnel by foreign companies. Moreover, they were not always satisfied with the quality of preparedness of Chinese personnel and equipment, which they were obligated to charter for Bohai's operations. The JCODC, in cooperation with the French, decided to open a technical training center for the Chinese at Tanggu in 1982. A relatively small number of Chinese technicians (several dozen men) were selected to undergo a one- to two-year training program.

In order to accommodate the increasing number of Japanese (and French) oil specialists employed in the Bohai projects, the Tianjin municipal government imported prefabricated housing units from the Nippon Sharyō Seizōgaisha and took only 110 days to build the Bohai Binguan in Tanggu in 1981.[31] Unlike the Boashan Binguan, which is a high-rise hotel, this one-story complex has 40 units for families and 70 two-room apartments for singles. It includes a swimming pool, tennis courts, restaurant, nursery, gift shop, post office, water tower, water treatment facility, automobile repair garage, and conference room. The Tianjin municipal government rented 60 units to the Japanese and 50 units to the French. On a rainy morning in June 1982 when I revisited Tanggu and saw the Bohai Binguan, I sensed a strange feeling of isolation and quiet despite the busy movement of Chinese receptionists and maids. My old friend Saitō Takashi, who had transferred from Tokyo to Tanggu as general manager of the Exploration Department in the Tianjin field office in early 1982, said that Japanese and French residents at this binguan did not socialize with each other except on the tennis courts, and in the winter they all were surrounded by the desolate, frozen salt fields.[32] On Sundays he and his colleagues often went to Tianjin City by company bus for a change of scene; he had left his wife and school-aged children in Japan. He expressed concern about the persistent problems of China's cumbersome bureaucratic system and low technical competence, which contributed to the slow pace of the Bohai operations.

The Chinese leaders were equally concerned about the bureaucratic problems that were affecting all aspects of China's oil diplomacy as well as other economic activities. In February 1982 the Chinese State Council announced issuance of regulations governing China's collaborative oil development with foreign companies; it also set up, under the Ministry of Petroleum Industry, the China National Offshore Oil Corporation headed by General Manager Qin Wencai (vice-minister of Petroleum Industry), who had played an important role in Bohai negotiations with Japan and France.[33] This corporation (as distinguished from the China National Oil and Gas Exploration and Development Corporation, which was charged with onshore oil projects) was responsible for centralizing all negotiations and management of offshore oil development with foreign companies and supervising the four operational oil companies—Bohai Sea, Yellow Sea, Eastern South China Sea, and Western South China Sea. The Bohai Sea Oil Company (*Bohai shiyougongsi*), headed by General Manager Wei Buren, absorbed the principal functions of the offshore branch at Tanggu; Zhong Yiming and Wu Xunze remained as its deputy general managers. As part of the nationwide bureaucratic reorganization measures, the China-Japan Cooperation Department and the China-France Cooperation Department in the offshore branch were merged into the Exploration and Development Department in the Bohai Sea Oil Company. In May 1982, Minister of Metallurgical Industry Tang Ke, who had previously served as vice-minister of petroleum and chemical industries during the 1960s and 1970s, replaced Kang Shien, who was appointed state councillor without explicit functional responsibilities. The MPI streamlined its top-heavy bureaucratic leadership by reducing the number of its vice-ministers from twelve to two; both Zhang Wenbin and Qin Wencai were removed from their subcabinet positions. However, all these legal and personnel changes did not have any substantive impact upon Sino-Japanese cooperation in the Bohai Sea.

The Japanese were concerned about oil transportation problems in the long run, because the shallow Bohai Sea was congested with Chinese and foreign vessels using Dalian, Tianjin, Qinhuangdao, and other ports. The Chinese planned to expand substantially Qinhuang-dao's port facilities to allow export of coal and Daqing oil to Japan. One possible solution to these problems was to ship Bohai's crude oil to Longkou on the Shandong peninsula and then to transport it via a 100-km pipeline, to be constructed from Longkou to Yantai, located in the Bohai Straits, so that large tankers could transport oil to Japan, or, alternatively, via a 200-km pipeline to be constructed across the Shandong peninsula from Longkou to Qingdao on the Yellow Sea.[34] The latter route would avoid the Bohai Straits, but more funds and time would be required for pipeline construction. Another option under active study was construction of a large concrete storage tank on oil production sites in the Bohai Sea for direct transportation of oil by tankers.[35] The Japanese expected to deal with this transportation problem prior to Bohai's full-scale oil production.

One of the most serious problems faced by Japan and China in their joint Bohai operations was the dramatic increase in their projected financial burdens. The JCODC was alarmed by this problem because the rental fee for a Chinese oil rig in 1982 had risen to $30,000 per day—twice as much as originally estimated—and because oil drilling was found to require a deeper descent and thus more days to complete than initially projected.[36] Furthermore, the oil exploration efforts in Bohai were expected to need two additional years. Hence the JCODC tripled its estimated exploration cost—from $210 million to $600 mil-lion—and decided to expand its current capital assets from 18.6 billion yen to 30 billion yen by the end of 1982.[37] However, the JCODC's private participants (particularly oil companies) resisted the request for addi-tional capital investment due to their own financial weaknesses. As the prices of oil equipment increased, the Chinese, too, became increas-ingly worried about the inevitably heavy burden of their oil develop-ment costs in Bohai. During his state visit to Tokyo in May 1982, Premier Zhao Ziyang asked the Suzuki government to increase the Japanese Eximbank's funds for China's Bohai oil projects.[38] Yet Ding Min, deputy director of the First Department of Asian Affairs in the Chinese Ministry of Foreign Affairs, expressed his satisfaction with the achievements of the Bohai oil projects and said that no OECD member-state had registered any objection to the Japanese Eximbank's financing commitments in Bohai.[39] The Sino-Japanese Joint Committee concern-ing the Bohai projects, which met in Tokyo in October 1982, agreed to increase the estimated exploration expense from $210 million to $599 million, to extend the exploration period for two more years (until May 1987), and to add a fourth drilling rig to the Bohai operations.[40] However, the French Société Nationale Elf Aquitaine, which had drilled two inconclusive test wells in the northern Bohai Sea, was anticipated to withdraw from the Bohai Sea and to concentrate its efforts on the Yellow Sea and South China Sea.[41] In spite of the rising costs of the Bohai project and the expected French withdrawal, the Japanese were determined to move ahead in their Bohai operations, and they received encouragement from the Reagan administration, which, in accordance with its imposition of anti-Moscow economic sanctions, prevented Japan's Sakhalin Oil Development Corporation from using U.S.-licensed equipment in 1982.

China's Oil Exports

○   While the Bohai oil exploration was under way, China continued to export Daqing crude oil to Japan. The way in which both sides negotiated the exact amounts and prices of oil exports each year, as well as the method of export, suggested the volatile nature of international oil diplomacy and the uncertain future of economic cooperation between China and Japan. The first major breakthrough in China's oil sales to Japan took place in the immediate aftermath of Beijing-Tokyo diplomatic normalization, when Kimura Ichizō (president of the Kansai Regional Headquarters of the Japanese Council for Promotion of International Trade), who had long played an important role in Sino-Japanese economic and political relations, was suddenly invited to Beijing (October 1972).[42] Premier Zhou Enlai told him that as a gift commemorating establishment of diplomatic relations, China had decided to accommodate Japan's repeated requests for oil purchases. Upon his return to Japan, Kimura and his associates promptly put together a consortium of four major oil companies, nine power companies, and six steel corporations that were interested in purchasing Chinese oil. In March 1973, this consortium established the International Oil Trading Corporation (IOTC) under President Matsubara Yosomatsu (chairman of the Kansai Petroleum Company and of Hitachi Shipbuilding) and Vice-President Kimura Ichizō and added two oil companies to its membership. In the spring of 1973, this consortium held a series of three negotiating sessions with the China National Chemicals Import and Export Corporation (CNCIEC) and agreed to buy 1 million metric tons of crude oil at the price of $3.93 per barrel during 1973 (see Table 22). A Chinese oil tanker (the Jinhuhao) left Dalian in the Bohai Sea and delivered the first shipment of 35,000 metric tons of Daqing oil to the Hyogo Refinery of the Idemitsu Industrial Corporation in May. It was treated as a historic occasion in Japan because Japan's high-growth economy required increasing imports of oil from diversified sources. A large number of

TABLE 22
CONTRACTS FOR CHINESE OIL EXPORTS TO JAPAN, 1973–1982
(in thousands of metric tons)

YEAR	TOTAL	INTERNATIONAL OIL TRADING CORP.			JAPAN-CHINA OIL IMPORT ASSOC.			AMOUNT PLANNED IN LONG-TERM TRADE AGREE.
		Base	Addition	Unfulfilled	Base	Addition	Unfulfilled	
1973	1,000	1,000						
1974	4,900	1,500	1,800		1,000	600		
	(−900)							
1975	6,900	5,400		300	1,500	600	600	
	(+900)							
1976	6,500–8,500	4,000–6,000	300	500	2,100	600	180	
	(−680)					400		
1977	4,700–5,500	2,800–3,300	200	60	1,900–2,200	250	20	
	(+450)		500			180		
	(+680)							
1978	7,100	4,300	60		2,800	20		7,000
	(+80)							
1979	7,640	4,640		90	3,000		30	7,600
	(−120)							
1980	8,000	5,000	90		3,000	30		8,000
	(+120)							
1981	8,300	5,236			3,064			9,500
1982	8,300							15,000

SOURCES: International Oil Trading Corporation; Japan-China Economic Association.

Japanese business and government leaders attended a party at the Hotel New Otani to celebrate the arrival of Chinese oil and the inauguration of the IOTC.

The IOTC's monopoly of importation of Chinese oil was broken in July 1974 when the Japanese Council for Promotion of International Trade, with China's blessing, brought seventeen non-IOTC oil companies and nine trading firms into another consortium called the Japan-China Oil Import Association (JCOIA) under President Hasegawa Ryūtarō of the Asia Petroleum Company. Whereas IOTC's six oil companies were known as Japan's indigenous or "national" industries (such as Mitsubishi Oil, Maruzen Oil, and Kyōdō Oil), JCOIA's seventeen oil companies were largely affiliates of foreign oil industries.[43] The CNCIEC usually conducted separate negotiations with the IOTC and the JCOIA either in Beijing or in Tokyo. This dual organizational setup meant an overlap of Japanese efforts, but the Chinese welcomed the obvious advantages of competitive elements and broad representation in their oil negotiations with Japan. (The practice of organizational dualism was reminiscent of China's utilization of the memorandum and friendship trade methods in the 1960s and early 1970s.) Kimura Ichizō admitted that Japanese oil and related industries failed to form a united front for the importation of Chinese oil, but he maintained that the IOTC and the JCOIA had a close cooperative relationship.[44]

For 1974 the CNCIEC agreed to sell 4.9 million metric tons of oil to Japan—3.3 million metric tons via the IOTC and 1.6 million metric tons via the JCOIA. This contracted volume represented a dramatic fivefold increase over the previous year; however, slightly less than 4 million metric tons were actually delivered during 1974 (see Table 23), and this constituted only 1.6 percent of Japan's total annual oil imports. In light of the Middle Eastern oil embargo and the worldwide oil price hike, China raised its oil price to $14.80 p/b (a price much higher than that of Indonesia's Minas oil, whose quality was quite comparable to Daqing's) for the first half of 1974, but in July adjusted the price downward so that it was close to the level of the Minas oil price (see Table 24). The Chinese proposed to export to Japan Shengli oil beginning in 1976 and Dagang oil beginning in 1977, but both the IOTC and the JCOIA declined them because of their low quality. Nevertheless, Minister of International Trade and Industry Nakasone Yasuhiro wished to have the assurance of a steady long-range oil supply from China, and in 1974 he dispatched members of the Agency of Natural Resources and Energy to Beijing for intergovernmental discussions. In 1975, the Chinese exported 8.14 million metric tons of oil to Japan, which constituted 3.5 percent of Japan's total oil purchases abroad. This substantial increase

TABLE 23
ACTUAL CHINESE OIL DELIVERIES TO JAPAN, 1973–1981
(in thousands of metric tons)

YEAR	AMOUNT CON-TRACTED	AMOUNT EX-PORTED	PERCENTAGE OF JAPAN'S TOTAL OIL IMPORTS	EXPORTED VIA INTERNATIONAL OIL TRADING CORP.	EXPORTED VIA JAPAN-CHINA OIL IMPORT ASSOC.
1973	1,000	1,000	0.4	1,000	0
1974	4,900	3,990	1.6	2,990	1,000
1975	7,800	8,140	3.5	5,740	2,400
1976	6,800	6,150	2.6	3,830	2,320
1977	5,950	6,540	2.8	3,930	2,610
1978	7,100	7,200	3.1	4,370	2,830
1979	7,640	7,560	3.1	4,590	2,970
1980	8,000	8,120	3.7	5,090	3,030
1981	8,300	8,320	4.2	5,250	3,070

Source: International Oil Trading Corporation.

reflected the impressive growth of China's total oil output. The Chinese also lowered their oil price below that for Minas. Moreover, they accepted the Japanese request to change a yuan-denominated payment procedure to one based on dollars and agreed to allow the international

TABLE 24
PRICE OF CHINESE OIL EXPORTED TO JAPAN,
1973–1982
(in dollars per barrel)

YEAR	MONTH(S)	CHINA'S DAQING OIL	MONTH(S)	INDONESIA'S MINAS OIL
1973	Apr.–Sept.	3.93	Apr.–Sept.	3.73
	Oct.	3.93	Oct.	4.75
	Nov.–Dec.	3.93	Nov.–Dec.	6.00
1974	Jan.–Mar.	14.80	Jan.–Mar.	10.80
	Apr.–June	14.80	Apr.–June	11.70
	July–Sept.	12.85	July–Sept.	12.60
	Oct.–Dec.	12.85	Oct.–Dec.	12.60
1975	Jan.–Sept.	12.10	Jan.–Sept.	12.60
	Oct.–Dec.	12.30	Oct.–Dec.	12.80
1976	Jan.–Dec.	12.30	Jan.–Dec.	12.80
1977	Jan.–June	13.15	Jan.–June	13.55
	July–Dec.	13.20	July–Dec.	13.55
1978	Jan.–Dec.	13.20	Jan.–Dec.	13.55
1979	Jan.–Mar.	13.73	Jan.–Mar.	13.90
	Apr.–May 14	16.36	Apr. 1–Apr. 30	15.65
			May 1–June 14	16.15
	May 15–June	16.96	June 15–July 14	18.25
	July–Sept.	21.80	July 15–Nov. 16	21.12
	Oct.–Dec. 15	24.00	Nov. 17–Dec. 16	23.50
	Dec. 16–Dec. 31	26.00	Dec. 17–Dec. 31	25.50
1980	Jan.	32.33	Jan.	32.50[a]
	Feb.–May 15	33.13	Feb. 4–Feb. 29	32.65[a]
			Mar. 1–May 20	32.50[a]
	May 16–Aug. 31	34.63	May 21–Aug. 31	33.50[a]
	Sept. 1–Nov. 30	33.13	Sept. 1–Nov. 30	32.50[a]
	Dec.	33.98	Dec.	33.35[a]
1981	Jan. 1–Mar. 31	37.15	Jan. 1–Jan. 31	35.60[a]
			Feb. 1–Apr. 30	36.00[a]
	Apr. 1–June 30	36.50	May 1–June 30	35.75[a]
	July 1–Dec. 31	34.90	July 1–July 31	35.63[a]
			Aug. 1–Aug. 31	35.38[a]
			Sept. 1–Nov. 20	35.25[a]
			Nov. 21–Dec. 31	35.00
1982	Jan. 1–Feb. 28	34.65	Jan. 1–Feb. 28	35.00
	Mar. 1–June 30	34.50	Mar. 1–June 30	35.00

SOURCE: International Oil Trading Corporation.
[a]Government sales price plus premium cost.

practice of usance (30 or 60 days) to Japanese buyers. The Soviet Union quickly accused China of damaging Indonesia's petroleum export policy.[45]

In 1976, however, Chinese oil exports to Japan drastically declined to 6.2 million metric tons, though the price remained constant at $12.30 p/b. The decline was caused by China's internal political turmoil and the resultant oil policy confusion and by Japan's economic slowdown. (The Japanese were also reluctant to buy too much of China's waxy, heavyweight Daqing oil.) Exports slowly increased in the latter half of 1977 when the new Chinese leadership under Premier Hua Guofeng stabilized the domestic political situation following the post-Mao succession struggle and adopted an aggressive economic modernization program that included a renewed emphasis on international economic cooperation. The opening of a new and deep port north of Dalian equipped with two large berths also facilitated China's oil exports. Negotiation of oil prices proved to be increasingly complex and difficult, however. When OPEC decided in December 1976 to adopt two-tiered oil price rates (namely, a 5 percent increase for Saudi Arabia and the United Arab Emirates and a 10 percent increase for Iran, Iraq, and nine other oil-exporting nations), it introduced an element of confusion to Sino-Japanese oil negotiations. Given OPEC's price hike decision and a 5.9 percent increase in the price of Indonesia's Minas oil (to $13.55 p/b), China and Japan settled on a 6.8 percent increase in the price of Daqing oil (to $13.15) for the first half of 1977. When OPEC reunified its oil price in July 1977, the Chinese demanded an increase of 10–20 cents per barrel, citing Minas oil's higher price (by 40 cents) and China's trade imbalance. The Japanese pointed to the easing of the shortage of world oil supplies and struck a compromise for a 5-cent increase, to $13.20 p/b. This price remained stable for the subsequent eighteen months. In spite of the other oil supplies (especially Minas oil) available to them, the Japanese agreed to buy more than the contracted amount from China in October 1977; this decision was probably prompted by Japan's desire to take part in China's new modernization projects. The Chinese delivered 6.5 million metric tons of crude oil to Japan during 1977. At the Association of Southeast Asian Nations (ASEAN) meeting in October 1977, Indonesian Minister of Mining and Energy Mohammad Sadli complained that the Japanese decision to favor Daqing oil over Minas oil was dictated by political considerations. Although Japan's oil imports from Indonesia were about double those from China, Daqing and Minas were competitive in Japan's nonrefinery oil markets and Indonesia's relative importance for meeting Japanese oil requirements decreased between 1973 and 1977. In their negotiations with Japan, the Chinese stated that the criteria or principles on which they based their pricing decisions were as follows: (1) to respect the spirit of OPEC decisions, (2) to take into account global oil prices, including Indonesia's, (3) to consider the quality and other characteristics (such as content) of Chinese oil, (4) to maintain special relations between China and Japan, and (5) to value the future of the two countries' economic cooperation.[46] Notwithstanding this policy elaboration, the shifting Minas oil prices remained a principal determinant of the course of Sino-Japanese oil negotiations.

In an attempt to guarantee China's long-range oil commitments, the Long-Term Trade Agreement (1978–1985) of February 1978 specified a minimum total amount of Chinese oil to be exported to Japan (47.1 million metric tons) through 1982. The exact distribution of imports by IOTC and JCOIA was agreed upon separately.[47] The Chinese promised to fulfill these commitments with Daqing oil or with other oil of comparable quality. The two sides agreed to negotiate the amount of China's post-1982 oil exports to Japan by 1981 and that these exports would exceed 15 million metric tons per year after 1982.

The Chinese met their commitments to Japan at a stable price during 1978. Although China's oil output reached a plateau during 1979 and domestic oil consumption increased by about 10 percent a year, the Chinese were faithful to the Long-Term Trade Agreement;[48] oil exports were a prerequisite for the importation of expensive foreign industrial plants and technology. Yet China's oil price doubled to $26 p/b in that year, reflecting the Iranian Revolution and OPEC oil price increases. The Japanese, who were losing 1 million barrels of oil a day due to the situation in Iran, were panicked into purchasing oil on the spot market. (Its price jumped as high as $37 p/b toward the end of 1979.) In 1980, despite a reduction in their oil output, the Chinese reversed their initial proposal to limit their oil export to Japan to 7 million metric tons and sold Japan more than 8 million metric tons, in part because they wanted to ensure the success of Premier Hua Guofeng's state visit to Japan, during which he planned to emphasize Sino-Japanese cooperation in oil and coal development.[49] However, the oil shipments were often held up or postponed during the summer of 1980 because Japan's fuel demand decreased considerably as a result of effective conservation measures, an economic slowdown, an unusually cool summer, and nuclear power generation.[50] In May 1980, in the wake of another OPEC price hike, which permitted $36.72 p/b for Libyan oil and $35.21 p/b for Algerian oil, the Chinese raised their oil price to a new peak ($34.625), $1.125 higher than Indonesia's. The price was readjusted downward in the last quarter of 1980.

Because of China's drastic economic readjustment measures and decreasing oil production, the Chinese were forced to tell their Japanese oil partners that they were simply unable to carry out their promise to export 9.5 million metric tons in 1981 and that they were prepared only to sell up to 8.3 million metric tons each year. In January 1981, the Chinese unilaterally notified the IOTC and the JCOIA that a new oil price had been set at $37.8 p/b—a $3.825 increase. The Japanese quickly responded with a counterproposal of $36.5—the same price paid for Minas oil. As a compromise, the negotiators split the difference between the two figures and agreed upon $37.15. In April 1981, the price for Minas oil decreased to $35.75, and the Japanese asked the Chinese to follow the Indonesian example; the Chinese consequently lowered the price to $36.5—about the same price reduction made by Minas. When asked about China's oil prices in June 1981, Kimura Ichizō (IOTC vice-president) readily admitted that they were "too high" because the international oil price, including the spot-market price, had declined.[51] In view of the competition from Indonesian oil, he maintained, the Chinese should reduce their oil price to a reasonable level. Subsequently the Chinese, in response to the worldwide oil price decrease, gradually reduced their oil price to $34.9 p/b for the latter half of 1981, $34.65 for the first two months of 1982, and $34.5 for the following four months.

Fluctuating volumes and prices were not the only issues in Sino-Japanese oil negotiations; a host of other issues emerged as the economic relations between the two nations became increasingly complicated. As a matter of equality, the Chinese insisted that 50 percent shipment of exported oil would be carried by Chinese tankers, and the Japanese grudgingly made a limited concession every year. The ratio of oil transported by Chinese ships slowly increased from 33.6 percent in 1974 to 38 percent in 1976; in 1977, the ratio was 40 percent for oil imported by the IOTC and 36 percent for oil imported by the JCOIA. The ratios have increased only slightly in subsequent years. The Chinese also conducted extensive negotiations with Japanese companies to import oil-related technology and machinery, which included drilling rigs and production platforms, several crude oil tankers, supply vessels, oil pipelines, and petrochemical plants and equipment.[52]

The geographical proximity of China and Japan meant that Japan saved on oil transport, and thus China enjoyed a distinct advantage over Indonesia and the Middle East. Yet the Chinese fees for port users and tonnage taxes were higher than those of other nations and were thus subject to negotiation. The particular quality of Daqing oil also presented a difficult problem for Japanese importers. Because of its waxiness, heavy weight, low sulfur content, and high pour point, it required structural changes and new investment in Japan's existing refineries, which had been tailor-made for the Middle Eastern oil. As a result, the Japanese tended to shift the use of Daqing oil from refineries to thermal power plants and steel mills. They faced a dilemma that although Japan's consumption of lightweight oil was increasing, Japan was importing a growing amount of heavyweight oil, such as Daqing and Minas. In order to resolve this dilemma, the Ministry of International Trade and Industry set up an advisory council on heavyweight oil in April 1978. On the council's recommendation, in June 1979 the MITI sponsored establishment of a technical research center to study the effective utilization of heavyweight or low-quality crude oil. Supported by a four-year fund of 24.2 billion yen, of which 75 percent was a government subsidy, it was joined by 26 companies (refineries, engineering firms, and power companies). In December 1979 the MITI also established a committee to study heavyweight oil as part of its Agency of Natural Resources and Energy.[53]

The continued export of Daqing oil to Japan depended upon its availability as well as upon Japan's technological advances in heavyweight oil utilization. Chinese oil exports to Japan fell far short of the targets set in the Long-Term Trade Agreement. Between 1978 and 1982 China failed to meet its export commitments by about 8 million metric tons, which meant a loss of several billion dollars in China's anticipated oil revenue. The main reason for this failure was China's inability to increase its oil output. In fact, China's oil production showed a negative growth rate during 1980 and 1981 (see Table 17). The Chinese were simply unprepared to fulfill their promise to sell 15 million metric tons of oil to Japan in 1982. Since China is unlikely to substantially increase its rate of oil production in the near future, it is unrealistic to anticipate fulfillment of Japan's expectation that China will export 30 million metric tons to Japan in 1985 and 50 million metric tons in 1990. The Chinese instead proposed in 1982 to set the volume of their oil exports to Japan at 8.3 million metric tons annually until 1985. If China's various offshore oil projects, including the Bohai Sea development, progress well and oil production begins in the late 1980s or early 1990s, China's ability to increase its oil exports to Japan may be improved.

The Chinese collaboration with Japan in the Bohai Sea oil projects and exportation of crude oil has constituted a valuable opportunity for China to learn the methods of international oil diplomacy. Until the mid-1970s, the Chinese had no concept of forming extensive joint ventures with foreign companies to exploit their seabed energy resources. Spurred by the imperatives of the four modernizations campaign and led by a pragmatic political leadership, they transcended a narrow ideological framework of economic self-reliance and sought foreign technology and capital to tap their vast offshore oil reserves, which were estimated at 10–20 billion metric tons (75–150 billion barrels).[54] Although the Chinese underwent a period of frustration and adjustment concerning the Bohai negotiations, they developed a sense of confidence in the process of dealing with the complex technical, financial, legal, and organizational issues involved in collaborative oil programs. They assured the Japanese that the growing multinational disputes over China's oil-drilling operations in the East China Sea (the Longjing oilfields) did not have any negative effect on Sino-Japanese cooperation in the Bohai Sea.[55] The Bohai model is a harbinger of China's ambitious plans for other vast offshore regions stretching from the Yellow Sea to the South China Sea and the Beibu Gulf.[56] The JNOC and the Idemitsu Oil Development Corporation (a participant in the JCODC), which joined 46 other foreign oil companies in vying for potentially lucrative development contracts in the Yellow Sea, the Pearl River estuary, and the Beibu Gulf during 1982, wished to exploit their Bohai involvement to influence China to make decisions favorable to Japan. The tangible achievements already registered by the Sino-Japanese cooperation at Bohai can be expected to facilitate similar joint ventures for the development of China's enormous seabed oil resources,[57] and China's cumulative experience in exporting oil to Japan is likely to facilitate its future oil salesmanship in the international market.

Economic Assistance: The Government Loans and Grant

FOUR

The Chinese long resisted the temptation to seek foreign government loans, for both ideological and historical reasons. The rigid Maoist principle of economic self-reliance, coupled with a sense of national pride, prevented them from accepting or participating in various methods of international economic cooperation (such as direct capital investment, joint ventures, free trade zones, and foreign government loans and grants-in-aid). They often reminded themselves that foreign countries had used government loans as an effective instrument for the rapid economic exploitation as well as the political manipulation of China in the nineteenth and twentieth centuries. The only exception was $1.5 billion in government loans that they had received from the "fraternal" socialist countries, the Soviet Union and East European nations, from 1953 to 1960. Whenever the Japanese raised the issue of possible government loans as a form of economic cooperation in the early 1970s, the Chinese unequivocally responded in the negative.[1] However, China's pursuit of pragmatic economic diplomacy overcame its ideological and historical misgivings in the late 1970s. Encouraged by the promise of close economic cooperation symbolized by the Long-Term Trade Agreement concluded in February 1978, its two signatories, Vice-Minister of Foreign Trade Liu Xiwen and JCEA President Inayama Yoshihiro, opened the first serious discussion of the possibility of Japanese government loans in September 1978.[2] At the time of his Tokyo visit in October 1978, Vice-Premier Deng Xiaoping publicly indicated China's interest in receiving such loans.[3] Soon the Chinese had gathered all the available information about Japan's ODA provided to developing nations.

Loan Negotiations

○   After deciding to request government loans (*daikuan* in Chinese or *shakkan* in Japanese) from Japan, the Chinese conducted extensive consultations with Japanese officials and businessmen and put together a package of eight construction projects requiring Japanese assistance in 1979. The package consisted of three hydroelectric power plants (Longtan in Guangxi Zhuang Province, Wuqiangxi in Hunan Province, and Shuikou in Fujian Province), three railroad lines (Yanzhou-Shijiusuo, Beijing-Qinhuangdao, and Hengyang-Guangzhou), and two ports (Shijiusuo on the Yellow Sea and Qinhuangdao on the Bohai Sea). As Table 25 shows, total construction costs were estimated at $5.54 billion (8.56 billion yuan or 1,200 billion yen), of which $2.81 billion (4.26 billion yuan) was earmarked for purchasing foreign machinery, generators, and

TABLE 25
LOAN NEGOTIATIONS
(in millions of dollars)

PROJECT	CHINA'S PRIORITY	CHINA'S ORIGINAL REQUEST	CHINA'S REVISED REQUEST	JAPAN'S ESTIMATE
Shijiusuo port	1	320	220	181
Yanzhou-Shijiusuo Railway	2	300	165	103
Longtan hydroelectric power plant	3	1,550	986	—
Beijing-Qinhuangdao Railway	4	650	375	375
Hengyang-Guangzhou Railway	5	910	660	108
Qinhuangdao port	6	160	104	104
Wuqiangxi hydroelectric power plant	7	810	530	530
Shuikou hydroelectric power plant	8	840	484	—
Beijing hospital	—	—	61	61
Total		5,540	3,585	1,462

SOURCES: *Asahi Shimbun*, September 1 and November 21, 1979; *Look Japan*, June 10, 1980.

construction materials.[4] All these projects were deemed part of an essential economic infrastructure for China's four modernizations program and for its trade expansion with Japan.

The Chinese decision to construct hydroelectric power plants was directly related to the Outline of the Ten-Year Plan for the Development of the National Economy (1976–1985), a goal of which was to double China's electric output (up to 500 billion kwh) by 1985 by construction of ten new large hydropower bases on the Changjiang (Yangzi) River, Huanghe (Yellow) River, and other rivers.[5] Because the Chinese suffered from a chronic power shortage (20–30 percent) in industries and agriculture, they relied heavily on coal-based thermal power generation (over 80 percent), neglecting to tap the great hydropower potential.[6] They estimated that the electric power potential of China's water resources was 580 million kw, of which 370 million kw was considered exploitable, but they actually utilized less than 3 percent (16 million kw) of the estimated reserve.[7] They correctly concluded that not only were the production costs of hydroelectric power plants one-fifth those of thermal power plants, but once constructed, they would also serve other purposes—flood control, irrigation, navigation, fishing, and control of ice formation. Construction of large-scale plants was planned at Longtan (3 million kw), Wuqiangxi (1.5 million kw), and Shuikou (1.4 million kw); the capacities of all would surpass that of China's largest operating plant at Liujiaxia in Gansu Province (1.2 million kw).[8] Since the Chinese lacked construction funds, the advanced technology required for large-scale operations, and machinery, they sought Japan's financial and technical assistance.

Coal was also featured as a major growth project in the Ten-Year Plan; the goal was to open eight major coal mines and to increase coal production from about 618 million metric tons in 1978 to 1,000 million metric tons in 1985. Moreover, as discussed in Chapter 1, the Long-Term Trade Agreement singled out Chinese exports of steam and coking coal as an important way of financing purchases of Japanese industrial plants and thus implementing the four modernizations program. The Chinese claimed that their known coal reserves were 600 billion metric tons, but their technical and financial ability to develop and transport this rich natural energy resource was limited.[9] According to official government statistics, China's coal production showed a moderate increase from 1976 to 1979, as follows: 483 million metric tons (1976), 550 million metric tons (1977), 618 million metric tons (1978), and 635 million metric tons (1979). After the Middle Eastern oil crisis forced the Japanese government to relax its traditional protectionist policy against coal imports, Chinese coal sales to Japan increased from

106 thousand metric tons in 1974 to 450 thousand metric tons in 1978 and 924 thousand metric tons in 1979. Qinhuangdao on the Bohai Sea was used as a trans-shipment point to Japan for steam coal from Datong (Shanxi Province) and coking coal from Kailun (Hebei Province); Lianyungang on the Yellow Sea was used to export steam coal from Huaibei (Anhui Province) and coking coal from Zaozhuang (Shandong Province).[10] Qinhuangdao could handle vessels of up to 25,000 tons, but Lianyungang's capability was limited to 10,000-ton vessels. Although China's initial coal exports to Japan did not constitute an important element either for meeting Japanese energy requirements or for increasing Chinese foreign trade, the Japanese agreed to cooperate with China to develop new coal mines with Eximbank loans and to increase imports of Chinese coal by 3.2 million metric tons in 1982 and by 10 million metric tons in 1985. The projects for Shijiusuo's construction and Qinhuangdao's expansion, as well as those for building the modern railroads linked to these ports, were expected to facilitate China's projected coal exports to Japan.

In the summer of 1979, Vice-Premier Gu Mu (also chairman of the State Capital Construction Commission and of the State Administrative Commission on Foreign Investment) submitted the details of the Chinese projects to Japanese Ambassador Yoshida Kenzō in Beijing; this was followed by further technical discussions between their respective deputies—Xie Beiyi, vice-chairman of the SCCC and of the State Administrative Commission on Foreign Investment, and Japanese Minister to China Ban Shōichi.[11] The four principal participants were eminently qualified to engage in loan negotiations. As director of the Bureau of Asian Affairs in the Ministry of Foreign Affairs during 1972, Yoshida had played a key role in the efforts to achieve Tokyo-Beijing diplomatic normalization. Ban had served as director of the Division of Technical Cooperation in *Gaimushō*'s Bureau of Economic Cooperation. Xie was a veteran technocrat with 25 years of administrative experience in economic agencies such as the SCCC and the State Economic Commission. In September 1979 Gu and Xie paid a twelve-day visit to Japan to negotiate loan-related issues with Japanese leaders, both governmental and private, and to inspect Japanese industries, including Nippon Steel's Kimitsu complex, a Mitsui petrochemical facility, a Toyota automobile plant, a Matsushita electric factory, a Hitachi machine factory, and a Mitsubishi heavy industrial facility. The Chinese visitors met with Prime Minister Ōhira and with other leaders of the Japanese political and financial communities. Gu explained China's overall economic policy and requested long-range, low-interest, yen-denominated loans administered by Japan's Overseas Economic

Cooperation Fund (OECF). In his press conference held in Tokyo, Xie stated China's new policy toward foreign government loans and urged Japan's favorable response to the proposed eight projects.[12] He argued that China and Japan had developed "special economic relations" because 28.5 percent of China's total imports and 60.5 percent of its foreign plant purchases had come from Japan by the end of 1978. Although China had received nongovernmental loan offers from several Western nations such as France ($7 billion), Britain ($5 billion), Sweden, and Canada, he said, Japan was the first nation with which China was prepared to discuss government loans. If yen loans were provided, he promised, China would buy the equipment and machinery required for the eight projects from Japan. Gu also declared: "The funds needed in China's construction are provided by ourselves while we seek foreign funds as an auxiliary. We will accept loans from all friendly nations as long as China's sovereignty is not impaired and the conditions are appropriate."[13]

Japanese government leaders responded sympathetically to the new Chinese policy but believed that the amount of the initial loan request ($5.54 billion) was beyond their financial ability. While trying to build a policy consensus among their diverse bureaucratic units, they dispatched a fourteen-member government survey team to China; led by Yanai Shinichi (director of *Gaimushō*'s Bureau of Economic Cooperation), it included representatives from the Ministries of Finance, International Trade and Industry, and Transportation and from the Economic Planning Agency. Their nine-day visit to China coincided with that of a 40-member delegation organized by the JCEA and led by its president, Inayama; the close government-business cooperation in China was unmistakable. The Japanese survey team inspected four of China's eight proposed construction sites, met with Vice-Premier Gu Mu, and held a series of technical consultations with Chinese officials. It also received a new Chinese loan request ($61 million) for building a large modern hospital equipped with 1,000 beds in Beijing. The Japanese explained the intricate procedural issues involved in loan negotiations and suggested that the Chinese make a clear distinction between required funds from foreign sources and local costs for Chinese labor and for domestically procured equipment and material.[14] Consequently, the Chinese reduced their loan request to $3.5–3.6 billion and estimated their local costs to be $1.9–2.0 billion.[15]

Using the survey team's detailed report and China's readjusted request, the Japanese government attempted to settle the issue of loans promptly so that Prime Minister Ōhira would be able to deliver the loans as Japanese "gifts" during his planned visit to China in December

1979. However, the Japanese government's attempt was constrained by a combination of domestic and foreign pressures. Although a loose coalition of Japan's mainstream business organizations, especially *Keidanren*, and opposition political parties, notably the JSP, strongly supported China's loan requests, pro-Taipei forces (such as the Asian Problems Study Group) within the LDP cautioned the Ōhira government against giving excessive economic assistance to Beijing.[16] Stronger pressure was exerted by the ASEAN, the EEC, the United States, and the Soviet Union, but with varying degrees of intensity. The ASEAN member-states were afraid that Japan's massive loan commitments to China would cause a possible reduction in their own proportion of Japanese ODA funds and that Japanese economic assistance would enable China to modernize its industries and to penetrate ASEAN's domestic markets.[17] It was noted that China, despite its overall trade deficits, had a surplus of $470 million in its ASEAN trade and was a rival to ASEAN members in light and consumer goods industries. The Japanese government pursued a concerted policy intended to woo ASEAN members, as demonstrated by Prime Minister Fukuda Takeo's promise of aid made to the ASEAN in August 1977 ($1 billion over ten years) and by Prime Minister Ōhira's Manila visit in May 1979; it also paid keen attention to the concern expressed by ASEAN members and assured them that their interests would be protected.[18] The EEC and the United States were equally apprehensive of the possibility that, under the umbrella of government loans, Japan might move to monopolize the China market or at least undermine vested economic interests of Western industrial nations.[19] Since the U.S. government, because of legal restrictions (no loans to communist states) and a fund shortage, found it impossible to compete with Japanese public loans to China, it insisted upon Japan's strict adherence to the principle of general "untied" loans, as specified in the joint communiqué issued by U.S. Commerce Secretary Juanita Kreps and her Japanese counterpart, Minister of International Trade and Industry Kōmoto Toshio, in January 1978.[20] The "untied" principle meant that recipients of Japanese government loans should be free to use these loans for buying non-Japanese goods, but in reality 14.9 percent of total Japanese yen credits was tied to purchases of Japanese products during 1978. At the U.S.-Japan consultative conference on economic aid policy held in Washington in October 1979, Yanai Shinichi, who had led the Japanese survey team to China, took great pains to stress that the Chinese would use Japanese loans freely in accordance with international competitiveness.[21] The United States threatened that if the untied principle were not honestly adhered to, it would join the EEC in adopting countermeasures against Japan. Already unhappy with the antihegemony clause in the Sino-Japanese Treaty of Peace and Friendship (1978), the Soviet Union issued a warning to Japan concerning loans to China and declared that "although the Chinese leadership publicly emphasized [economic] modernization in their loan applications to Japan, the underlying purpose of modernization is to increase their military capabilities and war preparedness."[22]

Notwithstanding all the pressures and warnings, the Japanese government decided to go ahead with the Chinese loans and adopted three principles for this purpose: to cooperate with Western nations, to implement a balanced loan policy in view of the interests of other Asian countries, especially the ASEAN, and to avoid making any loan to China's defense-related industries. The Japanese concluded that developmental project loans would be a convenient and useful way of enhancing Japan's long-range economic benefits—in particular, they would guarantee steady coal supplies from China, allow Japan to establish a firm foothold in China's economic infrastructure, and induce a spillover effect to other areas of Sino-Japanese economic cooperation. The fact that direct government loans had been an effective conduit for Japan's successful economic penetration of South Korea, Taiwan, Southeast Asia, and South Asia was well remembered. Japan's direct loan program started in 1958 with a loan of 18 billion yen to India; such loans totaled 3,937 billion yen by the end of 1980 (see Table 26). This amount included a loan of 54 billion yen ($150 million) that the Japanese government agreed to provide to Taiwan during the period 1966–1970. About 80 percent of all such assistance has been extended to Asian countries in the form of project and commodity loans. In fiscal year 1979, about 80 percent of Japan's direct loans (343 billion yen) went to low-income developing countries with a per capita GNP below $580. Major recipients of direct government loans have been (in descending order of amount) Indonesia, India, South Korea, Pakistan, Thailand, the Philippines, Malaysia, Burma, Egypt, and Bangladesh.[23]

Politically, the Japanese Ministry of Foreign Affairs, under the leadership of Sonoda Sunao and then Ōkita Saburō, held the view that government loans and other economic support should be used to encourage the Hua-Deng leadership's moderate and realistic policy, which was consistent with Japanese interests.[24] It is important to note that Sonoda was a key architect of the Sino-Japanese Treaty of Peace and Friendship in 1978, and Ōkita was an "old China hand" with wideranging personal experience and an intense interest in Chinese affairs. As suspected by the Soviet Union, it is conceivable that by strengthening its economic ties with China, Japan wished to pre-empt any prospect of a renewed Sino-Soviet alliance.[25] Undoubtedly Japan had a strong

TABLE 26
JAPAN'S DIRECT GOVERNMENT LOANS BY REGION, 1976–1980
(in billions of yen)

REGION	1976	1977	1978	1979	1980	CUMULATIVE TOTAL, 1958–1980	
						Amount	Percentage
Asia	208.8 (19.9)	308.6 (5.3)	281.6	258.4	399.3	3,256.9 (221.7)	82.7
Africa	15.6	44.0	33.7	42.2	33.9	342.8	8.9
Middle East	14.6	11.4	1.9 (1.7)	15.0	28.4 (1.3)	152.8 (3.0)	3.9
Latin America	9.6	13.0	19.3 (1.0)	27.7	14.7	164.9 (23.5)	4.2
Eastern Europe	0	0	0	0	0	11.0	0.3
Oceania	0	0	3.5	0	5.1	8.6	0.2
Total	248.6 (19.9)	376.9 (5.3)	340.1 (2.8)	343.2	481.3 (1.3)	3,936.9 (248.2)	100.0

SOURCE: *Look Japan*, May 10, 1981.
NOTE: Parentheses indicate amount of debt relief rescheduled and refinanced.

historic sense of competition with the United States and Western
Europe in China. The Japanese were shrewdly reminded by Xie Beiyi in
Tokyo that they fully understood the potential effects of Western
Europe's outstanding nongovernmental loan offers to China. They were
also conscious of Vice-President Walter Mondale's 1979 promise of $2
billion Eximbank credits for China's hydroelectric power development
and other projects. Moreover, at both the 27-nation Conference for
International Economic Cooperation and the OECD ministerial meetings in June 1977, Japan had been pressed to double its ODA funds over
five years. In terms of aid, Japan lagged behind most of the other industrialized nations; the annual allocation of its ODA funds was below the
annual growth rate of its governmental budget. At the Fourth Summit
Meeting of Industrialized Nations held at Bonn in July 1978, Prime
Minister Fukuda promised to double Japan's ODA funds in three years.
In this context, the Japanese regarded China as a new, appropriate
recipient of their increased ODA funds. In fact, they were successful in
including China in the list of less developed countries (LDCs) drawn up
by the eighteen-member Development Assistance Committee's Statis-

tics Commission (part of the OECD) so that Japan's loans to China could be counted as its ODA contribution.

Meanwhile, Japan's MITI prepared a response to the Chinese loan request—a plan to provide $1.5 billion (350 billion yen or about 40 percent of China's revised request) for five of China's proposed projects and a hospital over a period of five to six years (about 60 billion yen per year).[26] Four of the projects included in this plan were regarded as crucial to China's export of coal, which was projected to grow from 3 million metric tons in 1978 to 20 million metric tons in 1985. The MITI was reluctant to support three of China's eight proposals for the following reasons.

Longtan Hydroelectric Power Plant   The Chinese attached the third highest priority to this project to supply electricity to the world's largest aluminum-refining facility (600,000 metric tons a year), which was under construction in cooperation with the United States and some Western European countries. However, the MITI considered it too expensive and competitive with Japanese joint ventures for aluminum development in Indonesia and in Brazil.

Hengyang-Guangzhou Railway Expansion   Since the Chinese wanted to expand this railway system in order to transport Chinese exports to Southeast Asia, the MITI decided not to fund it because of ASEAN sensitivity.

Shuikou Hydroelectric Power Plant   The MITI was afraid that this plant's electricity would be used to develop a special industrial zone, financed by heavy investment by overseas Chinese, and to export Chinese industrial products to Southeast Asia.

The MITI also proposed that Japan give tied loans to China because the Japanese public would oppose the use of its taxes for supporting industries of a third country and because a genuine sense of *Nitchū Kyoryoku* ("Japan-China cooperation") would develop only when Japanese industries and technicians were directly involved. In response to mounting U.S. pressure against tied loans, the MITI pointed out that the United States allocated more than half of its own foreign aid using a "tied" formula—the buy-America policy.

The Ministry of Finance objected to the MITI plan as too costly, but the Ministry of Foreign Affairs proposed to add partial funding for the Hengyang-Guangzhou Railway expansion, already in progress. Yet the Finance Ministry and the Foreign Ministry agreed not to specify a total figure for multiyear government loans as did the MITI because loans were subject to annual budgetary decisions and because the $1.5 billion figure exceeded Fukuda's pledge made to the entire ASEAN region. Concerned about ASEAN's symbolic preoccupations, the Ministry of Foreign Affairs proposed that Japan's first-year loan to China should be limited to 50 billion yen—conspicuously less than the largest annual amount (55 billion yen) received by any one nation (Indonesia) in Southeast Asia. The Foreign Ministry plan called for a grant for a Beijing hospital project as a token of the new friendship between the two neighbors, but the economy-minded Finance Ministry was reluctant to support it.[27]

The Foreign Ministry further suggested that Japan heed the concern of the United States and the EEC by honoring the principle of untied loans. Ultimately, however, it was up to Prime Minister Ōhira to iron out the intrabureaucratic conflicts, strike a compromise solution that would be accepted in Japan, and present a unified loan policy to his Chinese host, Premier Hua Guofeng, during his visit to Beijing in December 1979. Ōhira was accompanied by Foreign Minister Ōkita Saburō, and Hua was assisted by Vice-Premier Gu Mu and Minister of Foreign Affairs Huang Hua.

Loan Agreements

O   The Ōhira-Hua summit meetings in Beijing resulted in agreement on Japan's first postwar governmental loan to China—up to 50 billion yen in fiscal year 1979 to assist six Chinese construction projects[28] (see Table 27); the principle of untied loans was adopted. This loan commitment represented more than 10 percent of Japan's total direct government loans. The Japanese prime minister promised a grant to assist the construction of a Beijing hospital. Regarding the possible extension of this loan in fiscal year 1980 and thereafter, the two sides agreed to hold working-level governmental consultations once a year and to reach a formal decision in accordance with China's construction progress and Japan's budgetary conditions. Yet they had an informal understanding that Japan would continue to appropriate loans for the six projects in the future unless a completely unexpected circumstance arose. In his Beijing press conference, Prime Minister Ōhira made it clear that Japan and China should look toward mutually beneficial cooperation into the twenty-first century, but that this bilateral cooperation should not be seen as constituting a bloc or as collusion against any third country.[29] In particular, the Japanese prime minister attempted to mollify Moscow's growing apprehension about Tokyo-Beijing ties and sent Assistant

TABLE 7
LOANS EXTENDED AND REVISED, FY 1979–1982
(in millions of yen)

PROJECT	FY 1979		FY 1980		FY 1981	FY 1982
	Original	Revised	Original	Revised	Original	Original
Shijiusuo	7,085	7,085	9,860	9,860	18,500	2,300
Yanzhou-Shijiusuo	10,100	10,100	3,110	3,110	3,200	11,800
Beijing-Qinhuangdao	2,500	2,500	11,200	11,200	9,200	30,900
Hengyang-Guangzhou	11,400	3,320	220	0	0	0
Qinhuangdao	4,915	4,915	13,770	13,770	9,100	0
Wuqiangxi	14,000	140	17,840	0	0	0
Subtotal	50,000	28,060	56,000	37,940	40,000	45,000
Commodity loans	0	21,940	0	18,060	20,000	20,000
Total	50,000	50,000	56,000	56,000	60,000	65,000

SOURCE: Overseas Economic Cooperation Fund of Japan.

Minister of Foreign Affairs Katori Yasue to five ASEAN countries.[30] The Japanese envoy assured his nervous Southeast Asian hosts that Japan had no intention of downgrading its ASEAN economic relations or monopolizing the China market; Japan's loans would be used to help develop China's economic infrastructure, not to contribute to industrial production that might compete with ASEAN interests.

The Japanese, in effect, decided to assist China largely to serve their own long-range economic interest. The construction of the Shijiusuo and Qinhuangdao port facilities and of the related transportation networks was directly related to Japan's projected imports of Chinese coal. The Wuqiangxi hydroelectric power plant was expected to develop China's nonferrous metals supplies whose export would help finance China's purchases of Japanese products. Since the Chinese government was determined to expand the Hengyang-Guangzhou Railway, even independently, the Japanese were willing to offer substantially reduced technical assistance to build certain portions of the railway line. Even though they decided to provide a grant to assist construction of the China-Japan Friendship Hospital (*Zhongri youhao yiyuan* in Chinese or *Nitchū yūkō byōin* in Japanese) in Beijing as a symbolic friendly gesture, they also hoped that the Japanese construction companies' experience in this project would be a catalyst leading to other potentially lucrative construction contracts with or projects in China. The two unfunded hydroelectric projects were not only unimportant to Japan but posed a sensitive economic and political problem for its Southeast Asian connections.

The six funded projects can be summarized as follows.[31]

Shijiusuo Port Construction   Located in Rizhao County, Shandong Province, along the Yellow Sea between two other ports (Qingdao and Lianyungang), the Shijiusuo port will have the largest deep-water wharf in China, one that can be used for vessels in the 100,000-ton class. *Renmin Ribao* (December 8, 1979) reported that this location has a relatively peaceful coastline and good geological conditions. The port will have a two-berth unit (one with a 100,000-ton capacity and the other with a 25,000-ton capacity) that can handle 15 million metric tons of coal a year for export (mainly to Japan) and another berth with a 100,000-ton capacity capable of handling 5 million metric tons of iron ore a year imported (mainly from Australia) for China's steel industry, including plants in Taiyuan (Shanxi Province) and Baotou (Inner Mongolian Autonomous Region). Administered by the Ministry of Communications, with an estimated total construction cost of $320 million, it will be completed by 1985.

Yanzhou-Shijiusuo (Yan-Shi) Railway Construction   The Yan-zhou-Shijiusuo Railway in Shandong Province will link the Shijiusuo port with Linyi (which is close to the Huaibei coal mines in Anhui Province) and with Yanzhou, a city on the trunk railway line from Tianjin to Shanghai. A single-track diesel rail line 300 km long, it will transport 10 million tons of cargo a year in each direction. It will be used to ship the coal produced in Yanzhou, Zaozhuang, Gujiao, Fengfeng, and Huoxian. The Chinese possess sufficient technical competence to build this rail line by themselves but need construction equipment, rails, bridges, and other materials from Japan and other industrialized nations. Administered by the Ministry of Railways, with an estimated total construction cost of $300 million, it will be completed by 1985.

Beijing-Qinhuangdao (Jing-Qin) Railway Expansion   Since the existing railway line is already congested and is expected to deteriorate by 1985, this double-track electric railway line, 280 km long, will link the capital to Qinhuangdao on the Bohai Sea by bypassing Tianjin and will transport coal produced in Datong (780 km from Qinhuangdao) in Shanxi Province and Kailuan (112 km from Qinhuangdao) near Tang-shan in Hebei Province. A new double-track railway line (127 km long) will connect Qinhuangdao with Langwopu, and the present single-track line (150 km long) between Langwopu and Beijing's Shuangqiao station will be expanded to a double-track system. Linked to Beijing by an electrified double-track railway, Datong has produced 24 million metric tons of coal a year; Kailuan has produced 21 million metric tons (with a 10 billion metric ton reserve). The expansion of the Beijing terminal complex and electrification of the Beijing-Shanhaiguan line will also be included in the project. Administered by the Ministry of Railways, it is to be completed by 1985 and will cost $650 million.

Qinhuangdao Port Expansion   Located in Hebei Province and linked to the Daqing oilfield by pipeline, the port at Qinhuangdao is the third largest port complex in China and is used to export crude oil and coal, largely to Japan. The new deep-water, ice-free wharf will be able to handle 20 million metric tons of coal a year. The first-phase construction of a 50,000-ton berth and a 20,000-ton berth was completed in 1982; the second-phase construction of two 50,000-ton berths, for which a Japanese loan has been granted, will be finished by 1985. The Ministry of Communications administers this project, whose total estimated cost is $160 million.

Hengyang-Guangzhou (Jing-Guang) Railway Expansion   As the only major link between the northern and southern parts of China, the railway from Beijing to Guangzhou (the Jing-Guang Railway) has a bottleneck problem. Hence a new parallel electric train line from Hunan Province to Guangdong Province is planned. When completed, it will increase the railway's transport capacity by 50 million metric tons a year in each direction. Sixty tunnels and 100 bridges are to be built across the mountainous areas. Japanese technical assistance is needed to help the Chinese build a tunnel 14.3 km long through Dayaoshan Mountain between Pingshi and Lechang in northern Guangdong Province; this tunnel, construction of which has already begun, will shorten the existing railway line by 19.3 km. The Ministry of Railways estimates total construction cost at $910 million, but Japan is only committed to a $108 million technical program.

Wuqiangxi Hydroelectric Power Plant   Located on the Yuanshui River (a tributary of the Changjiang River), in Hunan Province, which lacks coal, the hydroelectric power project at Wuqiangxi will result in construction of a dam 104 m high, 785 m wide, and 70–80 m deep, which will support five generators, each with a capacity of 350,000 kw. The plant will generate 7.1 billion kwh a year and will thus relieve serious power shortages in Wuhan and Changsha.[32] It will be particularly important for the development of rich nonferrous metal deposits—lead, zinc, tin, and antimony, as well as tungsten, which are expected to earn foreign exchange for China. The dam will be also useful for the timber industry and for flood control, irrigation, and navigation on the Yuanshui River. The project, which will require relocation of 200,000 local residents away from the dam areas, will provide employment for 18,000 workers. The project is administered by the Ministry of Water Conservancy and Power (before 1982, the Ministry of Power Industry) and will be completed by 1986. Total construction cost is estimated at $810 million.

The Ōhira-Hua agreement was followed by the return visit to Tokyo of Vice-Chairman of the SCCC Xie Beiyi toward the end of December 1979, the visit to China of three separate Japanese low-level survey teams (railways, ports, and hydroelectric power) in January and February 1980,[33] and the visit to Japan of China's high-level transportation delegation in February and March 1980. This last delegation was led by Guo Hongtao (vice-chairman of the State Economic Commission) and included Tao Qi (vice-minister of communications), Wang Xiaobin (vice-minister of railways), Li Kuisheng (vice-minister of coal industry), and Li Ziqing (deputy director of the Department of Communications, State Economic Commission). Sponsored by the JCEA, these Chinese visitors inspected port facilities, railroad stations, a bullet train factory, and other plants and industries.[34] They also visited the

United States in the spring of 1980 to learn from that nation's rich experience in building long-distance coal transportation systems. Other Chinese leaders who led their delegations to Japan during the spring of 1980 included Vice-Premier and Chairman of the SPC Yu Qiuli, Minister of Foreign Trade Li Qiang, Vice-Chairman of the SPC (and Vice-Chairman of the State Administrative Commission on Foreign Investment) Gu Ming, Vice-Chairman of the State Administrative Commission on Foreign Investment Wang Daohan, and Senior Vice-Minister of Foreign Affairs Han Nianlong. Like Foreign Minister Huang Hua, Han Nianlong (former ambassador to Pakistan and Sweden and vice-minister since 1964) was one of a few senior Chinese diplomats who had not been adversely affected by the Cultural Revolution; he had played a crucial role in normalization of diplomatic relations between Beijing and Tokyo and conclusion of the Sino-Japanese Peace and Friendship Treaty. Not all these visitors were directly concerned with the loan issues, but their discussions with Japan's governmental and business leaders contributed to the establishment of close political and economic ties between Tokyo and Beijing. It is interesting to note that upon the recommendation of Japanese Foreign Minister Ōkita, the Chinese asked Takiyama Mamoru (former Chief Engineer of the Japanese National Railways) to serve as a technical adviser for China's loan-assisted construction projects. In 1939, as a young engineer for the North China Railway (a subsidiary of the South Manchurian Railway), he had participated in the construction of a railroad line (which was not completed) between Datong and Tanggu and had worked at the Tanggu port's coal-handling facilities; he had also known another young Japanese engineer in China—Ōkita Saburō.[35] In January 1972 he organized the Japan-China Association for the Exchange of Civil Engineering Technology, which included Japanese engineers with experience in prewar China.[36]

As a result of their four months of consultations and negotiations, Japanese Ambassador Yoshida Kenzō and Chinese Vice-Minister of Foreign Affairs Han Nianlong signed the nine-paragraph Exchange of Notes on loans translated into three languages (Japanese, Chinese, and English) in April 1980; the ceremony was held in the Great Hall of the People and was attended by Vice-Premier Ji Pengfei (ex–foreign minister).[37] The terms for the Japanese loans were set as follows:

1. The repayment period will be twenty years after a grace period of ten years.
2. The rate of interest will be 3 percent per annum.
3. The disbursement period will be five years from the date of the signing of the relevant loan agreement, but it may be extended with the consent of the two governments.

Representatives of the Overseas Economic Cooperation Fund of Japan and the Chinese State Administrative Commission on Foreign Investment (set up in July 1979 under Vice-Premier Gu Mu) were authorized to sign the loan agreement for each of the six projects after the fund was satisfied of their feasibility. The last paragraph of the notes stipulated:

> The two Governments will jointly review from time to time the progress of the implementation of the Loan and take measures necessary to secure smooth and effective utilization of the Loan and otherwise consult with each other in respect of any matter that may arise from or in connection with the foregoing understanding.[38]

A few days after the Exchange of Notes was signed, SCCC Vice-Chairman Xie Beiyi and OECF President Ishihara Kaneo signed the loan agreements for all six projects during Minister of International Trade and Industry Sasaki Yoshitake's visit to China.[39] Under the principle of general untied loans, all 24 OECD member-states (including Japan, the United States, and the EEC member-states), and all the LDCs, including China, as determined by the OECD's Development Assistance Committee, were authorized to participate in the international bid for the supply of materials to China's six projects. The Soviet Union and other Warsaw Pact member-states were automatically disqualified because they were not participants in the OECD, nor had they been designated as developing nations.[40] An eligible supplier was permitted to import a certain proportion (up to 30 percent) of the materials from noneligible source countries. However, the principle of LDC-untying was adopted for the supply of ships, computers, cargo-handling equipment, and consultant and engineering services—that is, only the developing countries sanctioned by the Development Assistance Committee, plus Japan as the donor country, were eligible. Exceptions to the requirement concerning the international bid were allowed in the following cases: (1) the expected amount of a contract was less than 100 million yen; (2) the number of qualified suppliers was limited; (3) the specification of a particular trademark or contract was necessary for the sake of guaranteeing standardization or compatibility of equipment; or (4) a special situation was recognized by the OECF of Japan. None of these exceptions applied to Chinese suppliers.[41] The loan agreements specified documentary forms certifying a supplier company's nationality and eligibility, the origins of goods supplied, and the 30 percent limit on exports from noneligible source countries. The Chinese apparently estimated that Japanese government loans would be used for survey and other preparatory work (10 percent), vessels such as dredgers (20 percent), equipment (30 percent), and materials (40 percent).[42]

Accordingly, in July 1980, the CNTIC, in cooperation with the China National Machinery Import and Export Corporation and the China National Metals and Minerals Import and Export Corporation, announced international bids for the supply of 260 pieces of construction equipment, such as dump trucks, semitrailer trucks, cars, nine-seat jeeps, light buses, offroad station wagons, hydraulic truck cranes, bulldozers, dozer shovels, wheel loaders, mighty drills, battery locomotives, and crawler excavators. The advertisement, which appeared just once in *Renmin Ribao* (July 16, 1980), both in English and in Chinese, solicited letters requesting prequalification documents and bidding documents between July 20 and August 5 and set August 20, 1980, as the deadline for formal bids. In mid-September, the CNTIC joined the other two corporations in advertising for international bids to supply the construction materials: 58,000 tons of steel products (pipes, wire rods, sheets, bars, sections, window sections), 85,000 tons of Portland cement, and timber (red and white pine logs and fir logs). Initial letters of inquiry had to be received between September 22 and October 5, and the final deadline was October 30, 1980. The advertisement stated: "The payment for all purchases is to be made under the Loan. We hereby invite nationals of all the eligible source countries or well reputable and experienced manufacturers and/or trading companies organized and registered in and controlled by the eligible source countries to participate in the bid."[43] It also explained the untied nature of these bids. The prequalification documents requested the following information and documents, in English.[44]

1. The full name of the manufacturer and/or trading company and the country in which it is registered
2. Brief company history
3. The regulations of the company
4. The organizational structure and the names of the high-level executives of the company and the consortium to which it belongs
5. Paid-up capital and yearly total volume of business for the preceding three years and total net profit
6. Name of the bank reference and a certificate of financial standing issued by the bank reference
7. Name of the authorized agent and a letter of authority from the manufacturer (if it is an agent)
8. Data on manufacture and sale of similar equipment (or materials) by the company in the past three years, list of references, and a certificate of quality

9. Supply capacity, and time of expected delivery of the equipment and materials in item 8

About 50 companies participated in the first round of bids, worth about 5 billion yen, in August 1980, but the Chinese decisions and announcement were delayed several months. The United States and other OECD member-states complained that their companies did not have advance information or sufficient time to request and prepare prequalification and bidding documents on time, and that Japanese firms in reality enjoyed distinct advantages over foreign competitors. It was estimated that Japan and China captured about one-third of the contracts each, and the remaining third was shared by Hong Kong, Western Europe, and the other countries. Japan was the dominant supplier of construction machinery and equipment, and China awarded itself contracts mainly for the supply of materials.[45] The Bank of China was authorized to issue letters of credit to the manufacturers and trading companies that were awarded contracts and to use its yen account in the Bank of Tokyo, to which the OECF deposited funds. Financial settlements were made in yen or in dollars, but yuan were used for Chinese suppliers. The same procedures for competitive international bids and financial settlements were followed in 1981 and 1982.[46]

Progress on Loan-Supported Projects

O   The extension of government loans for fiscal year 1980 was assessed by the Japanese government's survey team that was dispatched to China in October 1980, and the amounts were agreed upon at the bilateral working-level meetings held in Tokyo in November; SCCC Vice-Chairman Xie Beiyi and *Gaimushō's* Bureau Director Yanai Shinichi represented their respective governments. The amount (56 million yen) was formally announced in the joint press communiqué issued by Vice-Premier Gu Mu and Minister of Foreign Affairs Itō Masayoshi on December 5, 1980, following the first regular Sino-Japanese ministerial conference in Beijing.[47] Foreign Ministers Itō and Huang Hua signed and exchanged the notes for this purpose and Ambassador to China Yoshida Kenzō and SCCC Vice-Chairman Xie Beiyi signed the accompanying minutes.[48] The loan agreements for China's six construction projects were signed a few days later and included the same terms as the fiscal year 1979 agreements. In an attempt to keep a "balance," according to a Japanese official, the amount of loans to China was set below the amount of Japanese loans to Indonesia (58 billion yen).[49]

In spite of Japan's eagerness to make loan commitments of 106 billion yen for fiscal years 1979 and 1980, the Chinese were very slow to utilize these loans for the construction of their six important projects; contracts totaling only about 300 million yen had been concluded by March 1981.[50] The Chinese had not developed concrete construction plans and were initially unfamiliar with the complexities involved in acceptance of foreign government loans—specifically, Japan's bureaucratic procedures and the international bidding system. The Japanese OECF conducted a seminar on government loans in China and set up a liaison office in Beijing[51] in June 1980 to assist Chinese loan administrators, but it was difficult for Japanese representatives to teach the ABCs of intergovernmental loan procedures in a short time.

At times the Chinese were confused and frustrated; for example, Vice-Chairman of the State Energy Commission (and Vice-Minister of Coal Industry) Wang Xinsan reportedly blamed Japan for the lack of progress in China's coal transport projects.[52] The Chinese failed to develop a well-coordinated, consistent policy regarding these projects because some die-hard advocates of strict economic self-reliance apparently insisted that a high priority be given to domestic procurements rather than to foreign purchases[53] and because a variety of bureaucratic units were involved in China's developmental projects. Both the SCCC and the State Administrative Commission on Foreign Investment were primarily responsible for overall decisions on construction projects and loan negotiations; the CNTIC and other functionally specific corporations under the Ministry of Foreign Trade handled international bidding and foreign procurements; and the Ministries of Railways, Communications, and Power Industry administered the construction of railways, ports, and hydroelectric power plants, respectively. The Ministries of Railways and Communications had a dispute over the procurement of coal-transporting trains because the Ministry of Railways relied upon China's local funds, whereas the Ministry of Communications used Japanese loans for port projects. The dispute was evidently resolved by Takiyama Mamoru's friendly mediation.[54]

Clearly, China's intrabureaucratic differences and factional rivalries tended to undermine efficient development administration. It is important to point out that the expensive Wuqiangxi hydroelectric power plant and the Hengyang-Guangzhou Railway expansion were reportedly criticized in China as CCP Chairman Hua Guofeng's mistakes.[55] Most important, as a result of China's economic readjustment policy, basic construction expenditures were dramatically cut, and this local fund shortage contributed to the postponement of these two projects, as well as many other industrial programs, such as Baoshan's second-phase construction, during 1981. Added to the Wuqiangxi project's financial difficulties were the extravagant scale of its initial construction design and the immense problems associated with the future relocation of 200,000 local residents away from the areas chosen for dam construction. Apparently the local farmers vehemently resisted the idea of leaving their traditional farmlands, and their acquisition of new land and housing facilities required substantial governmental expenditure. Yet in June 1981, Chinese Commercial Counselor to Japan Wu Shudong, a Japanese-trained veteran trade official, maintained that China was still interested in the eventual completion of the Hengyang-Guangzhou Railway and the Wuqiangxi project.[56]

As discussed in Chapter 2, in order to help finance Baoshan's first-phase construction and the building of the Daqing petrochemical complex, the Japanese government decided to intervene in the private contracts concluded between China and Japanese companies because the postponement or cancellation of these two projects, according to one MITI official, would have a "chilling effect" on Tokyo-Beijing relations.[57] Consequently, as part of the financing package totaling 300 billion yen ($1.3 billion), the two governments, at a working-level meeting in October and December 1981, agreed to transfer the unused portions of Japan's project loans to commodity loans (40 billion yen orginally earmarked for the Wuqiangxi and Hengyang-Guangzhou projects for fiscal years 1979 and 1980—21.94 billion yen and 18.06 billion yen, respectively). To relieve acute balance-of-payments difficulties, commodity loans, as distinguished from project loans, were designed to generate local counterpart funds from the domestic sale of foreign commodities paid for by Japan so that such funds could be used for China's top-priority steel and petrochemical projects. In an attempt to increase its local counterpart funds, the Chinese government was expected to sell these foreign commodities to provinces and cities at a high exchange rate, one that would double the official yen-yuan exchange rate.[58] The specific use of these funds was up to the Chinese government, which was required to submit an annual report to the OECF of Japan. For fiscal year 1981, the two sides set aside 20 billion yen (of Japan's 60 billion yen in government loans) for that purpose (see Table 28).[59] This arrangement was formalized at the second regular Sino-Japanese ministerial conference held at Tokyo in December 1981. Whereas the Hua-Ōhira joint press communiqué of December 7, 1979, and the joint press communiqué of December 5, 1980, issued by the first ministerial conference, had specifically mentioned the amounts of Japanese government loans, the joint press communiqué of December 16, 1981, issued by Vice-Premier Gu Mu and Minister of Foreign Affairs Sakurauchi Yoshio, was conspicuously silent on the amount of Japanese

TABLE 28
COMMODITY LOANS, FY 1980–1982

	FY 1980	FY 1981	FY 1982
Date of loan agreement	December 18, 1981	April 26, 1982	October 18, 1982
Chinese agency	State Administrative Commission on Foreign Investment	Ministry of Foreign Economic Relations and Trade	Ministry of Foreign Economic Relations and Trade
Amount (millions of yen)	40,000	20,000	20,000
Disbursement period	Until December 18, 1983	Until April 26, 1984	Until October 18, 1984
Interest rate per year	3 percent	3 percent	3 percent
Terms	30-year repayment; 10-year grace	30-year repayment; 10-year grace	30-year repayment; 10-year grace

SOURCE: Overseas Economic Cooperation Fund of Japan.

loans except to state that "notes were exchanged concerning commodity loans."[60] This contrast probably reflected the embarrassing diversion of the Japanese loan for fiscal year 1981. In March 1982, Foreign Minister Huang Hua and Japanese Ambassador to China Katori Yasue (who had replaced Yoshida Kenzō in September 1981) signed the Exchange of Notes regarding the loans for fiscal year 1981 (40 billion yen in project loans and 20 billion yen in commodity loans) in Beijing;[61] the loan agreements were signed in April 1982.[62]

Commodity loans had essentially the same terms as the project loans, but China was excluded from participation in competitive international bids. The OECF of Japan disliked China's preference for giving a higher priority to consumer goods (such as synthetic fibers and electric appliances) than to construction machinery in importing foreign commodities, but it eventually reconciled itself to the Chinese arguments that consumer goods were more easily absorbed into the domestic economy without competing with China's own industries.[63] Unlike the international bids for project loans that were advertised in *Renmin Ribao* (the Chinese-language daily), the invitations to bid for the commodity loans were required to be published in the *China Daily*—China's only English-language newspaper, whose inaugural edition appeared in May 1981.

The first invitation for international competition listed ten categories of commodities and materials: steel materials, timber, polypropylene resin, polyethylene, urea, chemical fiber, transparent plate glass, weed killer, cement, and plywood. The advertisement in the *China Daily* (February 18, 1982) read:

> We hereby invite manufacturers and trading companies
> organized and registered in and controlled by the eligible source
> countries (referring to all developing countries and all OECD
> member countries) to participate in the prequalification.
> Interested manufacturers and trading companies are kindly
> requested to submit relevant documents for prequalification to
> our corporation not later than March 20, 1982. The submitted
> documents shall be made in English language in quadruplicate,
> i.e., one original and three copies, and shall consist of brief
> history, financial state, production experiences and supply
> capacity of the manufacturers and trading companies and the
> time of delivery. After evaluation of the prequalification
> documents, we shall despatch inquiry information to the
> qualified manufacturers and/or trading companies.

Japanese applicants obtained about two-thirds of all the contracts.[64]

The Seventh Department of the CNTIC handled international bidding and contractual procedures for both project and commodity loans. The State Administrative Commission on Foreign Investment under Vice-Premier Gu Mu initially conducted loan negotiations with the OECF of Japan, but in the spring of 1982, as a result of China's central bureaucratic reorganization, this cabinet-level commission was transformed into the Bureau of Foreign Investment in the new Ministry of Foreign Economic Relations and Trade, which combined the Ministry of Economic Relations with Foreign Countries and the Ministry of Foreign Trade. Gu Mu, a principal architect of China's Japan connection, lost his vice-premiership as well as his functionally specific portfolios in the dramatic bureaucratic reshuffles, and he was appointed state councillor (without portfolio) in 1982, as were ex-Vice-Premiers Yu Qiuli, Kang Shien, Bo Yibo, and Ji Pengfei. Vice-Minister of Foreign Trade Liu Xiwen, an old Japan hand, retired, but he apparently retained his chairmanship of the China-Japan Long-Term Trade Committee. On the other hand, ex-Vice-Premier Chen Muhua, a female alternate member of the CCP Political Bureau, who was appointed state councillor as well as minister of foreign economic relations and trade, emerged as an influential new voice in Sino-Japanese economic diplomacy. Xie Beiyi was appointed vice-minister of urban and rural construction and environmental protection; his role in the loan negotiations was inherited by Chen Muhua's deputy, Wei Yuming, who was vice-minister of foreign economic relations and trade (former vice-chairman of the State Administrative Commission on Foreign Investment).

In contrast to the uneven progress of China's six construction projects, construction of the China-Japan Friendship Hospital in Beijing, China's most modern and largest multifunctional medical facility, was smoothly under way, financed by the Japanese government's grant of 16 billion yen. Unlike the OECF's project and commodity loans, this hospital project was administered by the Japanese International Cooperation Agency under the supervision of the Bureau of Economic Cooperation in the Ministry of Foreign Affairs. As promised in the 1979 Hua-Ōhira joint press communiqué, the Japanese government sent eight delegations to China during 1980 to make preliminary surveys, to develop and explain a construction layout, and to discuss contractual procedures. In January 1981, Ambassador Yoshida Kenzō and Vice-Minister of Public Health Tan Yunhe exchanged the notes on hospital design in Beijing.[65] A month later, the vice-president of the hospital, Liu Wenquan, and two Japanese architectural firms, Itō Kisaburō Architects and Engineers and Nikken Sekkei, signed a contract to prepare a hospital design (430 million yen).[66] In August 1981 Ambassador Yoshida and Vice-Minister Tan signed the notes on hospital construction expenditures (16 billion yen).[67] To be built on 9.7-ha site by the spring of 1984, this fourteen-story hospital (with one underground floor) is to have 1,000 beds, treat 2,500 outpatients a day, and have a staff of 1,700, including 297 doctors and 595 nurses.[68] It will include a center for clinical medical research with emphasis on traditional Chinese medicine (200 staff members), a nursing school (300 students, 30 teachers, and 20 staff members), and a rehabilitation center (300 beds, 126 medical staff members, and 234 additional staff members). The Japanese will not only provide construction machinery, medical equipment, and technical assistance, but will also train Chinese doctors, nurses, medical technicians, and hospital managers; twenty persons will be trained in Japan each year. For this technical training, the Medical School of Chiba University (which trained a large number of Chinese medical students in the 1910s and 1920s) signed an agreement with the China-Japan Friendship Hospital in November 1981.[69]

Raw materials and construction equipment are being procured in both countries. Six Japanese construction companies competed for the construction contract. Two of them (the Fujita Corporation and the Taisei Corporation) had hired Chinese workers for Japanese construction projects in Iraq. All six contractors wished to establish a foothold in China's construction industry in other areas in addition to hospital construction. In December 1981, the Takenaka Komuten Company, which had promoted technical interchanges with Chinese workers, underbid five other Japanese competitors and won the hospital construction contract.[70] The ground-breaking ceremony was held on December 2, 1981; a large number of Chinese and Japanese dignitaries were present.[71] On the same day, Premier Zhao Ziyang received an 80-member Japanese delegation and thanked it for its contribution. Minister of Public Health Qian Xinzhong emphasized that the China-Japan Friendship Hospital in Beijing and the China-Japan Center for Immunology, established in Shanghai in March 1982, symbolized the expansion of medical cooperation between China and Japan.[72] The two governments also had a preliminary discussion about another large-scale modern hospital to be built in China with a Japanese grant-in-aid.

All four construction projects related to coal exports moved ahead during 1982 because the Chinese recognized the projects' importance to China's economic development and because their familiarity with foreign loan administration had significantly increased. In June 1982 Ding Min, deputy director of the First Department of Asian Affairs in the Ministry of Foreign Affairs, expressed his complete satisfaction with the progress made in these projects and predicted that all of them would be completed by 1985.[73] Completion of the Qinhuangdao port expansion project in 1984 or 1985 will terminate Japanese loans for this particular purpose. Qinhuangdao's importance as China's coal-exporting outlet is expected to loom larger in the latter half of the 1980s because the Occidental Petroleum Company has agreed to invest $230 million to develop the Pingshou coal mines in Shanxi Province so that China can export 15 million metric tons of coal a year from these mines by 1986. In order to improve the railways to Qinhuangdao and to expand its facilities, China has decided to seek the assistance of U.S. technicians and advisers and to spend $270 million.[74] The Shijiusuo port project, despite some difficulties such as vandalism of construction materials by local commune members and dockworkers,[75] is expected to be completed by 1985.

The Chinese accelerated their work on the Yanzhou-Shijiusuo (Yan-Shi) Railway and the Beijing-Qinhuangdao (Jing-Qin) Railway systems and proudly reported that the Yan-Shi project was making rapid progress in the spring of 1981.[76] In mid-July 1982, they reported that about 30,000 workers assigned to the Jing-Qin project and dedicated to the four modernizations struggle had overfulfilled their main civil engineering works by 124 percent in the almost five months since March 1982.[77] *Renmin Ribao* (September 5, 1982) carried a report on the Jing-Qin project and included seven photographs showing the types of work in which Chinese workers were engaged. It claimed that the "good news" concerning the Twelfth National Party Congress of the CCP, which convened on September 1, 1982 (under Deng Xiaoping's leadership), encouraged these workers. It also reported that they had completed 40 percent of the bridges and 29 percent of the railway foundations by the end of August 1982. The two projects are expected to be completed in 1985, but the electrification of the Jing-Qin Railway may require an additional year.

Asked about the status of the Hengyang-Guangzhou Railway project, Rong Fengxiang (director of the Second Department of Regional Trade in the Ministry of Foreign Economic Relations and Trade) explained in his heavy Qingdao accent that construction of the Dayaoshan tunnel was under way and that China was relying upon its own construction funds plus the remainder (3.32 billion yen) of Japan's original loan commitments.[78] He said that China would request the resumption of Japanese government loans for this project in 1983 or 1984. In early 1982, the Chinese State Council had decided to expedite construction of the tunnel because it was of "great importance" to China's foreign trade and local economic activities.[79]

As to the future of the Wuqiangxi hydroelectric power plant project, Deputy Director Ding Min pointedly reminded me that China never intended to abandon it but rather planned to scale it down to a more manageable level.[80] He expected to start negotiations concerning Japanese yen credits for this project in 1984. The Japanese were not involved in China's overall redesign of the Wuqiangxi project; if the Chinese made a new loan application, said Yamada Masaharu (a China specialist in the OECF of Japan), the OECF would undertake its own feasibility study and then make a decision on the Chinese application.[81] Although the Japanese Ministry of Finance, always wary of foreign financial commitments, preferred to see the cancellation of the Wuqiangxi and Hengyang-Guangzhou Railway projects, it was the Japanese government's prevailing view that Japan should resume its yen loan programs for these two projects (estimated at 150 billion yen) in the future—probably after 1984. However, the Japanese government decided not to mention these two projects in any loan-related exchange documents.[82]

During his first six-day state visit to Japan (May 31–June 5, 1982), Premier Zhao Ziyang asked for 90 billion yen in loans for fiscal year 1982 (60 billion yen in project loans and 30 billion yen in commodity loans).[83] The Japanese regarded this request as too high but agreed to discuss it in the hope that the issue might be settled prior to Japanese Prime Minister Suzuki Zenkō's planned visit to China in September 1982. In order to fulfill its pledge to double its ODA contributions in the five-year period starting in April 1981 and to reverse the actual decline (4.1 percent) in its ODA funds that occurred between 1980 and 1981, the Japanese government was favorably disposed to increase its loan commitments to Asian countries—particularly China, Indonesia, and South Korea.[84] In September 1982, during Prime Minister Suzuki's China visit, Foreign Ministers Huang Hua and Sakurauchi Yoshio exchanged the notes on the 65 billion yen loan (45 billion yen in project loans and 20 billion yen in commodity loans) for fiscal year 1982; the loan agreements were signed a month later.[85] Although the initial Japanese government loans to China had produced mixed results, both sides expected to see the continuation of Japanese economic aid programs for China throughout the 1980s. In fact, Deputy Director Ding Min clearly indicated that China would request Japan's yen credits for other projects in 1983 or 1984. And Takeuchi Katsushi (chief of the OECF's liaison office in Beijing) candidly predicted that China would require and receive Japanese government loans throughout the rest of this century because it would remain a less developed country during that time.[86] Japan was the first noncommunist country to give government loans to the PRC; loans from other industrialized nations (such as Belgium and Denmark), OPEC member-states (such as Kuwait), and international financial institutions (such as the World Bank) were to follow.[87] Hence China's experience with Japanese loan programs proved to be useful for its increasing knowledge of international financial diplomacy.

Analysis
and Conclusions

FIVE

China and Japan are neighboring countries separated only by a
strip of water, and there was a long history of traditional
friendship between them. The two peoples ardently wish to end
the abnormal state of affairs that has hitherto existed between
the two countries. The termination of the state of war and the
normalization of relations between China and Japan—the
realization of such wishes of the two peoples will open a new
page in the annals of relations between the two countries . . .
Although the social systems of China and Japan are different, the
two countries should and can establish peaceful and friendly
relations.

Sino-Japanese Joint Statement, 1972

Since Zhou Enlai and Tanaka Kakuei agreed to issue this joint declara-
tion on September 29, 1972,[1] China and Japan have attempted to trans-
late this "new page" of their historical relationship into the tangible
reality of peaceful and friendly cooperation. As discussed in the preceding chapters, the record of cooperative efforts made in the field of
Sino-Japanese economic diplomacy is indeed remarkable. The governments of both countries successfully concluded a series of agreements
on economic issues as well as the Treaty of Peace and Friendship in the
1970s. The volume of bilateral trade has grown at a faster rate than
previously predicted, and technological and cultural exchange programs
have greatly expanded. In 1981 alone, China sent about 250 scientific
and technical delegations (altogether 1,100 persons) to Japan; between

1979 and 1982, 960 Chinese students entered Japanese universities and research institutes, and 480 Japanese students went to educational institutions in China.[2] The Chinese welcomed Japan's massive participation in the planning and construction of the Baoshan iron and steel complex, the Bohai oil development, and other large-scale economic projects in China. The Japanese government agreed to provide 261 billion yen in public loans and other grants-in-aid to China between 1979 and 1982; the total amount of private Japanese financing arrangements for China was even higher. Although these attempts have not always produced mutually satisfactory results, the range and magnitude of the new Sino-Japanese economic diplomacy attest to an increasing degree of economic interdependence between the two countries. Since the mid-1970s the Chinese have unmistakably achieved a significant conceptual breakthrough in their international economic policy. Gone is the extreme Maoist emphasis on xenophobic self-reliance and autarkic economic preferences. The Chinese are no longer reluctant to seek the involvement of Japan and other industrialized countries in a variety of industrial construction projects and resource development programs for the implementation of their four modernizations policy.

The political and diplomatic tensions that were evident in China's economic relations with Japan during the 1950s and 1960s have moderated considerably since 1972, and the two governments have cooperated to maintain an overall political environment conducive to their productive economic interaction. Yet China's changing domestic politics and shifting policy priorities have continued to influence the direction of Sino-Japanese economic diplomacy. And as seen in the cases of the Baoshan complex and the Wuqiangxi hydroelectric power plant, some aspects of Sino-Japanese economic cooperation have been both a stimulus to, and a victim of, China's intrabureaucratic debates and factional struggles. In contrast, the Japanese government, despite internal policy divisions, has sustained a reasonably stable economic approach toward China. The ruling Liberal-Democratic Party has enjoyed a comfortable majority in the National Diet, and the turnover of prime ministers (Tanaka Kakuei, Miki Takeo, Fukuda Takeo, Ōhira Masayoshi, Suzuki Zenkō, and Nakasone Yasuhiro) has not changed the substance of Sino-Japanese economic relations. All believed that Japan's pursuit of the important China market transcended partisan and factional differences and that it was in Japan's long-range national interest to support China's moderate and pragmatic political leadership economically. They also agreed on the general policy proposition that close economic cooperation with China was helpful to U.S. policy in Asia and detrimental to possible efforts at reconciliation between Beijing and Moscow. In effect, they discarded the celebrated principle of separation of political and economic matters. Consequently, the LDP government was able to iron out its internal policy differences regarding China and to actively support the Long-Term Trade Agreement, the Baoshan complex, the Bohai project, and economic assistance programs. Whereas the Japanese have tended to attach increasing political importance to their economic relations with China, the Chinese have deradicalized the politics of economic diplomacy and have conducted their relations with Japan primarily for the sake of intrinsic economic benefits rather than on the basis of political considerations.

As the Japanese government, in close cooperation with the *Keidanren* and the Japan-China Economic Association, gradually assumed a central role in planning, coordinating, and financing Japanese economic relations with China, the Chinese found the tactic of attempting to penetrate and manipulate Japan's pluralistic political and economic power structures and to take advantage of competitive and contradictory factors operating in Japan increasingly ineffective. The influence of the National Diet, *Sōhyō*, and opposition political parties, including the Japan Socialist Party, over Sino-Japanese trade gradually decreased, and the Japanese Council for Promotion of International Trade and former "friendly companies" were overshadowed by the powerful JCEA. The Japanese made modest progress in their attempts to influence China's intrabureaucratic dynamics because the substantial increase in economic interaction enabled them to identify a diversity of interests and channels existing in the Chinese bureaucracy and to develop shared interests with some Chinese organizations and individuals.

The two governments have been successful in containing actual and potential controversies over Taiwan's status, the Diaoyu (or Senkaku) Islands, the Longjing oilfields, and Japanese–South Korean oil drilling in the East China Sea; none of these issues has presented a serious threat to Sino-Japanese economic cooperation. A number of regional issues have been raised in the context of Sino-Japanese economic relations, such as the ASEAN's sensitivity to loan negotiations, Indonesia's interest in oil exports, and the Korean aspect of discussions concerning Baoshan and Bohai. Both China and Japan have deliberately avoided any manifestation of their regional rivalry as much as possible. In general, the United States has favored the stabilizing regional effects of a friendly relationship between Beijing and Tokyo but has attempted to restrain Japan's rapidly growing economic role in China. The United States government expressed reservations about Japan's government loans, the relaxation of COCOM regulations, and the generous financing terms made available to China, but some U.S. companies did take part in the Baoshan and Bohai operations. The Soviets, in order to prevent what they regarded as an anti-Moscow alliance consisting of the United States, Japan, and China, employed a "carrot-and-stick" approach toward Japan. The Soviet government warned Japan against accepting the antihegemony clause in the Treaty of Peace and Friendship and assisting in construction of the Baoshan complex, but it invited Japanese participation in the joint resource development projects in Siberia and on Sakhalin Island. However, neither the Soviet Union nor the United States has exerted much direct impact upon the dynamics of Sino-Japanese economic diplomacy since the early 1970s.

Sino-Japanese economic relations during the 1950s and 1960s were largely limited to a relatively simple process of buying and selling commodities; however, the new economic diplomacy represented a qualitative change because a host of complicated commercial, financial, legal, technological, and managerial issues required the sustained involvement of many negotiators, managers, and technicians on both sides. In the Baoshan and Bohai operations, total strangers from two different economic and political systems were suddenly thrown into a joint project and were required to have intensive daily contacts for an extended period. Their common tasks ranged from project design and field survey to data analysis, technical cooperation, and machine operation, but they quickly realized how different were their value systems, social customs, decision-making processes, managerial styles, and even accounting procedures. A common cultural heritage and geographic proximity undoubtedly helped them to appreciate each other's general tendencies, but such understanding was not always sufficient to overcome a number of specific difficulties (such as negotiating tactics, personal communication problems, contractual commitments, and policy coordination) encountered in both projects. The Japanese were accustomed to collaborating on international projects, but this was probably the first such experience for the Chinese since the departure of Soviet advisers in the early 1960s. Although the Japanese have a sense of superiority in technical competence and experience in international relations, their Chinese counterparts have a high degree of national pride and self-confidence. Under these circumstances it is understandable that the two nations were often frustrated and disillusioned in their initial cooperative experiment and that they were made keenly aware of each other's weaknesses and deficiencies. This process of mutual readjustment was undoubtedly desirable for the future improvement of relations between China and Japan.

It is important to recall that the Japanese were upset by the unilateral Chinese decisions to cancel contracts or to deviate from contractual terms or international business practices. The Baoshan case was a cause célèbre. The credibility of Chinese foreign economic policy fell sharply in the eyes of some Japanese, and they began to question whether their economic cooperation with China should continue. They did not fully comprehend the complex and inept Chinese bureaucratic system that made difficult the formulation of a rational and consistent economic policy toward Japan. The Baoshan experience and other collaborations with the Chinese taught the Japanese that their economic negotiators and advisers should have taken a more critical view of China's policy preferences and economic decisions in the first place. Japan's pro-China euphoria of the 1970s was replaced by an increasingly negative view of China in the early 1980s; some Japanese evidently despised China for its inefficiency and betrayal. A leading Japanese sinologist, Ishikawa Tadao, president of Keio University, warned against the danger that the pendulum of Japanese public opinion toward China might swing to the other extreme for sentimental reasons.[3] Another well-known China scholar, Professor Etō Shinkichi of Tokyo University, observed that "there are signs that the Japanese are taking a highhanded attitude toward the Chinese because of their technological supremacy and powerful economy."[4] And Professor Sakamoto Yoshikazu of Tokyo University reminded the Japanese that the Chinese had significantly helped Japanese economic development at two critical historical junctures—at the end of the Sino-Japanese War (1894–95), when Japan extracted 300 million yen in war reparations from China, and at the end of the Second World War, when China did not demand $50 billion in war reparations from Japan.[5] As a whole, however, the Japanese, both government officials and business leaders, have been able to persevere through many setbacks and frustrations in their new economic relations with China and to continue their constructive collaboration with the Chinese because of their own organizational abilities and hard-nosed realism. They have also succeeded in maintaining Japan's profitable number one position in the China market through a judicious mixture of innovative business practices and appropriate government actions, such as making available Eximbank funds, ODA loans, and grants.

The Chinese, too, have shown an appreciable change in their attitudes toward Japan since the early 1970s—from an emphasis on friendship and cooperation to critical and cautious reappraisal. The Baoshan controversy was followed in 1982 by heated disputes over Japanese textbooks, which were allegedly designed to whitewash the historical record of Japan's aggression against and exploitation of China. The Chinese lodged a formal protest with the Japanese Ministry of

Foreign Affairs, displayed ugly photographs of Japanese atrocities in *Renmin Ribao*, and widely publicized eyewitness accounts of Japanese imperialism.[6] In a confidential speech to Chinese students in Japan, Chen Kang (counsul-general in Sapporo) presented a negative assessment of Japan by stressing the evils of monopoly capitalism and the exploitation of working masses.[7] Speaking to the CCP Twelfth National Congress in September 1982, General Secretary Hu Yaobang pointed out that "some forces in Japan" were "carrying out activities for the revival of Japanese militarism" and poignantly admonished the Chinese people not to forget that "capitalist countries and enterprises will never change their capitalist nature simply because they have economic and technological exchanges with us."[8] In spite of this recurrence of unfortunate historical memories and ideological rhetoric, it is fair to say that the two governments have taken joint measures to restore the spirit of friendly cooperation, as exemplified by the exchange of state visits in 1982 by Premier Zhao Ziyang (June) and Prime Minister Suzuki Zenkō (September). They were particularly anxious to protect vested interests in Sino-Japanese economic cooperation and to nurture the legacy of the Zhou-Tanaka Joint Statement for the best long-range interests of both nations. However, it is clear that the emotionally charged Sino-Japanese love affair of the 1970s is over and that the Chinese and Japanese have reached the agonizing phase of groping for a more realistic, balanced, and productive partnership in the future.

Our study has demonstrated that one of the most serious obstacles to this partnership is the vast but inefficient Chinese bureaucratic system. If anyone still assumes that China has a highly centralized and effectively regimented monolithic system, in which a few top central leaders make all authoritative economic decisions and bureaucrats and cadres at lower organizational levels carry them out in an orderly and disciplined fashion, sufficient evidence has been presented here to refute this assumption. Nor do the Chinese themselves accept it. In his report to the Fifth National People's Congress in December 1981, Premier Zhao Ziyang attacked the pervasive "malady of bureaucratism" in China and pledged to alter the situation he described as being marked by "intolerably low efficiency resulting from overlapping and overstaffed administrations with their multi-tiered departments crammed full of superfluous personnel and deputy and nominal chiefs who engage in endless haggling and shifts of responsibility."[9] Moreover, General Secretary Hu Yaobang admitted that "many of our enterprises are backward in production techniques, operation and management."[10] It is indeed a monumental task for Hu and Zhao to reform and modernize their aging, privileged, underqualified, politically entrenched, and top-heavy administrative organization; they have started by taking bold steps to promote younger, better-educated, and technically competent persons to high-level positions. The Chinese have learned from their experiences with Japan that they must develop both efficient organizational channels and well-trained human resources if they are to absorb the advanced foreign technology necessary for implementation of their four modernizations program.

The remarkable continuity of office maintained by the top Chinese officials responsible for Japanese affairs has been an asset more than a liability. Such officials include Liao Chengzhi (president of the China-Japan Friendship Association and a member of the CCP Political Bureau), Liu Xiwen (chairman of the China-Japan Long-Term Trade Committee and former vice-minister of foreign trade), Xiao Xiangqian (director of the First Asian Department, Ministry of Foreign Affairs), Ding Min (deputy director of the First Asian Department), Sun Pinghua (secretary-general of the China-Japan Friendship Association), Wang Xiaoyun (minister of the Chinese Embassy in Japan), Wu Shudong (commercial counselor in Japan), Jin Sucheng (counselor in Japan), and Chen Kang (counsul-general in Sapporo). As a result of their long experience and their language competence, they have become thoroughly familiar with the intricacies of Japan's political and economic operations. They have also cultivated shared policy interests as well as deepening personal relationships with their Japanese counterparts in business circles. This appears to be a unique phenomenon, unparalleled in China's contemporary foreign relations, and it is likely to contribute to the further growth of individual and organizational ties between China and Japan.

There is no doubt that the intelligent and resourceful people of China and Japan can find a way to sustain their peaceful and friendly relations if they so wish and that they can obtain substantial economic benefits from each other in the future. Yet the exact course of their economic relationship is more likely to depend on China than on Japan. At the Twelfth CCP National Congress in September 1982, General Secretary Hu Yaobang made a commitment to quadruple the gross annual value of China's industrial and agricultural production by the end of this century. Although a moderate growth rate was projected by the Sixth Five-Year Plan (1981–1985) and the Seventh Five-Year Plan (1986–1990), he predicted a much faster "all-round upsurge" in China's economy during the 1990s.[11] As a requirement for this twenty-year commitment, Chen Muhua (minister of foreign economic relations and trade) reconfirmed China's "open-door" international economic policy and pointed out the continuing importance of the "mutual reliance" (*huxiang yilai*) between China and foreign countries.[12] In this context she praised the postwar economic recovery of Japan and West Germany, made possible by foreign trade, foreign capital, and importation of technology. The Chinese leadership appears to be irreversibly committed to accepting technology and capital from Japan and other industrialized nations. As long as the Chinese can sustain a stable domestic political basis for their four modernizations policy and can improve their bureaucratic and managerial performance, the normalization of economic and diplomatic relations between China and Japan suggests that both will be able to learn from their past achievements and mistakes and to work out a mature and viable system of mutually beneficial economic cooperation in the years to come. It is also conceivable that the experiences of both countries will move them closer together in terms of their economic and political policies in Asia and elsewhere.

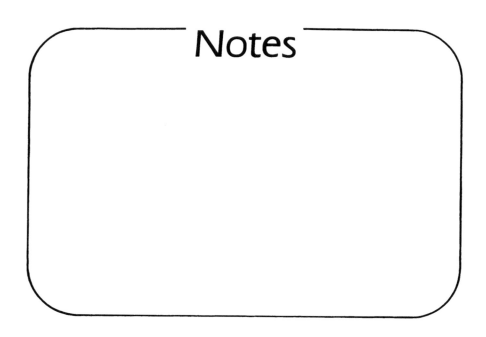

Notes

Chapter 1

1. Some of the material included in this chapter has been taken from my earlier work, *Japan Faces China: Political and Economic Relations in the Postwar Era* (Baltimore, Md.: Johns Hopkins University Press, 1976), pp. 134–83. For a succinct survey of Japan's pre-1945 economic relations with China, see Takahashi Shōgorō and Tanaka Shūjirō, *Nitchū bōeki kyōshitsu* [A classroom for Japan-China trade] (Tokyo: Seinen shuppansha, 1968), pp. 14–44.

2. For the texts of this treaty and its accompanying protocol, see *Nitchū kankei kihon shiryōshū* [Basic collected documents on Japan-China relations] (Tokyo: Kazankai, 1970), pp. 32–38.

3. In 1949 the United States and the Western European countries set up a Coordinating Committee (COCOM) to regulate exports of strategic commodities to the communist bloc. The COCOM established its China Committee (CHINCOM) in 1952 but disbanded it in 1957.

4. See the text in *Nitchū kankei*, pp. 43–44.

5. Ibid., pp. 57–59, 83–87.

6. Lee, *Japan Faces China*, p. 144.

7. *Nitchū kankei*, pp. 127–33.

8. For a discussion of the Nagasaki flag incident and its aftermath, see Lee, *Japan Faces China*, pp. 37–40.

9. Fujiyama's secret efforts to contact Mao Zedong's teacher, Zhang Shizhao, in Hong Kong, and Chinese Ambassador Wang Bingnan in Warsaw, are described by Fujiyama Aiichirō in *Seiji waga michi* [Politics—my way] (Tokyo: Asahi shimbunsha, 1976), pp. 172–77.

10. See the Japanese text of the Zhou-Matsumura agreement in *Nitchū kankei*, p. 214, or its Chinese text in *Ribenwenti wenjian huibian* [Collected documents on Japan questions] (Beijing: Shijie zhishi chubanshe, 1963), 4:16.

11. Lee, *Japan Faces China*, p. 144.

12. See *Renmin Ribao* [People's daily], September 10 and November 21, 1967.

13. For an account of these negotiations, see Tagawa Seiichi, *Nitchū kōshō hiroku* [Secret record of Japan-China negotiations] (Tokyo: Mainichi shimbunsha, 1973), pp. 71–108; and Furui Yoshimi, *Nitchū fukkō eno michi* [The road to Japan-China diplomatic normalization] (Tokyo: Kokusaimondai kenkyūjo, 1971).

14. See the Sato-Nixon joint communiqué in *Department of State Bulletin*, December 15, 1969, pp. 555–58. The excruciating political discussions, which lasted for one month in Beijing, are described in Tagawa, *Nitchū kōshō hiroku*, pp. 204–64.

15. *Peking Review*, October 6, 1972, pp. 12–13.

16. See *Renmin Ribao*, May 10, 1960.

17. The government's complete financing of the Interchange Association was mentioned by Tajima Takashi, director of the China and Mongolia Division of the Ministry of Foreign Affairs. Interview with Tajima, August 4, 1977, Tokyo.

18. See *Nihon Keizai Shimbun*, November 28, 1972.

19. *Asahi Shimbun*, January 19, 1973.

20. For a discussion of the processes and results of these negotiations, see *Nihon Keizai Shimbun*, June 16, August 17, and August 21, 1973; and *Asahi Shimbun*, June 19 and 27 and August 8, 12, 17, 22, and 31, 1973. Also see *Waga gaikō no kinkyō* [The recent state of our diplomacy] (Tokyo: Ministry of Foreign Affairs, 1974), 1:252–53.

21. For the text of the Sino-Australian trade agreement, see Gene T. Hsiao, *The Foreign Trade of China: Policy, Law, and Practice* (Berkeley and Los Angeles: University of California Press, 1977), pp. 199–201.

22. See ibid., pp. 196–98. In the final stages of the negotiations, Xi Yesheng (director of the Fourth Department of the Ministry of Foreign Trade) and Yanagiya Kensuke (minister of the Japanese Embassy) met more than twenty times in Beijing from September to December 1973. *Asahi Shimbun*, December 13, 1973.

23. The signing ceremony was witnessed by Vice-Premier Li Xiannian, Minister of Foreign Trade Li Qiang, Vice-Minister of Foreign Affairs Han Nianlong, Japanese Ambassador Ogawa Heishirō, Ministers Yanagiya Kensuke and Hayashi Yūichi, and Matsunaga Nobuo (director of the Bureau of Treaties). *Asahi Shimbun*, January 6, 1974; and *Renmin Ribao*, January 6, 1974.

24. *Renmin Ribao*, January 6, 1974. Mao gave Ōhira a copy of China's ancient literary text as a gift. As an official of the Japanese Ministry of Finance, he had worked in the Japanese-occupied area of China's Inner Mongolia in 1939.

25. For the Japanese ambassador's comment on Ōhira's China visit and achievements, see Ogawa Heishirō, *Pekin no yonen* [Four years in Peking] (Tokyo: Simul Press, 1977), pp. 39–41.

26. The text is reprinted in *Shin Chūgoku Nenkan* [New China yearbook], *1975* (Tokyo: Taishūkan shoten, 1975), pp. 177–81. Also see *Renmin Ribao*, April 21, 1974. The Japanese negotiators included Hashimoto Hiroshi (counselor of the Japanese Embassy in China and former director of the China and Mongolia Division in the Ministry of Foreign Affairs), Kunihiro Michihiko (director of the China and Mongolia Division), and Nakamura Tōru (director of the International Division, Bureau of Aviation, Ministry of Transportation). Their Chinese counterparts were Wang Xiaoyun (deputy director of the Department of Asian Affairs, Ministry of Foreign Affairs) and Liu Yuanxiong (deputy director of the International Department of the Civil Aviation Administration of China).

27. For the text, see *Shin Chūgoku Nenkan, 1975,* pp. 181–82. Also see *Renmin Ribao,* November 14, 1974.

28. See the texts in *Shin Chūgoku Nenkan, 1976,* pp. 152–55.

29. *Nihon Keizai Shimbun,* November 16, 1975. See also *Renmin Ribao,* November 16, 1975. Kōmoto also met with Li Qiang, minister of foreign trade, and Kang Shien, minister of petroleum and chemical industries.

30. *Nihon Keizai Shimbun,* January 9, 1976.

31. Ibid., January 23, 1976. The Inayama delegation's activities in China are reported in *Renmin Ribao,* January 19, 20, 22, and 23, 1976.

32. For representative examples of the anti-Deng articles, see those written by Fang Hai, by Li Zhang, and by Gao Lu and Chang Ge in *Hongqi* [Red flag], April 1976 (pp. 21–26), May 1976 (pp. 35–44), and July 1976 (pp. 25–30), respectively.

33. *Asahi Shimbun,* April 7, 1976.

34. See Michel Oksenberg and Sai-cheung Yeung, "Hua Kuo-feng's Pre–Cultural Revolution Hunan Years, 1949–66: The Making of a Political Generalist," *China Quarterly* 69 (March 1977): 3–53.

35. *Nihon Keizai Shimbun,* February 2 and 6, 1977. For an account of Inayama's discussions with Li Qiang and Gu Mu, see *Renmin Ribao,* February 5 and 6, 1977.

36. *Nihon Keizai Shimbun,* April 1, 1977.

37. Interview with Wu Shudong (commercial counselor of the Chinese Embassy in Tokyo), July 3, 1982, Tokyo. As deputy director of the Fourth Department of the Chinese Ministry of Foreign Trade, he was one of the key assistants to Liu Xiwen in 1977 and 1978.

38. *Asahi Shimbun,* January 18, 1978. For a complete list of the committee's leaders, see *Kokusai Sekiyu Repōto* [International petroleum report], no. 3 (Tokyo: Kokusai sekiyu kabushikigaisha, March 30, 1978), pp. 7–8.

39. *Kokusai Sekiyu Repōto,* p. 9.

40. For the text, see *Nitchū bōeki antei kakudai eno michisuji* [The road toward the stable expansion of Japan-China trade] (Tokyo: Nitchū keizai kyōkai, 1978), p. 40. See also *Renmin Ribao,* February 17, 1978. The signing ceremony was witnessed by Li Qiang (minister of foreign trade), Liao Chengzhi (president of the China-Japan Friendship Association), Wang Yaoting (chairman of the China Council for Promotion of International Trade), *Keidanren* President Dokō Toshio, and Japanese Ambassador Satō Shōji.

41. See Kim Woodard, *The International Energy Relations of China* (Stanford: Stanford University Press, 1980), pp. 121–22.

42. *Asahi Shimbun,* February 16, 1978.

43. For Hua's report to the National People's Congress, see *Peking Review,* March 10, 1978, pp. 7–40.

44. Whereas C. L. Sulzberger of the *New York Times* reported in 1974 that China would produce 400 million tons of crude oil annually by 1985, Julian Schuman (*Kansas City Times,* November 20, 1975) said that a "foreign estimate of a 200-million ton output of crude within five years is possible." Selig S. Harrison of the *Washington Post* observed that China had "better than fifty-fifty chance for a 400-million-ton-plus (3-billion-barrel-plus) production level by 1990." See Selig S. Harrison, *China, Oil, and Asia: Conflict Ahead* (New York: Columbia University Press, 1977), pp. 19–20. Even the most cautious estimate was that "doubling [oil] output in a decade

[by 1985] to 200 million metric tons is well within reach." See U.S., Congress, Joint Economic Committee, *Chinese Economy Post-Mao* (Washington, D.C.: Government Printing Office, 1978), 1:390.

45. *Asahi Shimbun*, February 11, 1978.

46. *Asahi Shimbun*. February 16, 1978.

47. See Chae-Jin Lee, "The Making of the Sino-Japanese Peace and Friendship Treaty," *Pacific Affairs* 3 (Fall 1979): 420–45.

48. *Nihon Keizai Shimbun*, September 14, 1978.

49. *Peking Review*, November 3, 1978, p. 15.

50. For the text, see *Nitchū keizai kōryū 1980* [Japan-China economic exchange] (Tokyo: Nitchū keizai kyōkai, 1981), p. 25.

51. See *Look Japan*, December 10, 1979, p. 3.

52. For example, Fujiyama first visited China in 1917 as a Keio University student; he met with Chiang Kai-shek in Nanjing in 1937 as a member of the Japanese business delegation. During the war he invested in a Shanghai flour mill and in a Hong Kong shipyard. See Fujiyama, *Seiji waga michi*, pp. 166–69. Whereas Mizukami (chairman of the Japanese Traders' Association in 1978) worked in China for seven years as a representative of Mitsui and Company in Beijing and Tianjin before 1945, Kimura (vice-president of the International Oil Trading Corporation in 1978) was one of the Japanese soldiers guarding the Yangzi River near Shanghai and was captured by the Chiang Kai-shek forces toward the end of the Pacific War. Okazaki worked as a wartime director of Shanghai's Kakō Shōgyō Bank.

Chapter 2

1. For the text of the party Constitution, see *Peking Review*, September 2, 1977, pp. 16–22.

2. See Hua's report in ibid., August 26, 1977, pp. 23–57.

3. As translated in ibid., January 6, 1978, pp. 6–12.

4. See Hua's report to the First Session of the Fifth National People's Congress in ibid., March 10, 1978, pp. 7–40, especially pp. 22–23.

5. For an analysis of China's steel industry, see Sekiguchi Sueo, *Chūgoku keizai o shindansuru* [To diagnose the Chinese economy] (Tokyo: Nihon keizai shimbunsha, 1979), pp. 164–67; Central Intelligence Agency, *China: The Steel Industry in the 1970s and 1980s* (Washington, D.C.: Central Intelligence Agency, May 1979).

6. Central Intelligence Agency, *China: The Steel Industry*.

7. Xue Muqiao, *Dangqian woguo jingji ruogan wenti* [Some questions about our country's present economy] (Beijing: Renmin chubanshe, 1980).

8. For a detailed report on the Baoshan project, see *Chōseiga no Chūgoku keizai to Nitchū kankei* [The Chinese economy under readjustment and Japan-China relations] (Tokyo: Nitchū keizai kyōkai, 1981), pp. 102–27.

9. Interview with Huang Jinfa, July 3, 1981, Baoshan, Shanghai, China. In his mid-40s, Huang is a graduate of Shanghai Jiaotong University, one of the most respected institutions of science and engineering in China.

10. Interview with Koguchi Motoichi, Steel Division, Bureau of Public Industries, MITI, June 25, 1981, Tokyo.

11. The exchange of steel delegations is described in *Nitchū bōeki antei kakudai eno michisuji* [The road toward the stable expansion of Japan-China trade] (Tokyo: Nitchū keizai kyōkai, 1978), pp. 313–19.

12. *Chōseiga no Chūgoku*, p. 111.

13. *Renmin Ribao*, May 24, 1978. The protocol had been initialed on April 19, 1978, in Beijing.

14. *Renmin Ribao*, May 25, 1978. Kang, ex-minister of petroleum and chemical industries, is a graduate of Qinghua University, another outstanding school of science and technology in China.

15. Jiang Zemin recalls that Deng Xiaoping, Nie Rongzhen, Li Lisan, and Fu Zhong worked at the Le Creusot mill in 1921 and 1922 and that their life was "very difficult"; the 30,000-man mill had about 10,000 Chinese workers, including about 100 work-study students. See *Tianjin wenshi ziliao xuanji* [Selections of Tianjin historical materials], no. 15 (Tianjin: Renmin chubanshe, 1981), p. 99.

16. See *Peking Review*, November 3, 1978, pp. 14–17.

17. *Renmin Ribao*, December 23, 1978.

18. See ibid., December 24, 1978; and *Asahi Shimbun*, December 24, 1978.

19. *Beijing Review*, January 5, 1979, p. 9.

20. Ibid., March 23, 1979, pp. 14–16.

21. *Yomiuri Shimbun*, April 24, 1980.

22. See *Shanhai Hōzanseitetsujo purojekuto repōto* [Shanghai Baoshan iron and steel complex project report] (Tokyo: Shinnihon seitetsu kabushikigaisha, June 1981), p. 4.

23. For analyses of China's emphasis on self-supply, see *Renmin Ribao*, January 23, 1980; and *Mainichi Shimbun*, June 4, 1980.

24. See *Nihon Keizai Shimbun*, April 23, 1980; and *China Business Review*, July–August 1980, p. 49.

25. *Nihon Keizai Shimbun*, June 7, 1980.

26. See *China Business Review*, July–August 1980, pp. 47–49; and *Business America*, August 11, 1980, pp. 12, 15.

27. *Renmin Ribao*, September 5 and 11, 1980. Due to a shortage of foreign exchange, the Chinese used the inflated exchange rate of 3.1 yuan to $1 (not the actual rate of 1.7–2.0 yuan to $1).

28. Interview with Odagawa Keisuke, senior assistant to the general manager, Business and Coordination Department, Shanghai–Baoshan Project Cooperation Bureau, China Projects Cooperation Division, Nippon Steel Corporation, June 30, 1981, Tokyo. See Ōgaki's cost estimate in *Nikkan Kōgyō Shimbun*, December 8, 1980.

29. See *Peking Review*, December 29, 1978, pp. 11–12; or *Hongqi* [Red flag] (Beijing), January 1, 1979, pp. 14–21.

30. *Asahi Shimbun*, March 19, 1979.

31. *Beijing Review*, March 23, 1979, pp. 9–13. This statement is in sharp contrast to his article in *Hongqi*, June 1, 1979, pp. 17–23. In his report dated November 27, 1979, Xue Muqiao, one of Chen Yun's economic allies and adviser to the State Planning Commission, complained that "some comrades" in China still opposed the economic readjustment policy on the ground that the Chinese economy would grow fast without readjustment. See Xue Muqiao, *Dangqian woguo jingji*, p. 75.

32. *Beijing Review*, May 11, 1979, pp. 15–18.

33. The eight characters adopted in 1979 were *diaozheng* (readjustment), *gaige* (reform or restructure), *zhengdun* (rearrangement or consolidation), and *tigao* (improvement or enhancement). The similar ones used in 1961 were *diaozheng, gonggu* (consolidation), *chongshi* (replenishment), and *tigao*.

34. As explained in "On Questions of Party History," a resolution adopted by the Sixth Plenary Session of the Eleventh CCP Central Committee on June 27, 1981. See *Beijing Review*, July 6, 1981, p. 27.

35. Ibid., April 20, 1979, p. 3.

36. Ibid., July 6, 1979, pp. 5–31.

37. As belatedly reported in *Renmin Ribao*, September 9 and 17, 1980.

38. For a discussion of Yao's distinguished family background, Christian upbringing, and radical Qinghua days, see John Israel and Donald W. Klein, *Rebels and Bureaucrats: China's December 9ers* (Berkeley and Los Angeles: University of California Press, 1976), p. 64. Another prominent radical student leader at Yenching (or Yanjing) University in 1935 was Huang Hua (who subsequently served as foreign minister).

39. Ibid., pp. 151 and 269.

40. The Chen-Xue relationship is analyzed by Dorothy J. Solinger in "Economic Reform via Reformulation in China: Where Do Rightist Ideas Come From?" *Asian Survey 9* (September 1981): 947–60. See also Xue Muqiao, *Shehuizhuyi jingji lilunwenti* [Theoretical questions of socialist economy] (Beijing: Renmin chubanshe, 1979); idem, *Zhongguo shehuizhuyi jingjiwenti yanjiu* [Studies of China's socialist economic questions] (Beijing: Renmin chubanshe, 1979); and Sun Yefang, *Shehuizhuyi jingjide ruogan lilunwenti* [Some theoretical questions of socialist economy] (Beijing: Renmin chubanshe, 1979).

41. See Yang Jianbai's article in *Renmin Ribao*, February 9, 1981; and Xue Muqiao's report of November 27, 1979, in *Dangqian woguo jingji*, p. 76.

42. See Feng Baoxing, Wan Xin, and Zhang Dajian, "Zai yiding shiqinei youxian fazhan qinggongyede keguan biranxing" [The objective necessity of giving a priority to the development of light industry during a certain period], in *Jingji Yanjiu* [Economic research] (Beijing), January 1980, pp. 17–22.

43. *Renmin Ribao*, October 22, 1979.

44. See Xue, *Dangqian woguo jingji*, pp. 34–35; and a commentary in *Hongqi*, November 16, 1980, pp. 2–4. Chairman Mao Zedong advocated the *yigang weimang* philosophy in the 1950s and Hua Guofeng repeated it in the 1970s. See Martin Weil, "The Baoshan Steel Mill," in U.S., Congress, Joint Economic Committee, *China Under the Four Modernizations*, pt. 1 (Washington, D.C.: Government Printing Office, 1982), p. 368.

45. *Beijing Review*, August 25, 1980, pp. 26–28.

46. Wang Dongxing was CCP vice-chairman and commander of Guard Unit 8341 in Beijing (and the security chief for Mao Zedong); Ji Dengkui was a vice-premier; Chen Xilian was a vice-premier and commander of the Beijing Military Region; and Wu De was mayor of Beijing. The CCP Secretariat consisted of Hu Yaobang, Wan Li, Wang Renzhong, Fang Yi, Gu Mu, Song Renqiong, Yu Qiuli, Yang Dezhi, Hu Qiaomu, Yao Yilin, and Peng Chong.

47. For the text of the communiqué, see *Beijing Review*, March 10, 1980, pp. 7–10.

48. *Asahi Shimbun*, July 4, 1980. *Renmin Ribao*, July 4, 1980, simply reported that Vice-Premier Bo explained China's economic reform measures to the Japanese economic delegation, led by Kanamori Hisao.

49. Wearing a pair of binoculars slung around his neck, Hua also held a discussion session with Japanese staff members. For an account of Hua's Baoshan visit, see *Renmin Ribao*, June 3, 1980.

50. *Nihon Keizai Shimbun*, July 14, 1980. The cheating charges are detailed in Okabe Tatsumi, *Chūgoku wa kindaika dekiruka* [Can China modernize itself?] (Tokyo: Nihon keizai shimbunsha, 1981), pp. 180, 217; and *Chūgoku no keizaikakumei* [China's economic revolution] (Tokyo: Yomiuri shimbunsha, 1981), pp. 54–60.

51. *Nikkan Kōgyō Shimbun*, August 18, 1980.

52. *Renmin Ribao*, September 5, 1980.

53. For extensive reports on the Baoshan project, see *Renmin Ribao*, September 9–17, 1980; see also Mu Zhi's article in *Dongxiang* (Hong Kong), October 1980, pp. 22–24.

54. See "On Questions of Party History," p. 26.

55. See *Asahi Shimbun*, March 18, 1981.

56. See Ke Yunlu, *Sanqianwan*, in *Renmin Wenxue* [People's Literature] (Beijing) 11 (November 1980): 3–20. This was selected as one of the best short stories written in 1980.

57. *Asahi Shimbun*, September 13, 1980.

58. *Nihon Keizai Shimbun*, November 24, 1980.

59. *Yomiuri Shimbun*, December 5, 1980. In August 1980, Vice-Premier Yu Qiuli was appointed chairman of the State Energy Commission, a new cabinet-level office.

60. *Asahi Shimbun*, December 6, 1980; and *Yomiuri Shimbun*, December 5, 1980.

61. About 100 persons—Political Bureau members, the premier and vice-premiers, economic ministers, and provincial party first secretaries—attended the conference. For its decisions, see *Hachijūnendai no Nitchū kankei* [Japan-China relations in the 1980s] (Tokyo), April 1981, p. 14; *Mainichi Shimbun*, December 14, 1980; *Asahi Shimbun*, December 23, 1980, and January 30, 1981; and *Zhengming* (Hong Kong), February 1981.

62. These statistics were taken from *Asahi Shimbun*, January 21, 1981; *Wenhuibao* (Shanghai), January 24–30, 1981; and *Renmin Ribao*, November 28, 1980.

63. *Mainichi Shimbun*, January 22, 1981.

64. *Mainichi Shimbun*, January 22, 1981.

65. *Yomiuri Shimbun*, January 28, 1981.

66. Inayama's and Ōgaki's reactions are described in *Asahi Shimbun*, February 18, 1981; see also Kakizaki Norio's report in *Ekonomisuto* [Economist] (Tokyo), February 24, 1981, pp. 54–59.

67. *Asahi Shimbun*, February 1, 1981.

68. Ibid., February 13, 1981.

69. *Renmin Ribao*, February 13, 1981. Vice-Premiers Gu Mu and Huang Hua, Vice-Minister of First Machine Building Zhou Jiannan (who was also vice-chairman of the State Administrative Commission on Foreign Investment), and Ambassador Yoshida Kenzō took part in the Deng-Ōkita meeting.

70. The Financial and Economic Commission was disbanded "to let the State Council

directly manage financial and economic operations and to promote governmental operational efficiency." See *Renmin Ribao*, March 7, 1981.

71. For an account of Okazaki's separate meetings with Li Xiannian and Gu Mu, Fujiyama's meeting with Deng Xiaoping, and Dokō's separate meetings with Deng and Zhao Ziyang, see *Renmin Ribao*, March 13, 14, and 15, 1981.

72. *Tōkyō Shimbun*, January 31, 1981.

73. Interview with Imamura Kōichi, deputy director, Shanghai Baoshan Office, Nippon Steel Corporation, July 3, 1981, Baoshan.

74. Interview with Huang Jinfa, Baoshan, July 3, 1981.

75. *Shanhai Hōzanseitetsujo*, pp. 23–24.

76. *Nihon Keizai Shimbun*, April 21 and May 31, 1981.

77. Ibid., June 25, 1981.

78. Ibid., February 13, 1981.

79. *Renmin Ribao*, March 29, 30, and 31, 1981.

80. Interview with Ikeda Tadashi, director, China and Mongolia Division, Bureau of Asian Affairs, Ministry of Foreign Affairs, June 18, 1981, Tokyo. At the Association of Southeast Asian Nations (ASEAN) meeting in Manila in June 1981, Japanese Foreign Minister Sonoda Sunao and Secretary of State Alexander Haig agreed to cooperate toward the goal of China's economic modernization. See *Asahi Shimbun*, June 20 and July 5, 1981.

81. Interview with Wu Shudong, June 16, 1981, Tokyo.

82. Interview with Hayashi Haruhiko, director, North Asia Division, Bureau of International Trade Policy, MITI, June 29, 1981, Tokyo.

83. *Japan Economic Journal*, September 15, 1981.

84. *Renmin Ribao*, September 24, 1981.

85. *Asahi Shimbun*, June 19, 1981.

86. *Yomiuri Shimbun*, March 19, 1981; and *Nihon Keizai Shimbun*, April 24, 1981.

87. *Japan Economic Journal*, September 1, 1981.

88. *Renmin Ribao*, September 24, 1981.

89. See *Nihon Keizai Shimbun*, January 9, 1982. The final settlement, which allowed China to extend the three-year freeze to five years, is described in *Mainichi Shimbun*, March 3, 1982.

90. For a discussion of China's chemical construction projects, see *Jitsumu kyōryoku eno kisogatame o mezashite* [Aiming at the basic consolidation of practical cooperation] (Tokyo: Nitchū keizai kyōkai, 1982), pp. 187–212.

91. *Beijing Review*, October 12, 1981, pp. 6–7. Also see *American Metal Market*, November 18, 1981.

92. For a description of Beilun, see *China Business Review*, July–August 1980, p. 49.

93. Interview with Odagawa Keisuke of Nippon Steel, July 1, 1982, Tokyo.

94. Interview with Jian Wensheng, May 31, 1982, Baoshan.

95. Ding Min, son of Korean parents, was in Shanghai during the Japanese Occupation and probably learned the Japanese language there. He graduated from Qinghua University and served as director of the Division of Japanese Affairs in the Ministry of Foreign Affairs from 1978 to 1981. Interview with Ding Min, June 16, 1982, Beijing.

96. A premier, two vice-premiers, and ten state councillors constituted the Standing Committee of the State Council. Wan Li was a regular member of the Political Bureau; Yao Yilin was one of its three alternate members. They were both regular members of the Party Secretariat. At the Twelfth CCP National Congress, Hu Yaobang gave up the party chairmanship, which was abolished, but he retained his position as general secretary. He joined Ye Jianying, Deng Xiaoping, Zhao Ziyang, Li Xiannian, and Chen Yun as a member of the Standing Committee of the Political Bureau. Hua Guofeng was demoted from the Political Bureau to the Central Committee. Gu Mu and Kang Shien were elected to the Central Committee; Gu was also a member of the Party Secretariat. See *Renmin Ribao*, September 11, 13, and 14, 1982.

97. See *Nihon Kōgyō Shimbun*, July 15, 1982.

98. See *Nihon Keizai Shimbun*, July 21, 1982; and *Shanhai Hōzanseitetsujo*, p. 20.

99. The organizations directly involved in the *Baogang* project included the State Planning Commission; the State Economic Commission; the Ministries of Metallurgical Industry, Foreign Economic Relations and Trade, Machine Building, Communications, Coal Industry, Urban and Rural Construction and Environmental Protection, and Water Conservancy and Power; the People's Liberation Army; the CNTIC; and local governments (Shanghai and Jiangsu and Zhejiang provinces).

100. *Renmin Ribao*, August 21, 1982.

101. See *Renmin Ribao*, October 16 and November 22 and 24, 1982.

102. See *Nikkei Sangyō Shimbun*, April 7, 1982.

103. Interview with Ding Min, June 16, 1982, Beijing.

104. See the statements made by Bo Yibo and Ma Hong (president of the Chinese Academy of Social Sciences) in *Asahi Shimbun*, September 23, 1982.

105. *Renmin Ribao*, December 13, 1982.

106. As revealed in my discussions with economists of the Economic Research Institute of Nankai University, July 8, 1981, Tianjin, China.

Chapter 3

1. For a succinct description of the history of China's oil experience, see *Chūgoku no shigen kaihatsu* [Resource development of China] (Tokyo: Nitchū keizai kyōkai, 1980), pp. 143–70.

2. The activities of these delegations are described in *Nitchū bōeki antei kakudai eno michisuji* [The road toward the stable expansion of Japan-China trade] (Tokyo: Nitchū keizai kyōkai, 1978), pp. 321–26. In March 1978, the Ministry of Petroleum and Chemical Industries was split into the Ministry of Petroleum Industry under Minister Song Zhenming (former secretary of the Daqing City Committee of the CCP) and the Ministry of Chemical Industry under Minister Sun Jingwen.

3. See Premier Hua's report to the First Session of the Fifth National People's Congress in *Peking Review*, March 10, 1978, pp. 7–40.

4. Interview with Saitō Takashi (deputy general manager, Exploration Department, Japan-China Oil Development Corporation), June 22 and 25, 1981, Tokyo; and with Wu Xunze (deputy general manager, offshore branch, Petroleum Company of China), July 10, 1981, Tanggu, Tianjin, China.

5. As quoted in Kim Woodard, *The International Energy Relations of China* (Stanford: Stanford University Press, 1980), p. 390.

6. My reconstruction of the negotiation processes is largely based upon the following sources: Saitō Takashi, "Bokkai ni okeru Nitchū kyōdō sekiyu kaihatsu" [Japan-China joint oil development of the Bohai Sea], in *Chūgoku Keizai Kenkyū Geppō* [Chinese economic research monthly] (Tokyo), September 1980, pp. 1–20, and October 1980, pp. 1–11; Matsuzawa Akira, "Chūgoku tono sekiyu kaihatsu kōshō" [Negotiations for oil development with China], in *Keiei Kondankai Geppō*]Management consultative society monthly] (Tokyo), June 1980, pp. 38–41, and July 1980, pp. 58–62; Kojima Sueo, "Japanese Cooperation in the Development of Chinese Offshore Oil," *China Newsletter* (Tokyo), December 1979, pp. 27–31; and Dori Jones, "China's Offshore Oil Development," *China Business Review* 4 (July–August 1980): 51–56.

7. The Hiroshima Shipbuilding Yard of Mitsubishi Heavy Industries constructed this rig, originally called "Fuji," in 1969. It was first used in the shallow waters surrounding Indonesia and Singapore. The offshore branch of the Petroleum Company of China bought it from Japan in 1972 at a cost of 2.6 billion yen ($12 million) and renamed it "Bohai No. 2" in 1973. See *Nihon Keizai Shimbun*, September 9, 1972. For Minister of Petroleum Industry Song Zhenming's revealing self-criticism for his failure to prevent the accident, see *Renmin Ribao*, August 26, 1980. A highly publicized trial was held in the Tianjin Intermediate People's Court; three officials of the Ministry of Petroleum Industry and the captain of the towing vessel were given jail sentences ranging from one to four years. See *Renmin Ribao*, September 3, 1980; and *Beijing Review*, September 1980, pp. 7–8.

8. See *Renmin Ribao*, December 7, 1979; and *Nihon Keizai Shimbun*, December 6, 1979.

9. *Asahi Shimbun*, February 9, 1980.

10. *Sankei Shimbun*, May 30, 1980; and *Renmin Ribao*, May 30, 1980. On the same day in Beijing, Deputy General Manager of the Petroleum Company of China Qin Wencai (vice-minister of petroleum industry) signed contracts for joint oil development with two French oil companies—the Société Nationale Elf Aquitaine for development of the northern Bohai Sea and the Compagnie Française des Pétroles for development of the northeastern zone (10,190 km^2) of the Beibu Gulf (Gulf of Tonkin). See *Renmin Ribao*, May 30, 1980.

11. See *Beijing Review*, June 9, 1980, pp. 8–9; or *Renmin Ribao*, May 30, 1980.

12. Jones, "China's Offshore Oil Development," p. 52; and *Petroleum Economist*, November 1981, p. 490.

13. Saitō Takashi, "Bokkai ni okeru," in *Chūgoku Keizai Kenkyū Geppō*, September 1980, p. 17.

14. *Nihon Keizai Shimbun*, September 5, 1979.

15. *Beijing Review*, September 14, 1979, pp. 4–5.

16. Ibid., September 14, 1979, pp. 4–5.

17. For a discussion of these companies, see *Kaisha gaiyō* [Corporation outline] (Tokyo: Nitchū sekiyu kaihatsu kabushikigaisha, September 1980); and *Introduction to Japan-China Oil Development Corporation and Chengbei Oil Development Corporation* (Tokyo: Nitchū sekiyu kaihatsu kabushikigaisha, n.d.).

18. Interview with Saitō, June 22, 1981, Tokyo.

19. My translation. See Matsuzawa, "Chūgoku tono," July 1980, pp. 60–61.

20. Interviews with Wu and Li, July 10, 1981, Tanggu.

21. See *Jigyō gaiyō* [Operational outline] (Tanggu: Tenshin kōgyōjo, May 15, 1981).

22. The operational progress is described in Matsuzawa Akira, "Ichiyaku kyakkō abiru Bokkai yuden kaihatsu" [Sudden limelight on oilfield development in the Bohai Sea], in *Shūkan Daiyamondo* [Weekly diamond] (Tokyo), June 6, 1981, pp. 42–44; and his "Bokkai no sekiyu kaihatsu" [Oil development in the Bohai Sea], *Energy* (Tokyo), July 1981, pp. 36–41.

23. See *Beijing Review*, June 1, 1981, p. 9; *Yomiuri Shimbun*, April 7, 1981; and *Nihon Keizai Shimbun*, May 14, 1981.

24. *Nihon Keizai Shimbun*, April 12, 1981.

25. See *Japan Economic Journal*, October 27, 1981; *Petroleum Economist*, November 1981, p. 490; *Beijing Review*, October 26, 1981, p. 7; and *Renmin Ribao*, October 12, 1981.

26. *Renmin Ribao*, November 14, 1981. Also see *Jitsumu kyōryoku eno kisogatame o mezashite* [Aiming at the basic consolidation of practical cooperation] (Tokyo: Nitchū keizai kyōkai, 1982), pp. 56–63.

27. *Renmin Ribao*, December 2, 1981. For an account of the successful French operations in the Beibu Gulf, see *Renmin Ribao*, May 29, 1981.

28. *Wenhuibao* (Shanghai), May 31, 1982; and *Asahi Shimbun*, June 1, 1982.

29. *Renmin Ribao*, October 3, 1982.

30. See *Jitsumu kyōryoku*, pp. 60–61.

31. See *Nikkan Kōgyō Shimbun*, August 10, 1981.

32. Interview with Saitō Takashi, June 21, 1982, Tanggu.

33. The regulations were reprinted in *Renmin Ribao*, February 11, 1982. In August, China announced passage of a law for the protection of marine environments. See *Renmin Ribao*, August 25, 1982.

34. Interview with Sasaki Masaaki (director, Management Department, Tianjin field office), July 10, 1981, Tanggu.

35. Interview with Yoshida Yoshitaka (general manager of the Exploration Department, JCODC), July 5, 1982, Tokyo.

36. See *Nikkei Sangyō Shimbun*, March 13, 1982.

37. See *Nihon Keizai Shimbun*, July 12, 1982.

38. Ibid., June 2, 1982.

39. Interview with Ding Min, June 16, 1982, Beijing.

40. *Nikkei Sangyō Shimbun*, November 6, 1982.

41. *Sankei Shimbun*, November 10, 1982. The French personnel started to leave the Bohai Binguan in November 1982.

42. Interview with Kimura Ichizō, June 22, 1981, Tokyo.

43. For a history of these two organizations, see *Kokusai Sekiyu Repōto* [International petroleum report], no. 4 (Tokyo: Kokusai sekiyu kabushikigaisha, August 22, 1980), pp. 16–18.

44. Interview with Kimura, July 5, 1982, Tokyo.

45. See Kim Woodard, *International Energy Relations*, p. 128.

46. *Nitchū bōeki*, p. 195.

47. *Kokusai Sekiyu Repōto*, no. 4, pp. 4–8.

48. *Mainichi Shimbun,* January 23, 1980.
49. *Asahi Shimbun,* March 19, 1980.
50. See *Nitchū keizai kōryū 1980* [Japan-China economic exchange] (Tokyo: Nitchū keizai kyōkai, April 1981), p. 350.
51. Interview with Kimura, June 22, 1981, Tokyo.
52. See Kim Woodard, *International Energy Relations,* pp. 136–37.
53. See *Nitchū keizai kōryū 1980,* pp. 364–66.
54. *China Daily,* April 10, 1982.
55. For a discussion of the Longjing disputes, which involved China, Japan, South Korea, and Taiwan, see Selig S. Harrison, "Oil Rush in East Asian Waters," *Asia* 2 (July–August 1982): 8–10. For an analysis of China's successful operations at Longjing, see *Renmin Ribao,* August 6 and September 18, 1982.
56. China's collaborative programs with foreign companies in other offshore areas are described in *Chūgoku no sekiyu kaihatsu to shogaikoku no kyōryoku* [China's oil development and cooperation with various foreign countries] (Tokyo: Nitchū keizai kyōkai, 1982), pp. 74–88.
57. In November 1982 the Idemitsu Oil Development Corporation joined four other Japanese oil companies in undertaking a $50 million oil exploration project in the Beibu Gulf. See *Nihon Keizai Shimbun,* November 11, 1982.

Chapter 4

1. For example, see *Keidanren* President Uemura Kogorō's report in *Nihon Keizai Shimbun,* August 15, 1972.
2. See ibid., September 29 and 30, 1978.
3. See *Peking Review,* October 25, 1978, pp. 15–17.
4. *Asahi Shimbun,* September 1, 1979.
5. See Premier Hua Guofeng's report to the First Session of the Fifth National People's Congress in *Peking Review,* March 10, 1978, pp. 7–40.
6. For a succinct discussion of China's electrical programs, see *Chūgoku no shigen kaihatsu* [Resource development of China] (Tokyo: Nitchū keizai kyōkai, 1980), pp. 109–40.
7. See *Beijing Review,* December 14, 1979, p. 6, and August 4, 1980, p. 6.
8. Other major hydroelectric power plants under construction or completed during the late 1970s and early 1980s include: Gezhouba (Hubei Province), 2.7 million kw; Longyangxia (Qinghai Province), 1.6 million kw; Baishan (Jilin Province), 900,000 kw; Ankang, 800,000 kw; and Wanan, 600,000 kw.
9. *Beijing Review,* December 14, 1979, p. 6.
10. See *Nitchū keizai kōryū 1980* [Japan-China economic exchange] (Tokyo: Nitchū keizai kyōkai, 1981), pp. 367–86.
11. As mentioned by Xie Beiyi in *Nihon Keizai Shimbun,* September 5, 1979.
12. Ibid.
13. *Beijing Review,* September 14, 1979, pp. 4–5; or *Asahi Shimbun,* September 7, 1979.
14. See *Asahi Shimbun,* October 9, 1979; and Isozaki Masao's article in *Look Japan,* June 10, 1980, pp. 17–18.

15. *Nihon Keizai Shimbun*, October 10, 1979.

16. See the account of Ōhira's meeting with Dietman Machimura Kingo, chairman of the Asian Problems Study Group, in *Asahi Shimbun*, November 30, 1979.

17. *Asahi Shimbun*, September 21, 1979.

18. See the joint communiqué issued by Fukuda and ASEAN leaders in Kuala Lumpur, *Waga gaikō no kinkyō* [The recent state of our diplomacy] (Tokyo: Ministry of Foreign Affairs, 1978), pp. 362–66. For an analysis of Japan-ASEAN relations, see Donald C. Hellmann, "Japan and Southeast Asia: Continuity Amidst Change," *Asian Survey* 12 (December 1979): 1189–98.

19. See *Nihon Keizai Shimbun*, October 25, 1979; and *Asahi Shimbun*, December 2, 1979.

20. See *Waga gaikō no kinkyō*, 1978, p. 213.

21. *Tokyo Shimbun*, November 1, 1979.

22. Radio Moscow broadcast to Japan on November 23, 1979, as reported in *Asahi Shimbun*, November 24, 1979.

23. See *Look Japan*, May 10, 1981, p. 12.

24. *Asahi Shimbun*, November 26, 1979.

25. Discussion with Dr. Dmitry Petrov of the Institute of the Far East, USSR Academy of Sciences, October 23, 1981, Moscow.

26. *Nihon Keizai Shimbun*, November 4, 1979; and *Asahi Shimbun*, December 1, 1979.

27. *Asahi Shimbun*, November 22, 1979.

28. See the texts of the joint press communiqué (December 7, 1979), in *Renmin Ribao*, December 8, 1979; and *Yomiuri Shimbun*, December 7, 1979.

29. *Asahi Shimbun*, December 8, 1979.

30. *Nihon Keizai Shimbun*, December 17, 1979. Katori had served as director of *Gaimushō*'s Bureau of Economic Cooperation. In September 1981, he was appointed Japanese ambassador to Beijing.

31. This information is taken from *Asahi Shimbun*, September 1, 1979, and December 1, 1979; *Beijing Review*, January 21, 1980, p. 8; *Nitchū keizai kōryū 1980*, p. 81; *Chūgoku no shigen kaihatsu*, pp. 62–66; and Isozaki, *Look Japan*.

32. *Dempa Shimbun*, April 17, 1980.

33. Each Japanese team was headed by a division director (*kachō*) of the ministry concerned. See *Nihon Kōgyō Shimbun*, January 14, 1980; and *Nikkan Kōgyō Shimbun*, January 28, 1980.

34. *Nihon Keizai Shimbun*, January 25, 1980.

35. *Sankei Shimbun*, January 27, 1980.

36. See Takiyama's report in *Nitchū Keizai Kyōkai Gaihō* [Report of the Japan-China Economic Association], June 1982, pp. 2–3.

37. See *Renmin Ribao*, April 26, 1980; and *Nihon Keizai Shimbun*, April 26, 1980. For the texts of the notes and accompanying letters, see *Jōyakushū* [Collection of treaties], no. 3234 (Tokyo: Ministry of Foreign Affairs, December 1980). The two sides agreed that "in case there is any divergence of interpretation of the said Exchange of Notes which is done in the Japanese, Chinese and English languages, the English text shall prevail."

38. *Jōyakushū*, p. 12.

39. *Asahi Shimbun*, May 1, 1980; and *Renmin Ribao*, May 1, 1980. For an account of

Sasaki's meetings with Premier Hua, Vice-Premiers Yu Qiuli and Kang Shien, Minister of Foreign Trade Li Qiang, and Minister of Metallurgical Industry Tang Ke, see *Renmin Ribao,* April 29 and May 1, 1980.

40. The list of qualified countries is given in *Chūgoku enshakkan no gaiyō* [Outline of China's yen loans] (Tokyo: OECF, April 1982), pp. 20–21.

41. Ibid., p. 5.

42. This information is based on *Shakkan kyōtei no gaiyō* [Outline of loan agreements] (Ministry of Foreign Affairs internal document with no dates); and *Nitchū Nisso Bōeki Hannenpō* [Semiannual report on Japan-China and Japan-USSR trade], Spring 1981 (Tokyo: Bōeki tsūshinsha, April 1, 1980), p. B/74.

43. *Renmin Ribao,* September 16, 1980.

44. For this list, see *Renmin Ribao,* June 12, 1982.

45. Interview with Takeuchi Katsushi, chief of the OECF's Beijing liaison office, June 17, 1982, Beijing.

46. See *Renmin Ribao,* September 10, 1981; January 17, 1982; June 12, 1982; and July 29, 1982.

47. For the text, see *Renmin Ribao,* December 6, 1980; and *Yomiuri Shimbun,* December 5, 1980. The Chinese participants in the conference included Vice-Premiers Gu Mu (chairman of the SCCC), Yao Yilin (chairman of the SPC), and Huang Hua (minister of foreign affairs); Minister of Foreign Trade Li Qiang; Minister of Coal Industry Gao Yangwen (vice-chairman of the State Energy Commission); Minister of Railways Guo Weicheng; Minister of Finance Wang Bingqian; Vice-Chairman of the SPC Gu Ming; Vice-Chairman of the State Economic Commission Ma Yi; Vice-Chairman of the State Agricultural Commission Du Runsheng; Vice-Chairman of the SCCC Xie Beiyi; Vice-Minister of Communications Tao Qi; and Chinese Ambassador to Japan Fu Hao. The Japanese counterparts were Minister of Foreign Affairs Itō Masayoshi; Minister of Finance Watanabe Michio; Minister of Agriculture, Forestry, and Fisheries Kameoka Takao; Minister of International Trade and Industry Tanaka Rokusuke; Minister of Transportation Shiokawa Masajurō; Director-General of the Economic Planning Agency Kōmoto Toshio; and Japanese Ambassador to China Yoshida Kenzō.

48. *Renmin Ribao,* December 6, 1980.

49. Interview with Ikeda Tadashi, director of the China and Mongolia Division, Bureau of Asian Affairs, Ministry of Foreign Affairs, June 18, 1981, Tokyo.

50. *Asahi Shimbun,* March 3, 1981.

51. The liaison office, which occupied a two-room suite in the Beijing Hotel, consisted of two Japanese officials and two Chinese interpreters. Takeuchi Katsushi talked about the frequent turnover of Chinese interpreters; in the second half of 1980, he trained five different Chinese individuals, who left his office to serve in the increasing number of joint ventures.

52. For Wang's complaint to MITI Vice-Minister Yano Toshihiko, see *Mainichi Shimbun,* September 11, 1980.

53. *Nihon Keizai Shimbun,* August 5, 1980.

54. See *Kokusai Bōeki* [International trade], July 21, 1981.

55. *Mainichi Shimbun,* February 5, 1981.

56. Interview with Commercial Counselor Wu Shudong, June 16, 1981, Tokyo.

57. See the report by Ueda Haruyoshi of the Division of Economic Cooperation,

Japanese Ministry of International Trade and Industry, in *Look Japan,* January 10, 1982, pp. 17–18.

58. *Nihon Kōgyō Shimbun,* January 12, 1982.

59. In fiscal year 1980, commodity loans constituted only 8 percent of Japan's government loans to other countries; recipients were Pakistan, Sri Lanka, Burma, Egypt, and Turkey. See *Look Japan,* May 10, 1981, pp. 12–13.

60. For the English text, see *Beijing Review,* December 28, 1981, pp. 15–16. The Chinese text appeared in *Renmin Ribao,* December 17, 1981. The Chinese participants in the second Sino-Japanese ministerial conference were Vice-Premiers Gu Mu and Huang Hua (also minister of foreign affairs), Chairman of the State Economic Commission Yuan Baohua, Chairman of the SCCC Han Guang, Minister of Foreign Trade Zheng Tuobin, Minister of Agriculture Lin Hujia, Minister of Finance Wang Bingqian, Vice-Chairman of the SPC Duan Yun, Vice-Chairman of the State Administrative Commission on Import and Export Affairs Gan Ziyu, and Ambassador to Japan Fu Hao. The Japanese side included Minister of Foreign Affairs Sakurauchi Yoshio, Minister of Finance Watanabe Michio, Minister of Agriculture, Forestry, and Fisheries Tazawa Kichirō, Minister of International Trade and Industry Abe Shintarō, Minister of Transportation Kosaka Tokusaburō, Director-General of the Economic Planning Agency Kōmoto Toshio, and Japanese Ambassador to China Katori Yasue.

61. *Tōkyō Shimbun,* March 27, 1982.

62. *Nihon Keizai Shimbun,* April 30, 1982.

63. See ibid., October 9 and 25, 1981.

64. Interview with Yamada Masaharu, a China specialist in the OECF of Japan, July 5, 1982, Tokyo.

65. *Mainichi Shimbun,* January 26, 1981.

66. *Renmin Ribao,* February 19, 1981.

67. *Renmin Ribao,* August 16, 1981. Minister of Public Health Qian Xinzhong was present at the occasion.

68. See Horiuchi Nobusuke's report in *Kokusai Kyōryoku Tokubetsu Jōhō* [Special report on international cooperation], May 1981, pp. 1–6.

69. See *Nihon Keizai Shimbun,* November 20, 1981; and *Renmin Ribao,* November 20, 1981.

70. *Japan Economic Journal,* December 15, 1981.

71. *Renmin Ribao,* December 3, 1981.

72. See *Mainichi Shimbun,* March 13, 1982.

73. Interview with Ding Min, June 16, 1982, at the Chinese Ministry of Foreign Affairs, Beijing.

74. See *Mainichi Shimbun,* March 26, 1982.

75. A report published in China's *Gongren Ribao* [Worker's daily] (September 19, 1981) included an urgent appeal to stop rampant vandalism at the Shijiusuo construction site. According to this report, local commune members and dockworkers loaded gravel from the construction areas in tractors and carts and sold it elsewhere. In the first eight months of 1981, the loss amounted to 600,000 yuan.

76. *Renmin Ribao,* April 9, 1981.

77. *Renmin Ribao,* July 17, 1982.

78. Interview with Rong Fengxiang, June 18, 1982, at the Chinese Ministry of Foreign Economic Relations and Trade, Beijing.
79. See *Renmin Ribao*, August 13, 1982.
80. Interview with Ding Min, June 16, 1982, Beijing.
81. Interview with Yamada Masaharu, July 5, 1982, Tokyo.
82. These intrabureaucratic developments are described in *Asahi Shimbun*, July 5 and 29, 1981; and *Tōkyō Shimbun*, August 29, 1981.
83. *Nihon Keizai Shimbun*, June 8, 1982.
84. See *Japan Economic Journal*, March 30, 1982; and *Nihon Keizai Shimbun*, July 6, 1982.
85. The Exchange of Notes is described in *Renmin Ribao*, September 28, 1982; and *Nihon Keizai Shimbun*, September 27, 1982. The loan agreements were signed by Aoki Shinzan (vice-president of the OECF of Japan) and Wei Yuming (vice-minister of foreign economic relations and trade); Minister Chen Muhua and Ambassador Katori Yasue were present at the signing ceremony. See *Renmin Ribao*, October 19, 1982; and *Sankei Shimbun*, October 19, 1982.
86. Interview with Takeuchi Katsushi, June 17, 1982, Beijing.
87. See the CNTIC's advertisement that invited international bids for the Lubuge hydroelectric power project, funded by the International Bank for Reconstruction and Development (IBRD), in *Renmin Ribao*, September 6, 1982. As stipulated by the loan agreement with the Kuwait Fund for Arab Economic Development, the CNTIC opened an international bid for the equipment required to construct the Hunan wood-based panel plant. See *Renmin Ribao*, December 14, 1982.

Chapter 5

1. For the text of the Zhou-Tanaka Joint Statement, see *Peking Review*, October 6, 1972, pp. 12–13.
2. See *Renmin Ribao*, September 28, 1982.
3. Interview with Ishikawa Tadao, June 30, 1981, Tokyo.
4. *Look Japan*, September 10, 1982, p. 3.
5. See *Renmin Ribao*, October 9, 1982.
6. For example, see the reproduced photographs of the "Rape of Nanking" in ibid., August 2, 1982; or the interview with Li Yanlu (a former commander of anti-Japanese guerrilla forces in Manchuria) in ibid., August 9, 1982.
7. See *Yomiuri Shimbun*, February 19, 1982.
8. See the English text of his speech in *Beijing Review*, September 13, 1982, pp. 11–40.
9. See the English text of his report in ibid., December 21, 1981, pp. 6–36.
10. See the English text of his speech in ibid., p. 16.
11. According to this twenty-year projection, the gross annual production would increase from 710 billion yuan in 1980 to 2,800 billion yuan in 2000; this increase would require an average annual growth rate of 7.2 percent. The estimated growth rates were 4–5 percent in the Sixth Five-Year Plan, 6–8 percent in the Seventh Five-Year Plan, and 8–9 percent in the 1990s.
12. See Chen's article in *Renmin Ribao*, September 20, 1982.

Selected
Bibliography

Newspapers and periodicals published in China and Japan were one important documentary source for my research. They include *Renmin Ribao* [People's daily], *Hongqi* [Red flag], *Peking Review* (and *Beijing Review*), *Asahi Shimbun*, *Nihon Keizai Shimbun*, *Yomiuri Shimbun*, *Look Japan*, *Ekonomisuto* [Economist], *China Newsletter*, *Japan Economic Journal*, and *Chūgoku Keizai Kenkyū Geppō* [Chinese economic research monthly].

Chinese- and Japanese-Language Sources

CHEN MUHUA. "Dakai duiwaijingji maoyi de xinjumian" [Open the new phase for foreign economy and trade]. *Renmin Ribao* [People's daily]. September 20, 1982.

Chōseiga no Chūgoku keizai to Nitchū kankei [Chinese economy under readjustment and Japan-China relations]. Tokyo: Nitchū keizai kyōkai, 1981.

Chūgoku enshakkan no gaiyō [Outline of China's yen loans]. Tokyo: Overseas Economic Cooperation Fund, April 1982.

Chūgoku no keizaikakumei [China's economic revolution]. Tokyo: Yomiuri shimbunsha, 1981.

Chūgoku no shigen kaihatsu [Resource development of China]. Tokyo: Nitchū keizai kyōkai, 1980.

DONG FURENG. "Woguo jingji fazhanzhong jilei he xiaofeide guanxiwenti" [Concerning the relationship between accumulation and consumption in the development of our economy]. *Wuhan Daxuebao* [Wuhan University journal] 41 (1981): 44–52.

FANG HAI. "Pipan yangnu zhexue" [Criticize the philosophy of servility to foreign things]. *Hongqi* [Red flag] 4 (1976): 21–26.

FENG BAOXING, WAN XIN, and ZHANG DAJIAN. "Zai yiding shiqinei youxian fazhan qinggongye de keguan biranxing" [The objective necessity of giving a priority to development of light industry during a certain period of time]. *Jingji Yanjiu* [Economic research] 1 (1980): 17–22.

FUJIYAMA AIICHIRŌ. *Seiji waga michi* [Politics—my way]. Tokyo: Asahi shimbunsha, 1976.

FURUI YOSHIMI. *Nitchū fukkō eno michi* [The road to Japan-China diplomatic normalization]. Tokyo: Kokusaimondai kenkyūjo, 1971.

HAN GUANG. "Tantan jiben jianshe de diaozheng wenti" [Discussions on the readjustment problems in basic construction]. *Hongqi* [Red flag] 6 (1979): 17–23.

Jitsumu kyōryoku eno kisogatame o mezashite [Aiming at the basic consolidation of practical cooperation]. Tokyo: Nitchū keizai kyōkai, 1982.

KAKIZAKI NORIO. "Hōzan shoku no shinkoku na yukue" [The serious direction of the Baoshan shock]. *Ekonomisuto* [Economist] 7 (1981): 54–59.

KE YUNLU. *Sanqianwan* [30 million yuan]. *Renmin Wenxue* [People's literature] 11 (November 1980): 3–20.

MU ZHI. "Baogang shejian zhongyu tongchu laila" [The end of the Baogang affair is exposed]. *Dongxiang* [Trend] 25 (1980): 22–24.

Nitchū bōeki antei kakudai eno michisuji [The road toward the stable expansion of Japan-China trade]. Tokyo: Nitchū keizai kyōkai, 1978.

Nitchū kankei kihon shiryōshū [Basic collected documents on Japan-China relations]. Tokyo: Kazankai, 1970.

Nitchū keizai kōryū 1980 [Japan-China economic exchange]. Tokyo: Nitchū keizai kyōkai, 1981.

OGAWA HEISHIRŌ. *Pekin no yonen* [Four years in Peking]. Tokyo: Simul Press, 1977.

OKABE TATSUMI. *Chūgoku wa kindaika dekiruka* [Can China modernize itself?]. Tokyo: Nihon keizai shimbunsha, 1981.

Ribenwenti wenjian huibian [Collected documents on Japan questions]. Vol. 4. Beijing: Shijie zhishi chubanshe, 1963.

SEKIGUCHI SUEO. *Chūgoku keizai o shindansuru* [To diagnose the Chinese economy]. Tokyo: Nihon keizai shimbunsha, 1979.

Shanhai Hōzanseitetsujo purojekuto repōto [Shanghai Baoshan iron and steel complex project report]. Tokyo: Shinnihon seitetsu kabushikigaisha, June 1981.

Shin Chūgoku Nenkan [New China yearbook]. Tokyo: Taishūkan shoten, 1975–76.

SUN YEFANG. *Shehuizhuyi jingjide ruogan lilunwenti* [Some theoretical questions of socialist economy]. Beijing: Renmin chubanshe, 1979.

TAGAWA SEIICHI. *Nitchū kōshō hiroku* [Secret record of Japan-China negotiations]. Tokyo: Mainichi shimbunsha, 1973.

Tianjin wenshi ziliao xuanji [Selections of Tianjin historical materials], no. 15. Tianjin: Renmin chubanshe, 1981.

Waga gaikō no kinkyō [The recent state of our diplomacy]. Tokyo: Ministry of Foreign Affairs, 1974–1978.

Xue Muqiao. *Dangqian woguo jingji ruogan wenti* [Some questions about our country's present economy]. Beijing: Renmin chubanshe, 1980.

————. *Shehuizhuyi jingji lilunwenti* [Theoretical questions of socialist economy]. Beijing: Renmin chubanshe, 1979.

————. *Zhongguo shehuizhuyi jingjiwenti yanjiu* [Studies of China's socialist economic questions]. Beijing: Renmin chubanshe, 1979.

Zhongguo Jingji Nianjian [China's economic yearbook]. Beijing: Beijing jingjiguanli zazhishe, 1981.

English-Language Sources

Central Intelligence Agency. *China: The Steel Industry in the 1970s and 1980s.* Washington, D.C.: Central Intelligence Agency, May 1979.

Harrison, Selig S. *China, Oil, and Asia: Conflict Ahead.* New York: Columbia University Press, 1977.

————. "Oil Rush in East Asian Waters." *Asia* 2 (July–August 1982): 8–10.

Hellmann, Donald C. "Japan and Southeast Asia: Continuity Amidst Change." *Asian Survey* 12 (December 1979): 1189–98.

Hsiao, Gene T. *The Foreign Trade of China: Policy, Law, and Practice.* Berkeley and Los Angeles: University of California Press, 1977.

Introduction to Japan-China Oil Development Corporation and Chengbei Oil Development Corporation. Tokyo: Nitchū sekiyu kaihatsu kabushiki-gaisha, n.d.

Israel, John, and Klein, Donald W. *Rebels and Bureaucrats: China's December 9ers.* Berkeley and Los Angeles: University of California Press, 1976.

Jones, Dori. "The Baoshan Contracts." *China Business Review* 4 (1980): 47–49.

————. "China's Expanding Offshore Oil Fleet." *China Business Review* 6 (1980): 50–52.

————. "China's Offshore Oil Development." *China Business Review* 4 (July–August 1980): 51–56.

Kojima, Sueo. "Japanese Cooperation in the Development of Chinese Offshore Oil." *China Newsletter* 24 (1979): 27–31.

Koshiro, Keiichi. "Another Look at the Baoshan Complex." *China Newsletter* 32 (1981): 8–13.

Lee, Chae-Jin. *Japan Faces China: Political and Economic Relations in the Postwar Era.* Baltimore, Md.: Johns Hopkins University Press, 1976.

————. "The Making of the Sino-Japanese Peace and Friendship Treaty." *Pacific Affairs* 3 (Fall 1979): 420–45.

Oksenberg, Michel, and Sai-cheung Yeung. "Hua Kuo-feng's Pre–Cultural Revolution Hunan Years, 1949–66: The Making of a Political Generalist." *China Quarterly* 69 (1977): 3–53.

Solinger, Dorothy J. "Economic Reform via Reformulation in China: Where Do Rightist Ideas Come From?" *Asian Survey* 9 (September 1981): 947–60.

U.S., CONGRESS, JOINT ECONOMIC COMMITTEE. *Chinese Economy Post-Mao.* Vol. 1. Washington, D.C.: Government Printing Office, 1978.

WEIL, MARTIN. "The Baoshan Steel Mill." In U.S., Congress, Joint Economic Committee, *China Under the Four Modernizations,* pt. 1. Washington, D.C.: Government Printing Office, 1982, pp. 367–93.

WOODARD, KIM. *The International Energy Relations of China.* Stanford: Stanford University Press, 1980.

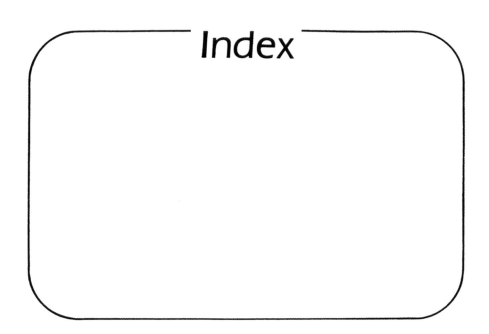

Index